## UNIVERSITY OF NORTH CAROLINA AT CHAPEL HILL
DEPARTMENT OF ROMANCE LANGUAGES

## NORTH CAROLINA STUDIES
## IN THE ROMANCE LANGUAGES AND LITERATURES

*Founder:* URBAN TIGNER HOLMES

*Distributed by:*

UNIVERSITY OF NORTH CAROLINA PRESS
CHAPEL HILL
North Carolina 27514
U.S.A.

NORTH CAROLINA STUDIES IN THE
ROMANCE LANGUAGES AND LITERATURES
Number 217

ARTFUL ELOQUENCE
Jean Lemaire de Belges and the Rhetorical Tradition

# ARTFUL ELOQUENCE
## Jean Lemaire de Belges and the Rhetorical Tradition

BY

MICHAEL F. O. JENKINS

CHAPEL HILL

NORTH CAROLINA STUDIES IN THE ROMANCE
LANGUAGES AND LITERATURES
U.N.C. DEPARTMENT OF ROMANCE LANGUAGES

1980

Library of Congress Cataloging in Publication Data

Jenkins, Michael F    O
  Artful eloquence.

  (North Carolina studies in the romance languages and literature; 217)
  Based on the author's thesis, Cornell University, 1971.
  Bibliography: p.
  Includes index.
  1. Lemaire de Belges, Jean, 1473-1515 or 16—Criticism and interpretation.
2. Rhetoric—History.  3. French orations—History and criticism.  I. Title.
II. Series.

PQ1628.L5J46      841'.3      80-17150
ISBN 0-8078-9217-3


I S. B. N. 0-8078-9217-3


DEPÓSITO LEGAL: V. 981 - 1980    I. S. B. N. 84-499-3671-3

ARTES GRÁFICAS SOLER, S. A. - OLIVERETA, 28 - VALENCIA (18) - 1980

# TABLE OF CONTENTS

|  | Page |
|---|---|
| INTRODUCTION | 11 |
| ABBREVIATIONS | 13 |

CHAPTER

| | | Page |
|---|---|---|
| I. | RHETORIC FROM CLASSICAL ANTIQUITY TO THE SIXTEENTH CENTURY | 15 |
| II. | JEAN LEMAIRE: THE TYPE OF THE RENAISSANCE ORATOR | 45 |
| III. | JEAN LEMAIRE'S CONCEPTION OF THE WRITER AND HIS CRAFT | 71 |
| IV. | THE DISTRIBUTION AND FUNCTION OF ORATIONS IN THE WORKS OF JEAN LEMAIRE | 92 |
| V. | A STUDY OF SOME SELECTED ORATIONS | 113 |
| VI. | SOME RHETORICAL ASPECTS OF JEAN LEMAIRE'S PROSE STYLE | 141 |
| VII. | AN OVERVIEW OF PRE-RENAISSANCE RHETORIC: "LA PLAINTE DU DÉSIRÉ" | 163 |

| | Page |
|---|---|
| BIBLIOGRAPHY | 176 |
| INDEX | 182 |

# INTRODUCTION

"Artful Eloquence," the title of this essay, speaks for itself. It is a direct translation from Jean Lemaire's phrase "leloquence artificielle" in *Les Illustrations de Gaule et Singularités de Troie,* which conveys the notion of a skillful or artistic use of language, as well as the generally pejorative meaning the word "artificial" has in current English parlance. In Lemaire's case, I hope it will soon be apparent that the former connotation is the appropriate one.

The book is based on my doctoral dissertation (Cornell University, 1971), which was directed by Prof. Edward P. Morris, to whom I owe my deepest gratitude. For a grant which enabled me to complete the revision of the manuscript I must express my appreciation to Angelo State University. My thanks are also due to Prof. Jean Parrish, who most obligingly served on my graduate committee, to Prof. Giuseppe Mazzotta, who originally suggested the topic to me, and to the ever-helpful staff of the Olin Graduate Library at Cornell. Two persons deserve particular mention. The first is my wife Georgia, who has cheerfully typed her way through seemingly innumerable drafts and who has been my copy editor, proofreader, and first critic. Finally, I here gladly follow what has become well-nigh a tradition in the field of Renaissance scholarship in America by extending my heartfelt thanks to Professor emeritus James Hutton of Cornell University, who has throughout our acquaintance been unfailingly kind and encouraging. Prof. Hutton's emendations, suggestions, and observations — all freely offered — have been of immeasurable assistance to me, as to so many others before me.

In conclusion, I wish merely to note that, like many researchers in the field of letters, I have found my topic to be of much greater scope than I had at first anticipated. Accordingly, there are some avenues which I have perforce left relatively unexplored, though indicating them in passing so that others might continue where I have left off.

SAN ANGELO, TEXAS
January 1976

# ABBREVIATIONS

| | |
|---|---|
| AM | *The Art of Memory* (Yates) |
| AP | *Les Arts poétiques du XII⁰ et du XIII⁰ siècle* (Faral) |
| APG | *The Art of Persuasion in Greece* (Kennedy) |
| ARP | *Ancient Rhetoric and Poetic Interpreted from Representative Works* (Baldwin) |
| Concorde | *La Concorde des deux langages* (Lemaire) |
| CREP | *Classical Rhetoric in English Poetry* (Vickers) |
| ELLMA | *European Literature and the Latin Middle Ages* (Curtius) |
| FPT | *Three Centuries of French Poetic Theory* (Patterson) |
| Genre humain | *La Concorde du genre humain* (Lemaire) |
| HP | *Histoire de la Pléiade* (Chamard) |
| HP15 | *Histoire poétique du XV⁰ siècle* (Champion) |
| HPF16 | *Histoire de la poésie française au XVI⁰ siècle* (Guy) |
| JL | *Jean Lemaire, der erste humanistische Dichter Frankreichs* (Becker) |
| "JLB" | "Jean Lemaire de Belges" (Lefranc) |
| JLB | *Jean Lemaire de Belges, sa vie, son œuvre et ses meilleures pages* (Spaak) |
| JLBEFB | *Jean Lemaire de Belges, écrivain franco-bourguignon* (Jodogne) |
| JLBR | *Jean Lemaire de Belges et la Renaissance* (Doutrepont) |
| LLP | *Literary Language and Its Public in Late Latin Antiquity and in the Middle Ages* (Auerbach) |

| | |
|---|---|
| MAJLB | *Marguerite d'Autriche et Jean Lemaire de Belges* (Thibaut) |
| MRP | *Medieval Rhetoric and Poetic (to 1400) Interpreted from Representative Works* (Baldwin) |
| RGRE | *Rhetoric in Greco-Roman Education* (Clark) |
| RLC | *Renaissance Literary Criticism* (Hall) |
| RPR | *Rhetoric and Poetry in the Renaissance* (Clark) |
| RPRH | *Rhetoric and Philosophy in Renaissance Humanism* (Seigel) |
| WMA | *The Waning of the Middle Ages* (Huizinga) |

Chapter I

RHETORIC FROM CLASSICAL ANTIQUITY
TO THE SIXTEENTH CENTURY

Many otherwise valuable studies in the field of sixteenth-century literature are seriously flawed by their failure to take into account the paramount importance of rhetorical precept and practice to the Renaissance. Nowhere is this more apparent than in the works devoted to Jean Lemaire de Belges, and in fact it is none other than Ph. Aug. Becker, the first modern scholar to recognize Lemaire's true significance, who most vividly demonstrates this underlying misapprehension. Becker is, for example, persuaded that the oratorical developments in the second book of *Les Illustrations de Gaule et Singularités de Troie* are to be viewed as an infallible indicator of the author's uneasiness when dealing with "unsympathetic" matters such as the adultery of Paris and Helen. Seen from this standpoint, Lemaire can only really do himself justice when his subject matter is congenial to him; hence the striking contrast between Book I of *Les Illustrations,* where Paris's love for Pegasis Oenone is depicted as idyllically innocent, and Book II, whose subject is the hero's moral and physical downfall. When Lemaire is in his constrained, moralizing vein, writes Becker, "so hält er sich fremd und nimmt seine Zuflucht zu den äusseren Mitteln der Rhetorik, zu Exclamationen, Apostrophen, Aposiopesen usf. Er verleiht der Erzählung an Glanz, was er ihr an Innigkeit nicht zu geben vermag." [1] Thus Lemaire's recourse to rhetorical devices is categorically equated with lack of conviction and indeed with outright

---

[1] *Jean Lemaire, der erste humanistische Dichter Frankreichs* (Strassburg, 1893), 225.

artistic failure. One can only reject so bland an assumption that rhetorical and literary creation are somehow irreconcilable.[2] In any case, the facts in no way support this theory, because although the "Glanze der Redekunst" of which Becker speaks is much in evidence in *Les Illustrations* II — as cannot be gainsaid — it is not a whit less so in Book I.

If the doyen of Lemaire scholars could commit so basic an error, it is perhaps no great wonder that others after him have been similarly misled, the problem of rhetorical influence on literary evolution having been, until very recently, sadly neglected. Of especial interest to *seiziémistes* has been the appearance (in 1969 and 1970) of at least two studies dealing precisely with the close interrelationship between rhetoric and poetry: Robert Griffin's *Coronation of the Poet: Joachim Du Bellay's Debt to the Trivium*, and Alex. L. Gordon's *Ronsard et la Rhétorique*. It is doubtless to be expected that the two greatest poets of the French Renaissance would be chosen as the first subjects for so refreshingly new an approach.[3] However, this still leaves many writers of the earlier part of the sixteenth century languishing under the cloud of contemporary critical disapproval. In fact, an entire school, the much-maligned Grands Rhétoriqueurs, was, with the notable exception of Jean Lemaire, for many years dismissed with contempt and derision by critics who, quite uninhibited by their ignorance of the facts, rarely scrupled to treat the rhétoriqueur poets with anything but undisguised hostility.[4] The deplorable narrowness of their views may be excused in part insofar as they were formulated before the

---

[2] Cf. Northrop Frye, *Anatomy of Criticism* (New York, 1968 [1957]), 245: "Rhetoric has from the beginning meant two things: ornamental speech and persuasive speech. These two things seem psychologically opposed to each other, as the desire to ornament is essentially disinterested, and the desire to persuade essentially the reverse. In fact ornamental rhetoric is inseparable from literature itself, or what we have called the hypothetical verbal structure which exists for its own sake." And again (*ibid.*), "... if the direct union of grammar and logic is characteristic of non-literary verbal structures, literature may be described as the rhetorical organization of grammar and logic."

[3] New, that is, for French literature, English literature having hitherto been far better served in this respect.

[4] For a comprehensive review of critical opinion on Jean Lemaire de Belges and the Rhétoriqueurs from the sixteenth century through the present day, I refer the reader to M. Pierre Jodogne's masterly study *Jean Lemaire de Belges, écrivain franco-bourguignon* (Brussels, 1972), Chapter I. (Cited hereafter as *JLBEFB*).

publication of Ernst Robert Curtius's epoch-making *European Literature and the Latin Middle Ages,* a study which has contributed immeasurably to our comprehension of the centrality of rhetoric to literature.

Now, Lemaire was undeniably affiliated with the Rhétoriqueurs, and indeed proudly boasts of his discipleship; see, *inter alia,* the title-page of *Le Temple d'Honneur,* his first published work, where he proclaims himself "disciple de Molinet." This affiliation is perhaps the one hard fact about him known to everyone who has perused the usual rather cursory "pre-Renaissance" chapters of the literary histories. There it is generally *de rigueur* to state that Lemaire, being — unlike Molinet, Cretin, Octovien de Saint-Gelais and the rest — a genuine poet, frequently transcends the many appalling limitations of his school. Yet he is all too often held back by the stifling weight of rhétoriqueur precept, from which, alas, he never fully escapes.[5] In the specialized studies devoted to him, one keeps coming across lamentations over his bad luck at being born in an age so unpropitious for poetry. "S'il était né trente ans plus tard, quelles pages nous aurions de lui!" exclaims Henry Guy in a moment of enthusiasm, adding sadly: "Mais il faut avouer qu'il n'a pas tenu, à cause de la sottise ambiante et des chaînes qui le liaient au passé, autant que promettait sa nature."[6] To me, this

---

[5] As recently as 1972, Prof. John A. McClelland could criticize Lemaire for preferring "the arid precept of rhetoric... to 'the imitation of an action.'" (Unpubl. paper read before the 1972 MLA convention: "*La Plainte du Désiré*: Rhetoric and Catharsis in the Early Renaissance.")

[6] *Histoire de la poésie française au XVI$^e$ siècle* (Paris, 1910), I, 176. Cf. Francisque Thibaut, *Marguerite d'Autriche et Jean Lemaire de Belges* (Paris, 1888), 246: "Que ne parut-il 50 ans plus tard!" Charles Fétis, in his *Mémoire sur Jean Lemaire* (publ. 1870, and cited by P. Jodogne in *JLBEFB*, 18), takes the opposing standpoint, namely that the poet "eût été heureux de naître un demi-siècle plus tôt," which would have made him a contemporary of François Villon and Charles d'Orléans instead of the disciple of the Rhétoriqueurs. Jean Stecher (writing 3 years later than Thibaut and 19 before Guy) rightly disapproves of such futile outbursts: "Qu'on cesse donc de dire que l'enthousiaste érudit de Bavay est venu ou trop tôt ou trop tard; il est fort opportunément arrivé à son heure." *Notice sur la vie et les œuvres de Jean Lemaire de Belges,* in Stecher's edition of Lemaire's *Œuvres* (Louvain, 1891), IV, xcii. Cf. also Abel Lefranc: "Le premier ouvrage de Jean Lemaire fut le *Temple d'Honneur et de Vertus*... c'est un poème sans valeur, tant il est empreint des défauts les plus graves que l'on reproche aux rhétoriqueurs." "Les Grands Rhétoriqueurs," in *Revue des Cours et Conférences* 19 (1$^{re}$ série, 1910-1911), 729.

is quaintly reminiscent of Voltaire's equally vain regrets over Shakespeare's misfortune in not arriving on the scene during the age of Addison: "Que peut-on conclure de ce contraste de grandeur et de bassesse, de raisons sublimes et de folies grossières, enfin de tous les contrastes que nous venons de voir dans Shakespeare? qu'il aurait été un poète parfait s'il avait vécu du temps d'Addison." [7] In short, when Lemaire is acknowledged to be in "poetic" vein, he is hailed by all as the harbinger of the Pléiade; when writing in his rhétoriqueur manner, on the other hand, he is — in the not altogether infallible consensus of the critics — simply not being true to himself and to his finer instincts.

If Jean Lemaire is nevertheless widely accepted as a pivotal figure in the history of French literature, it is not due merely to the fact that his life happens to span that transitional epoch between 1475 and 1525 which is designated as the "pre-Renaissance," but because things in the French domain of letters are no longer quite the same after him as they were before. Jean Stecher's *Notice sur la Vie et les Œuvres de Jean Lemaire de Belges* does not hesitate to credit Lemaire with being "l'instaurateur de la Renaissance," a phrase which is echoed almost word for word by Paul Laumonier in his *Ronsard, poète lyrique*.[8] Undoubtedly, Lemaire is a stylist of no mean rank in both prose and poetry, yet it is true that since the sixteenth century very little attention has been focused upon his prose works, which form by far the greater part of his opus. While we possess excellent critical editions of his finest poetry (including the charming *Épîtres de l'Amant Vert* and *La Concorde des deux langages,* whose linking passages are in prose), the only complete edition to be published in modern times is that of Jean Stecher, which is fast approaching the ripe old age of ninety. Only now are *seiziémistes* beginning to do justice to this author's prose works.[9] Jean Lemaire was much taken up with problems of literary form; and it is my contention that, far from acting as a needless and

---

[7] In his "Article sur l'Art Dramatique" (*Dictionnaire philosophique* I, in *Œuvres Complètes* [Paris, 1878], 403).

[8] Stecher, *Notice,* lxxxiii; Laumonier, *Ronsard, poète lyrique* (Paris, 1909), 647.

[9] The two major works, *Les Illustrations de Gaule* and *La Couronne Margaritique,* are reportedly in preparation by, respectively, M. Jacques Abélard and Mlle Hélène Naïs, but have not as yet appeared in print.

positively harmful encumbrance to his art — an almost unchallenged assumption hitherto— it is on the contrary rhetoric which to a large extent makes him what he is.

Lemaire was not, of course, a unique phenomenon in the history of French literature, nor was he the first French writer consciously and systematically to adopt rhetorical techniques.[10] Rather was he a link in an evolutionary chain which connects him, via Jean Molinet and Georges Chastellain, to Alain Chartier, "lointaing immitateur des orateurs"[11] and acknowledged founder of French *prose oratoire* (see below, Chap. II). Nevertheless it was in Jean Lemaire that this gradual and steady growth attained, precisely during the pre-Renaissance period in France, its earliest full flowering.

The rhetorical element in Lemaire's works is so strikingly apparent that one might well be forgiven for asking why it has thus far been passed over virtually without comment. One major reason is doubtless the plain fact that rhetoric, which held undisputed sway in the field of Greco-Roman pedagogy, and again for some four hundred years from the high Renaissance to the time of Goethe (d. 1832),[12] has during the greater part of the nineteenth and twentieth centuries been pretty thoroughly ignored. The term itself has become well-nigh pejorative; the arguments of one's opponents are often automatically dismissed as "mere," "cheap," "empty," or "irresponsible" rhetoric, as observers of the contemporary political scene are only too painfully aware. But in the literary domain, our recent neglect of rhetoric is attributable to a confusion between it and "rhétorique" — the fundamental misconception, so widespread throughout the Middle Ages, that rhetoric consists in the artificial embellishment superadded by the writer to a commonplace and perhaps otherwise unpalatable matter, much in the fashion of the sugar coating on the pill. This is by no means the prime function

---

[10] I hope I may be forgiven for arbitrarily making a Frenchman out of the staunch Hainault-born and Burgundian-oriented Lemaire. Linguistically speaking, the more so in view of his studies at Paris (cf. *Œuvres*, ed. Jean Stecher [Louvain, 1882-1891], I, 106), Lemaire belongs with France.

[11] *Le Quadrilogue Invectif* (Paris, 1950 [1422]), Prologue, 1. 6.

[12] "...down to the Revolution of 1830, Europe remained convinced that it could not do without a constantly renewed presentation of rhetoric which should keep pace with contemporary literary production." Ernst R. Curtius, *European Literature and the Latin Middle Ages*, trans. Willard R. Trask (New York, 1963 [1948]), 78. (Hereafter cited as *ELLMA*).

of rhetoric as conceived by classical antiquity and as revived during the humanistic period. To clarify the question, there now follows a brief outline of the history and chief tenets of the rhetorical tradition. Needless to say, I make no claim to originality in this summary, its purpose being simply to refresh the reader's memory and establish a convenient frame of reference.

The formal study of rhetoric originated in Greece, where oratory was fundamental to the lives of the inhabitants of the city-states.[13] The Athenian of the fifth and fourth centuries B.C. lived in an age when litigation was pursued with a passion. A man was expected to be his own attorney, and the customary penalty for failure to win over a jury of one's peers was death, or banishment and confiscation of property. So much for the judicial aspect of rhetoric. There was also the deliberative type, by the skillful employment of which an orator might very well alter the course of history. One has only to think of the orations of Pericles (which unfortunately have not survived except by repute) and those of Demosthenes, who, by convincing the Athenians (in his *Philippics*) that the only honorable course open to them was unremitting hostility to Philip of Macedon, unintentionally hastened the decline of his own city.

The art of rhetoric was not invented during the Athenian Golden Age: it has a much more venerable history, going back at least as far as Homer, whose *Iliad* and *Odyssey* are both highly rhetorical in character (nearly one-half of the *Iliad* and more than two-thirds of the *Odyssey* are given over to orations of various kinds). For this reason, Homer has ever since classical times been acclaimed as the father of rhetoric. Thus, Quintilian in the *De institutione oratoria* declares that Homer is "supreme not merely for poetic, but for oratorical power as well. For, to say nothing of his eloquence, which he shows in praise, exhortation and consolation, do not the ninth book containing the embassy to Achilles, the first describing the quarrel between the chiefs, or the speeches delivered by the

---

[13] The distinction between the terms "rhetoric" and "oratory" is concisely made by Donald C. Bryant, "Rhetoric: Its Function and Scope," in *The Province of Rhetoric*, ed. J. Schwartz and J. A. Rycenga (New York, 1965), hereafter cited as *PR*. Says Bryant (p. 11): "Traditionally *rhetoric* and *oratory* have been the standard terms for the theory and the product." ·

## RHETORIC FROM CLASSICAL ANTIQUITY

counsellors in the second, display all the rules of art to be followed in forensic or deliberative oratory?"[14]

Nevertheless, it was from the fifth century B.C. on that the primacy of rhetoric was assured, and it was thenceforth subjected to a most searching and thorough analysis, carried out with ever-increasing refinement and subtlety. (Ironically enough, this intensive study of rhetoric got under way at the very moment when the Greek city-states were beginning to decline, and by the time the Hellenistic rhetoricians had attained their highest influence — with Cicero — on Republican Rome, democracy was doomed there also, to be succeeded by the tyranny of the early Empire. Deliberative rhetoric no longer had any reason to exist and in fact practically disappeared. Forensic rhetoric, however, continued to flourish, as did epideictic, and rhetorical studies became the very foundation of the Imperial educational system.)

But the age of Socrates was also the age of the sophists (traveling teachers, rhetoricians, and philosophers), who were frequently accused of making "the worse appear the better argument,"[15] as Aristotle puts it. Socrates himself was charged with being a sophist, and it is in Plato's *Phaedrus* that he first introduces the term "lovers of wisdom or philosophers" as the "modest and befitting title"[16] of the truly wise man, as opposed to what Plato alleges are the sophists' arrogant claims to outright wisdom. (Pythagoras is credited with the actual coining of the term "philosopher.") Plato's views on rhetoric are chiefly to be found in the two dialogues *Gorgias* and *Phaedrus*, the former representing a debate between Socrates and the eminent Sicilian rhetorician and sophist Gorgias of Leontini, the latter containing the famous characterization of love as a divine madness. In *Gorgias*, rhetoric is attacked because it deals not in truth — the object of the Socratic dialectic — but with mere probability, with the manipulation of arguments. In short, as Gorgias himself is made to admit, rhetoric is "the ability to persuade with speeches."[17] In

---

[14] Quintilian, *Institutio Oratoria*, trans. H. E. Butler (Cambridge, Mass., and London, 1963-1968 [1920-1922]), Loeb Classical Library, X.i.46-47.

[15] *The "Art" of Rhetoric*, trans. John H. Freese (Cambridge, Mass., and London, 1959 [1926]), Loeb Classical Library, II.xxiv.11.

[16] In *The Dialogues,* ed. and trans. Benjamin Jowett (New Lork and London, 1892 [1871]), Vol. I, *Phaedrus,* 278.

[17] Trans. W. R. M. Lamb (London and New York, 1932 [1925]), Loeb Classical Library, 452 E.

the hands of a skillful yet unprincipled practitioner, such a discipline might indeed make "the worse appear the better argument." In *Phaedrus,* Socrates again criticizes rhetoric for being concerned with opinion and plausibility rather than with knowledge and truth, but on this occasion he is much more interested in postulating an ideal form of oratory, which he himself proceeds to demonstrate, contrasting it — to the latter's disadvantage — with the "sophistic" type, in the well-known series of speeches about love.

It is worth noting that ancient rhetoricians after Plato earnestly insist that the orator must be both wise *and* virtuous, fully cognizant of his awesome responsibility to his fellow citizens. Quintilian cites (XII.i.1) the most lapidary definition of the ideal orator, Cato's "Vir bonus dicendi peritus." Cicero's introductory lines to *De inventione,* written — unlike the work itself — in his maturity, include the following: "Wisdom without eloquence does too little for the good of states, . . . eloquence without wisdom is generally highly disadvantageous and is never helpful." [18]

Aristotle's *Rhetoric,* the most thorough-going scientific analysis of the art, is to a large degree taken up with developing in detail points which Plato had raised only to drop almost immediately (e.g., the vital question of audience psychology, touched upon very briefly by Socrates [*Phaedrus,* 277], is a major theme throughout the *Rhetoric*). As for Plato's fundamental objection to rhetoric on the grounds that it is liable to be abused by clever scoundrels, Aristotle simply retorts that "this objection applies equally to all good things except virtue, and above all to those things which are most useful, such as strength, health, wealth, generalship" (I.i.13). Rhetoric itself he defines as "the faculty of discovering the possible means of persuasion in reference to any subject whatever" (I.ii.1). Yet the *Rhetoric,* for all its profound and subtle insights, had very little influence on the actual teaching of the art. It is a commonplace of the history of rhetoric that Demetrius Phalereus — reputedly the author of a famous treatise on style: *Peri Hermeneias* — was the sole distinguished orator to be produced by the school of Aristotle (despite the careful attention which the philosopher devoted to

---

[18] Trans. H. M. Hubbell (Cambridge, Mass., 1960 [1949]), Loeb Classical Library, I.i.1. Cf. Quintilian I.Pr. 9: "The first essential for [the perfect orator] is that he should be a good man."

rhetorical instruction), whereas the rival establishment of Isocrates turned out what D. L. Clark calls "an amazing number of honorable and useful statesmen and generals, orators and historians."[19] Isocrates is also an extremely influential figure in the domain of letters, since he appears to have originated the doctrine of imitation of selected models, which was to become so momentous to Renaissance literary theory and practice. Werner Jaeger goes so far as to claim that: "Historically, it is perfectly correct to describe [Isocrates] . . . as the father of 'humanistic culture.' "[20]

It was to the Hellenistic period that rhetoric owed the proliferation of numerous handbooks, known as *technai*, or "arts" (in the ancient sense of "a body of rules" or "a craft"). Most of these have long since been lost, but their doctrine has not, thanks to its embodiment in two Roman manuals of the first century B.C.: Cicero's youthful essay *De inventione* (often claimed to be no more than a reworking of notes taken during his student days) and the anonymous *Rhetorica ad Herennium*, itself long ascribed to Cicero (until the early Renaissance, in fact).[21] The significance of these treatises will be discussed more fully in connection with medieval rhetoric. Cicero's mature writings on rhetoric, of which the most important are *De oratore, Orator, Brutus,* and *Partitiones oratoriae* (with *De oratore* the acknowledged masterpiece), are not "arts" of rhetoric at all, but — and this is especially true of the first two works — what C. S. Baldwin calls "fine encomia of the higher function of

---

[19] *Rhetoric in Greco-Roman Education* (New York, 1959 [1957], hereafter referred to as *RGRE*), 58. In the preceding paragraph, Clark — himself a distinguished professor of rhetoric — characterizes Isocrates as "the earliest, noblest example of the teacher of rhetoric, the teacher who is master of the art he teaches, who is devoted to the true advantage of his pupils, who envisages education in rhetoric as the training of young people to take their place in a human society where all transactions are conducted through the medium of language."

[20] "The Rhetoric of Isocrates and Its Cultural Ideal" (in *PR*, 84).

[21] Prof. Harry Caplan, in the Introduction to his edition of the *Ad Herennium*, credits Lorenzo Valla in the mid-fifteenth century with casting doubt on Cicero's authorship of the treatise. *Ad C. Herennium de Ratione Dicendi (Rhetorica ad Herennium)* (Cambridge, Mass., and London, 1939), Loeb Classical Library, p. ix. James J. Murphy says the work was "universally regarded as Cicero's until Erasmus questioned [its] authorship." *Rhetoric in the Middle Ages* (Berkeley, 1974; cited hereafter as *RMA*), 109.

oratory, and of the orator as leader... Without very original or even very specific doctrine they are eloquently persuasive."[22]

Cicero's death in 43 B.C. coincides more or less with the end of the Roman Republic and the subsequent decline of deliberative oratory. Well over a hundred years later (c. 95 A.D.) appeared one of the greatest and most influential of all educational manuals, Quintilian's *De institutione oratoria*. Writing at a time when almost the only practical application of oratory was to the law courts and to the highly formalized epideictic genres,[23] Quintilian distilled the quintessence of a great tradition into one monumental treatise, which is in effect classical antiquity's last authoritative word on rhetoric. James J. Murphy remarks that it has been described as "four major works blended into one: a treatise on education, a manual of rhetoric, a reader's guide to the best authors, and a handbook on the moral duties of the orator."[24] In the prologue to Book VIII, Quintilian formulates what remains perhaps the single most comprehensive definition of rhetoric: "I desired to make it clear that rhetoric is the science of speaking well, that it is useful, and further, that it is an art and a virtue. I wished also to show that its subject matter consists of everything on which an orator may be called to speak, and is, as a rule, to be found in three classes of oratory, demonstrative, deliberative, and forensic; that every speech is composed of matter and words, and that as regards matter we must study invention, as regards words, style [*elocutio*], and as regards both, arrangement, all of which it is the task of memory to retain and delivery to render attractive" (VIII.Pr.6). He continues (VIII.Pr.7) by stating that "the duty of the orator is composed of instructing, moving and delighting his hearers" (*Oratoris officium docendi, movendi, delectandi partibus contineri*).

---

[22] *Renaissance Literary Theory and Practice*, ed. D. L. Clark (Gloucester, Mass., 1959 [1939]), 45.

[23] Curtius lists "funeral orations, birthday orations, consolatory orations, orations of greeting, of congratulation, etc." (*ELLMA*, 69), as well as official eulogies of the reigning Emperor, a genre rejoicing in the name of *basilicos logos*.

[24] In the Introduction to his edition of *On the Early Education of the Citizen-Orator*, John Selby Watson's translation of *De inst. orat.*, I and II (Indianapolis and New York, 1965), p. xi. Cf. George Kennedy: "The twelve books *De institutione oratoria* are the finest statement of ancient rhetorical theory." *The Art of Rhetoric in the Roman World* (Princeton, 1972), 496.

Having surveyed the history of the art to its fullest development in the ancient world, let us now briefly examine the elements of rhetorical theory and practice at the beginning of the Empire.

There are — as we have seen — three modes or types of rhetoric: deliberative, demonstrative or epideictic, and forensic. As classified by Aristotle (*Rhetoric,* I.iii.3-4), the first is concerned with the discussion before the assembled citizenry of some proposed future action; the second deals with a present occasion (funeral, Emperor's birthday, etc.); and the third involves the legality (or illegality) of some deed already committed.

Rhetoric is divided qualitatively into five parts, *inventio, dispositio, elocutio, memoria, pronuntiatio* (or *actio*), of which *inventio* is at once the most important and the hardest to define. "Invention is the discovery of valid or seemingly valid arguments to render one's cause plausible," states Cicero (*De inventione,* I.vii.9); he is echoed by *Ad Herennium* (I.ii.3): "Invention is the devising of matter, true or plausible, that would make the case convincing." Martianus Capella — writing in the early fifth century A.D. — puts it somewhat differently: "*Invention* is the wise investigator — the comprehension, as it were — of points and arguments ... *invention,* whose task it is to dig out the points of the case, and discover arguments suitable for demonstration." [25]

*Dispositio* is the arrangement of the subject matter, in the sense of the overall plan of composition. *Elocutio* (not to be confused with our "elocution") has to do with the selection of suitable words and figures with which to clothe one's thought, and also deals with such things as rhythm and harmony. In short, as C. S. Baldwin suggests, the term is best rendered by "style." [26] Also considered

---

[25] *De Nuptiis Philologiae et Mercurii et de Septem Artibus Liberalibus* Book V (*De Rhetorica*), trans. Lou W. Conklin, unpubl. M. A. thesis (Cornell, 1928), 41-42. Among commentators of our own time, C. S. Baldwin says that *inventio* is concerned with "the investigation, analysis, and grasp of the subject-matter," with, "in Aristotelian language, the discovery of all the intrinsic means of persuasion, or more simply, survey of the material and forecast." *Ancient Rhetoric and Poetic Interpreted from Representative Works* (New York, 1924), 43 and 67 (hereafter cited as *ARP*). For an extremely well-documented account of what *inventio* meant to Renaissance literary theory, see Grahame Castor, *Pléiade Poetics* (Cambridge, England, 1964), particularly chapters 8-12 and 16-17.

[26] *ARP,* 67.

under this heading are the so-called three styles, the grand, the middle, and the plain or simple (*gravis, mediocris, extenuata* [*Ad Herenn.,* IV.viii.11]). Quintilian calls them "grand and forcible" (*grande atque robustum*), "plain" (*subtile*), and "intermediate or florid" (*medium, floridum*). His term for style in this context is simply *dicendi genus* (XII.x.58). For him, as for Cicero,[27] the grand style is best suited to moving the audience, the plain to instructing or proving, and the intermediate to delighting or charming (*movere, docere, delectare*).

The fourth part of rhetoric, *memoria,* does indeed include memory, but a great deal more besides. The author of *Ad Herennium,* whose treatment of the subject is apparently the oldest mnemonic system extant, calls it "the treasure-house of the ideas supplied by Invention, . . . the guardian of all the parts of rhetoric" (III.xvi.28). Quintilian (XI.ii.1) terms memory an "animating principle" (*spiritus*) and regards it as being of cardinal importance to extempore eloquence (a topic to which he devotes much thought in X.vi and vii),[28] maintaining that "it is memory which has brought oratory to its present position of glory" (XI.ii.7). As D. L. Clark has it, the art of memory was to the ancients not "the art of learning by heart a written speech, but rather the art of keeping ready for use a fund of argumentative material, together with the features of the case which the speaker might be pleading."[29]

The fifth and last subdivision, *pronuntiatio,* deals with the delivery of the finished oration; and, as usual, the *Rhetorica ad Herennium* has a neat, methodical, and concise section on the subject (III.xi-xv), discussing such aspects of delivery as voice quality (*vocis figura*), physical movement (*corporis motus*), the four kinds of conversational tone (*sermo*), i.e., the Dignified, the Explicative, the Narrative, and the Facetious (III.xiii.23). Even the bodily attitude, movement, and gestures best befitting the vocal tone employed are carefully described, all in the interests of rendering "what is de-

---

[27] *Orator,* trans. H. M. Hubbell (Cambridge, Mass., and London, 1939), Loeb Classical Library, xxi.69.

[28] Cf. XI.ii.3. For a fascinating, if perhaps somewhat idiosyncratic, treatment of mnemotechnical theory from antiquity through the Renaissance, see Frances A. Yates, *The Art of Memory* (London, 1966).

[29] *Rhetoric and Poetry in the Renaissance* (New York, 1922), 30. (Cited hereafter as *RPR.*)

livered more plausible" (III.xv.26). For example: "For the Broken Tone of Debate, one must extend the arm very quickly, walk up and down, occasionally stamp the right foot, and adopt a keen and fixed look" (III.xv.27). The longest and most painstaking analysis of delivery is supplied by Quintilian (XI.iii, *passim*), copiously illustrated with splendid examples drawn from the great masters, above all, as one might expect, from Cicero and Demosthenes. Like the author of the *Ad Herennium,* Quintilian stresses the fact that delivery "has an extraordinarily powerful effect in oratory" (XI.iii.2). "For my own part," he says, "I would not hesitate to assert that a mediocre speech supported by all the power of delivery will be more impressive than the best speech unaccompanied by such power" (XI.iii.5).

Turning now to the quantitative analysis of rhetoric, we find that the forensic oration — with which the rhetorical theorists chiefly concern themselves — typically comprises five divisions: introduction (*exordium* or *prooemium*); *narratio,* or exposition of the facts in the case; *confirmatio* (also called *argumentatio, probatio*) or proof; *confutatio* (*refutatio*) or rebuttal of the opening arguments; and *peroratio* (*conclusio, epilogus*), the conclusion. Sometimes (as, e.g., *Ad Herenn.,* I.iii.4) a sixth part (*divisio* or *partitio*) is recommended, in which the orator enumerates the main points of his argument. This five- or six-fold division, also used in the epideictic and deliberative modes, was to become the basic organizational principle of literary composition.

It is worth noting that special conventions evolved for certain of the rhetorical subdivisions, in particular the exordium and peroration. E. R. Curtius has written some enlightening pages on what he calls the "affected modesty topos," taking examples from Cicero, Quintilian, Tacitus, St. Jerome, etc., and defining the two chief elements of such protestations: first, that the author would never have ventured to write this work at all if he had not been expressly directed or requested to do so; second, that he is totally unworthy to undertake such a task. One is reminded of the semi-facetious "unaccustomed as I am to public speaking" of the contemporary after-dinner speaker; and, on a higher level, of Mark Antony — at the climax of a most brilliant piece of deliberative oratory — disclaiming any oratorical power:

> I am no orator, as Brutus is;
> But, as you know me all, a plain blunt man,
> That love my friend; and that they know full well
> That gave me public leave to speak of him.
> For I have neither wit, nor words, nor worth,
> Action, nor utterance, nor the power of speech,
> To stir men's blood: I only speak right on.[30]

Mark Antony's placing of the affected modesty topos near the end of his oration is rather unorthodox, as such protestations of unworthiness are usually reserved for the proem; in the peroration it is more common to find equally insincere expressions of concern lest the reader become satiated or bored with the author's prolixity. Curtius cites as an illustration Milton's "Time is our tedious song should here have ending" (*ELLMA*, 83 ff.).

On the subject of the rhetorical organization of literary compositions, Quintilian consistently maintains that the budding orator can scarcely hope to succeed unless his eloquence has first been cultivated by assiduous practice in *writing* (a point all too often overlooked nowadays in the teaching of English). "It is the pen which brings at once the most labour and the most profit. Cicero is fully justified in describing it as the best producer and teacher of eloquence ... We must therefore write as much as possible and with the utmost care ... It is in writing that eloquence has its roots and foundations, it is writing that provides that holy of holies where the wealth of oratory is stored, and whence it is produced to meet the demands of sudden emergencies" (X.iii.1-3). In other words, exercises in written composition are of the utmost value in developing facility in — *inter alia* — extempore speaking. (Cf. also Northrop Frye on the indivisibility of rhetoric and literature, n. 2 above.)

Such then are the basic elements of classical rhetoric as codified during the declining years of the Roman Republic and under the early Empire. With modifications of greater or less importance, this body of doctrine remains at the center of rhetorical theory through-

---

[30] William Shakespeare, *Julius Caesar*, III, ii, 221-227. Note Antony's overt use of rhetorical terminology in ll. 225-227. "Wit nor words" would seem to be an allusion to *inventio,* whereas the phrase "Action, nor utterance, nor the power of speech" comprises *actio* in its various aspects of verbal power and of florid gesture (see above, pp. 26-27).

out the later Imperial period and the Middle Ages. The only aspect of the so-called Second Sophistic (i.e., the rhetoric of the second, third, and fourth centuries) with which we need concern ourselves is the fact that as the epideictic mode attained to unparelleled popularity, and the stylistic considerations of *elocutio* gradually encroached upon the previously unchallenged primacy of *inventio*, the techniques of description grew ever more complex, more refined, and more formalized.

Description constitutes a rhetorical figure in itself, and one whose terminology is somewhat more confusing than is necessary, owing to the vast proliferation of Latin and Greek synonyms [31] for the various subdivisions of the figure, i.e., vivid description of an event (*demonstratio*,[32] *illustratio*, *evidentia*, *representatio*, *enargia*), the detailed portrait of a human subject (*effictio*)[33] and the "separable decorative description, usually of a stock subject" (*ecphrasis*).[34] Ecphrasis is then systematically broken down into representations of the seasons, the dawn, etc. (*ecphrasis chronôn, chronographia*),[35] of places (*topographia*), trees (*dendrographia*), water (*hydrographia*), and so on. (For the purposes of this study, I shall so far as possible restrict myself to the basic terms "description" and "portrait.")

---

[31] This tendency towards creating ever-more-subtle distinctions in rhetorical terminology never did cease, so that by the sixteenth century a student might well be confronted with such a catalogue as, e.g. (under the generic term *metaplasm*), *Prosthesis, Aphaeresis, Epenthesis, Syncope, Paragoge, Apocope, Systole, Diastole, Ellipsis, Synaloepha, Synaeresis, Diaeresis, Antisthecon, Metathesis* (v. Richard A. Lanham, *A Handlist of Rhetorical Terms* [Berkeley and Los Angeles, 1969], 66); or at least with *Mycterismus, Subsannatio, Fleering Frumpe* — the final pleasingly vigorous term being the brainchild of George Puttenham in his *Arte of English Poesie* of 1589 (cited in Lanham, 52).

[32] "Demonstratio est cum ita verbis res exprimitur ut geri negotium et res ante oculos esse videatur" (*Ad Herenn.* IV. 1v.68). Cf. John of Garland, *Exempla honestae vitae*, ed. Edwin Habel, in *Romanische Forschungen* 29 (1910-1911), 152, 1. 260: "Demonstratio est rerum gestarum narratio cum circumstantiis suis."

[33] See *Ad Herenn.*, IV.xlix.63.

[34] Charles S. Baldwin, *Medieval Rhetoric and Poetic (to 1400) Interpreted from Representative Works* (Gloucester, Mass., 1959 [1928]). He continues: "The orator turns on, as it were, a storm, a feast, the prospect of a city. The essentially artificial character of the ecphrasis is obvious in the favorite exercise of word-painting a peacock" (17-18). (Cited hereafter as *MRP*.)

[35] See, e.g., Jean Lemaire's "Annotation de la saison Estiuale" (I, 184); also his evocation of "froidure hyuernalle" (I, 193-194). (Unless otherwise identified, all passages cited from Lemaire are taken from *Les Œuvres* edited by Stecher, cited n. 10 above.)

In the Imperial period, description was highly esteemed as an indispensable means of developing the powers of graphic presentation. "It is a great gift to be able to set forth the facts on which we are speaking clearly and vividly. For oratory fails of its full effect, and does not assert itself as it should, if its appeal is merely to the hearing." Thus Quintilian (VIII.iii.62), who insists on the necessity of not merely narrating the facts of the case, but of displaying them "in their living truth to the eyes of the mind." Naturally, he is concerned with the spoken word of judicial oratory rather than the written word of literature, but given the immense prestige and influence enjoyed by the epideictic mode in the literary sphere, the rhetoricians of the later Empire continued greatly to elaborate the theory of description. Aphthonius, for example, who flourished at the turn of the fourth and fifth centuries A.D., devotes the twelfth chapter of his *Progymnasmata,* or Prefatory Exercises, to this subject alone: "One must describe persons and things, times and places, dumb animals and, in addition, plants; persons, as Homer describes . . .; things, like battles on land and sea, just as the historian describes them; times, like spring and summer, in recounting as many kinds of flowers as come forth from them; [36] places, as Thucydides himself speaks of Chimerium . . . in telling exactly what shape it has. And it is necessary for those who describe persons to go from the first elements to the last, that is to say, from head to foot; . . . in describing times and places, from those surrounding and those within them." [37] After distinguishing between "simple" and "compound" descriptions, Aphthonius recommends adorning the representation with different figures of speech. His *Progymnasmata* were destined to be exceedingly influential in European educational theory of the sixteenth and seventeenth centuries (even more so than those of his predecessor Hermogenes of Tarsus), thanks to his practice of appending model themes to each topic discussed. Now the earliest known Latin translation of Aphthonius is dated 1507 at Bologna, [38] but, as Curtius informs us, the

---

[36] Cf. Jean Lemaire's enumerations of birds, beasts, trees, plants, fruits, etc. (I, 135, 154, 158, 159, 174, 201, 202, 215, 253, and *passim*).

[37] *Progymnasmata,* trans. Roy Nadeau, in *Speech Monographs* 19 (1952), 264-285; this citation p. 279.

[38] See D. L. Clark, "The Rise and Fall of Progymnasmata in Sixteenth and Seventeenth Century Grammar Schools," in *Speech Monographs* 19 (1952), 259-263.

*Progymnasmata* of Hermogenes (whose doctrine Aphthonius sedulously reproduces) "were translated by the grammarian Priscian under the title *Praeexercitamina* and in this form descended to the Latin Middle Ages."[39] Erich Auerbach believes that the earliest known specimen of verbal portraiture according to the precepts of the *Progymnasmata* (i.e., not merely the methodical head-to-foot delineation, but also the *portrait moral*) is that of the Visigothic monarch Theodoric II found in the correspondence of Sidonius Apollinaris (c. 430 - c. 487).[40]

During the Middle Ages, the art of description was — if possible — even more systematized by the authors of the *Arts poétiques* edited by E. Faral. One such theorist, Matthieu de Vendôme, enumerates eleven distinct attributes to be taken into account when describing a person, and the inviolable order to be followed when depicting a garden: first the flowers, then the trees, finally the birds.[41] The stylized garden is, needless to say, of great consequence to medieval and Renaissance literature in the guise of the *locus amoenus* (two of the most celebrated examples being those of *Le Roman de la Rose*, passim; and of Dante's *Purgatorio*, Cantos XXVIII and XXIX of which evoke the Earthly Paradise). The *locus amoenus* descends in unbroken line from the idyllic scenes of classical bucolic poetry and, as Curtius observes, "from the Empire to the sixteenth century, it forms the principal motif of all nature description."[42]

---

[39] *ELLMA*, 159. Clark ("Rise and Fall," 260) mentions that Priscian — the *Praeexercitamina* included — went through thirteen editions between 1470 and 1500.

[40] *Epistolae* I.ii (to Agricola). Auerbach, *Literary Language and Its Public in Late Latin Antiquity and in the Middle Ages*, trans. Ralph Manheim (London, 1965 [1958]), 197. (Cited hereafter as *LLP*.)

[41] In Edmond Faral, *Les Arts Poétiques du XII<sup>e</sup> et du XIII<sup>e</sup> siècle* (Paris, 1923), 77-78, 81-82. (Cited hereafter as *AP*.)

[42] *ELLMA*, 195. In his chap. 10 ("The Ideal Landscape"), Curtius shows how rules for description originated on the one hand in the inventional topics of forensic oratory, which is largely concerned with finding arguments to answer the questions Why? Where? When? How? The question Where? for instance, necessitates an *argumentum a loco*, whose function it is to discover "proofs in the character of the place where the matter in question occurred. Was it mountainous or level? by the sea or inland? cultivated? frequented? lonely?" etc. (193-194). Similarly there are *argumenta a persona* and *a tempore*, and, owing to a "blurring and mingling of the several oratorical genres" in late antiquity, they turn up again in medieval poetics. On the other hand,

Closely akin to the question of descriptive techniques is the famous Horatian dictum *ut pictura poesis*.[43] It is notorious that, until the publication in 1766 of G. E. Lessing's aesthetic study *Laokoon,* most scholars had from the early sixteenth century on unquestioningly assumed *ut pictura poesis* to affirm that, as Plutarch puts it, "poetry is vocal painting, and painting, silent poetry."[44] The responsibility for the propagation of this essentially false analogy is not to be laid at Horace's door, however, as D. L. Clark (*RPR,* 22) remarks when he claims that later critics, by taking the phrase out of context, completely — and predictably — missed the point of Horace's statement. This is concerned with but one aspect of the similarity between a picture and a poem, namely, that "one strikes your fancy more, the nearer you stand; another, the farther away."[45]

Medieval theory of rhetoric is to a very high degree preoccupied with two areas which could well strike the modern reader as not being particularly rhetorical at all, namely, on the one hand the new epistolary art (*dictamen, ars dictaminis*) engendered by the needs of the chanceries, and, on the other, poetics (i.e., in the domain of medieval *Latin,* not vernacular, poetry). But before these matters are considered, a word must be said on the subject of the sermon,

---

Curtius says (194), "the description of landscape could also start from the rules of *inventio* for epideictic oratory... Among things that can be praised, places form one category. They can be praised for their beauty, for their fertility, for their healthfulness..." Geoffrey of Monmouth's twelfth-century *Historia Regum Britanniae* (I, ii) contains a charming illustration of the *locus amoenus* in the form of a eulogy of Britain, "best of islands."

[43] Horace, *Ars Poetica,* trans. H. Rushton Fairclough (Cambridge, Mass., and London, 1961 [1926]), Loeb Classical Library, 1. 361.

[44] *De audiendis poetis III,* quoted in D. L. Clark, *RPR,* 20.

[45] The complete text is "Ut pictura poesis: erit quae, si propius stes, / te capiat magis, et quaedam, si longius abstes." For a suggestive account of the considerable influence exerted by rhetorical theory on the history of art in the Quattrocento, see John R. Spencer's "Ut Rhetorica Pictura" (in *Journal of the Warburg and Courtauld Institutes* 20 [1957], 26-44), which examines Leon Battista Alberti's *Della pittura* of 1436. Spencer demonstrates that, whereas the erroneous interpretation of *ut pictura poesis* was due in large measure to sixteenth-century art academies, in the fifteenth century humanists "turned rather to Cicero and Quintilian as the source for their theories on the arts of painting and poetry... Alberti's treatise, then, was composed in an ambience that favoured rhetorical rather than poetical bases for all the arts" (*op. cit.* 26).

which was in effect the only formal discourse, as such, known to the period, or at least to its earlier centuries.[46]

The sermon is particularly interesting in that a serious preoccupation with *inventio* in the Middle Ages survives in homiletics alone. (In the medieval *arts poétiques, inventio* had been displaced by an almost obsessive concern with *elocutio* and *dispositio*; in other words, manner had become preeminent at the expense of matter, at least in principle.) Professor Harry Caplan demonstrates the very strong influence of classical rhetoric on the authors of the *Artes praedicandi*, particularly as regards "the inventional use of the *topos* or commonplace, the artistic finding of the right argument communicable to the right audience in the right circumstances, . . ." a principle "admirably suited to the scholastic method and to . . . preaching."[47] Thus to the three classical modes of forensic, deliberative and epideictic oratory, the Middle Ages added a fourth, the sacred. It is, however, noteworthy that the preaching discussed by Caplan and Th. M. Charland differs markedly in one significant respect from the popular — not to say downright earthy — kind so graphically recorded in Étienne Gilson's invaluable essay, "Rabelais franciscain."[48] The authors of the *Artes* almost without exception have in mind "la composition du sermon savant, à prononcer devant

---

[46] An enlightening discussion of these three most characteristically medieval branches of rhetoric may be found in Murphy's *RMA*, comprising a detailed outline of the ways in which theorists made "pragmatic adaptations of ancient materials to shape special genres for their own purposes" (362). Murphy's edition of *Three Medieval Rhetorical Arts* (Berkeley, 1971) provides one example of each class: epistolary, poetic, and preaching. Reflecting the relative absence of oratory proper in the Middle Ages, Charles Homer Haskins has drawn attention to the curious fact that the word which formerly denoted an address of the most public kind, *oratio*, "came ordinarily to mean the most private sort of discourse, the prayer of man to his Maker" (*The Renaissance of the Twelfth Century* [Cleveland and New York, 1967 (1927)], 138). For a comprehensive study of medieval homiletics, see *Artes Praedicandi* (Paris and Ottawa, 1936), by Th. M. Charland, O.P., who includes a *catalogue raisonné* of the principal treatises, examines the theory of preaching and analyzes its application in two fourteenth-century *Artes*, representing respectively the schools of Paris and of Oxford, the *Forma praedicandi* of Robert de Basevorn and the *De modo componendi sermones* of Thomas Waleys.

[47] From "Classical Rhetoric and the Mediaeval Theory of Preaching," in *Classical Philology* 28 (1933), 73-96; this reference p. 86. This does not mean that *elocutio* and *dispositio* were neglected in the art of the sermon, as Caplan later makes abundantly clear (p. 91).

[48] In *Les Idées et les lettres* (Paris, 1955 [1931]), 197-241.

l'Université; ce n'est qu'incidemment qu'ils parlent du sermon au peuple." [49]

What the *ars praedicandi* was to the spiritual life of the Middle Ages, the *ars dictaminis* was to the temporal. It too is squarely based upon the arts of persuasion. *Pronuntiatio* and *memoria* are plainly irrelevant to letter-writing, but the three remaining qualitative parts of rhetoric are just as plainly essential to the art; and as for the five divisions of discourse, all were appropriated to *dictamen* with little alteration. The exordium is now subdivided into the *salutatio,* or greeting, and the exordium proper, by means of which the writer hopes to ingratiate himself with the intended recipient (hence the term *captatio benevolentiae*). *Narratio* remains unchanged, then comes *petitio* (the request, the very heart of the letter), and finally *conclusio*. The *salutatio* in particular is the beneficiary of endlessly infinitesimal distinctions, as, with characteristic medieval insistence on the hierarchical scheme of things, the *dictatores* instruct their disciples in the correct mode of addressing a Pope, an Emperor, an Archbishop, a Duke, a Master of Arts, etc. [50]

In the domain of poetry, things were not quite so cut and dried. To begin with, ever since the earliest period of classical antiquity there had been much interaction between poetics and rhetoric, the distinctions between them often becoming either very blurred or simply nonexistent. In *Gorgias,* Plato has Socrates say: "If we strip any kind of poetry of its melody, its rhythm and its metre, we get mere speeches as the residue, do we not?" (502C). Cicero's celebrated comparison of poet and orator — with just a hint of condescension toward the former — cannot be ignored: "The truth is that the poet is a very near kinsman of the orator, rather more heavily fettered as regards rhythm, but with ampler freedom in his choice of words, while in the use of many sorts of ornament he is

---

[49] Charland, 110.

[50] See, e.g., the twelfth-century *Ars dictandi Aurelianensis* ascribed to Raoul de Tours (in Ludwig Rockinger's *Briefsteller und Formelbücher* [New York, 1961 (1863-64)], I, 103-114), with its "Salutaciones pape ad seculares personas," "Salutaciones ecclesiasticarum personarum ad papam," "Archiepiscopus ad castellanum," etc. And cf. John of Garland's *Poetria* (c. 1270), which includes a section on the *ars dictandi* (pp. 58 ff.), complete with specimen letters (page references are to *The* Parisiana Poetria *of John of Garland,* ed. Traugott Lawler [New Haven and London, 1974]). There is even, John tells his readers (58), an *Ars Inueniendi Litteras sine Salutatione!*

his ally and almost his counterpart."[51] Quintilian, on the other hand, sternly warns his students not to be a party to the popular misconception that "in composing speeches we should imitate the poets and historians, and in writing history or poetry should copy orators and declaimers. Each branch of literature has its own laws and its own appropriate character" (X.ii.21-22). Yet at the same time, *De institutione oratoria* contains countless examples from the poets, which are then used by Quintilian to make valuable observations in the field of rhetoric.[52]

We have noted previously how the epideictic mode became predominant in later antiquity and extended its sphere of influence to include poetry. Rhetorical theory, as described by Baldwin (*MRP*, chap. I), was reduced by and large to a concern with style for its own sake. Already, classical treatises on rhetoric had been virtually unanimous in giving over a major portion of their space to stylistic matters, and in the Middle Ages style was to be the exclusive preoccupation of the theorists, with the emphasis now on literary, rather than on oral, science.[53] Here originates the medieval notion

---

[51] *De oratore*, trans. E. W. Sutton and H. Rackham (Cambridge, Mass., and London, 1959 [1942]), Loeb Classical Library, I.xvi.70. Cf. Joachim Du Bellay, *La Deffence et Illustration de la Langue Françoyse*, ed. Henri Chamard (Paris, 1966 [1948]), I.xii: "Il est tens de clore ce pas, afin de toucher particulierement les principaux poinctz de l'amplification & ornement de notre Langue. En quoy (Lecteur) ne t'ebahis, si je ne parle de l'orateur comme du poëte. Car outre que les vertuz de l'un sont pour la plus grand' part communes à l'autre [etc.] . . ."

[52] Erich Auerbach notes that the rhetoricization of Latin poetry was halted for a while by the "first generation of Augustan poets, among whom Virgil and Horace were the most prominent . . . This antirhetorical reaction was far from radical . . . Nevertheless Virgil and his contemporaries preferred the great literature of the earlier Greeks to the highly rhetorical Hellenistic works, and he himself wrote the only Latin epic with a lofty style in which rhetoric does not play a preponderant part. The reaction was brief; despite his wonderful gift for form, Ovid allowed himself to be beguiled by rhetorical devices and tricks . . . Seneca in tragedy, Statius in the epic, and the short-lived Lucan created a kind of rhetorical sublimity" (*LLP*, 193).

[53] Cf. Brunetto Latini, *Li Livres dou Tresor*, ed. Francis J. Carmody (Berkeley, 1948), III.iv.1-4. Latini, whose rhetorical theory is broadly based on the *De inventione* (see Faral, *AP*, 49), is concerned simultaneously with oratory proper and the *ars dictaminis*, but recognizes that the principles involved are common to both: "Or dist li mestres que la science de rectorique est en .ii. manieres, une ki est en disant de bouche et une autre que l'om mande *par letres*; mais li enseignement sont commun, car il ne puet chaloir que l'on die un conte ou que on le mande par letres" (ital. in original). More important for

that rhetoric consists uniquely in the ornate embellishment, the gilt overlay, the "colors" or "flowers" which the writer as it were grafts on to his subject matter.[54] Rhetorical decoration is especially called for if the matter is in itself unpleasant or forbidding or if, on the other hand, it lacks weight or is simply too short. Brunetto Latini, analyzing a speech of Julius Caesar's to the Senate, shows how Caesar makes the most of a weak case by bedecking his exordium in a florid style so as to win the good will of his audience (*Li Livres dou Tresor,* III.xxxvi.5-8): "... Julle Cesar ... se torna ... as moz dorés, por ce ke sa matire estoit contraire, car il savoit bien ke li cuer des oïeurs estoient commeu contre sa entention, et por ce li covient il aquerre la lor bienweillance [in other words, an adroit use of *captatio benevolentiae*]." When the matter is "briés et legiere, tu le dois eslongier briefment et aorner avenablement... Car matire est samblable a la cire, ki se laisse mener et apeticier et croistre a la volenté du mestre" (III.xii.7-13), a passage which proves that for Brunetto at least, embellishment and amplification are one and the same. Of great interest are two other strikingly concrete images used in the *Tresor,* where Brunetto teaches that, whether in prose or in poetry, language must be "replain de jus et de sanc, c'est a dire de sens et de sentence," and insists that it be free of "laidures nules, mais la bele coulour soit dedens ou dehors, et la science *de rectorique soit en toi peinturiere* ki mete la coulour en risme et en prose" (III.x.17-25; italics in original).

Yet despite Brunetto's eloquent plea for "sens et sentence," by far the greater part of medieval literary theory has to do with style rather than content. This is as true of the *Arts poétiques* of, e.g., Matthieu de Vendôme, Geoffroi de Vinsauf, and John of Garland

---

our purposes is another passage, in which Latini strikes a familiar note by declaring that the precepts of rhetoric are common to both prose and poetry, "sauve ce que la voie de prose est large et pleniere ... mais li sentiers de risme est plus estrois et plus fors" (III.x.1-5).

[54] Cf. the famous allegorical figure of Rhetoric (much admired and imitated in the Middle Ages) in the fifth book of Martianus Capella's *De Nuptiis Philologiae et Mercurii* (para. 426): "... lo! a form of celestial beauty and more than regal bearing, with shining countenance of womanly splendor, advances on her way, her head and helmet's crest wreathed in royal majesty. In her hand she bears her weapons ... they shine refulgent in the light. Beneath her armor she wears a robe, girt about her shoulders in the Latin way; broidered with many a painting in the rainbow's varied hues, her breast begemmed with many an exquisite jewel."

as it is of the third book of Brunetto's own *Livres dou Tresor* (on Rhetoric), wherein the author's overriding concern is not literary at all, but overtly political. Thus it is no surprise to learn that the *Arts poétiques* are above all handbooks dealing with such topics as the several ways of beginning and ending a work, descriptive techniques and amplificatory devices, *ornatus,* and colors of rhetoric in general.

Faral enumerates the methods of amplification commonly approved by medieval rhetoricians (*AP,* 62-63) as *interpretatio* and *expolitio,* periphrasis, comparison, apostrophe, prosopopoeia, digression, description, *oppositum*. He remarks earlier (p. 61) on a significant shift in emphasis away from the strictly classical meaning of the term *amplificatio*. "Par 'amplifier,' les anciens entendaient 'rehausser (une idée), la faire valoir'.... Mais les théoriciens du XII$^e$ et du XIII$^e$ siècle entendent par là 'développer, allonger (un sujet).'" C. S. Lewis puts his finger squarely on this lop-sided approach to *amplificatio* when he writes, with regard to the influential Geoffroi de Vinsauf: "On *Amplificatio* he is almost embarrassing. He calls the various methods of 'amplifying' your piece, quite frankly, *morae* (delays); as if the art of literature consisted in learning how to say much when you have little to say."[55] And if the poet's major function is to amplify, the chief goal of medieval poetry, according to Faral, is description. "Il est visible que Matthieu [de Vendôme] considère la description comme l'objet suprême de la poésie" (*AP,* 75).

Another facet of classical rhetoric destined to be rather drastically modified was the doctrine of the three levels of style. Whereas

---

[55] *The Discarded Image* (Cambridge, England, 1967 [1964]), 192. Revealingly enough, Brunetto Latini entitles the thirteenth chapter of Book III (*Tresor,* 330): "Comment on puet acroistre son conte en .VIII. manieres." Brian Vickers, *Classical Rhetoric in English Poetry* (London, 1970), emphasizes the *creative* aspect of amplification, noting that "when in the Preface to *Bérénice* Racine writes that 'toute l'invention consiste à faire quelque chose de rien' he is testifying to the power of amplification" (79-80). And, enlightening as always in his presentation of the problem, C. S. Baldwin (*ARP,* 55) adduces as a "brilliant instance of what the ancients meant by amplification" Cicero's entire section on style in the third book of *De oratore*. "Cicero is an admirable example," Baldwin continues, "of his own definition of the eloquent as those 'who speak with clear distinctions, lucid order, amplitude, brilliance of matter and manner, and in prose weave something of the spell of verse — in a word, who enhance.'"

for the ancients the distinction between them was a purely aesthetic matter, the Middle Ages transformed it into an affair of social standing, of rank in the feudal hierarchy — "interprétation nouvelle et maladroite," in Faral's words (*AP*, 88). The misunderstanding appears to have its origins in ancient commentaries on Virgil, which treated his *Eclogues, Georgics,* and *Aeneid* as illustrations, respectively, of the simple, middle, and sublime styles. This basic notion reappears in the Middle Ages in the guise of a formalized device known as the *Rota Virgilii,*[56] which prescribes for each of the three styles a corresponding social condition, proper name, animal, domicile, plant, etc. For example, the appropriate categories under the heading of the *gravis stilus* are: warrior, Hector, horse, city or camp, laurel, and so on.[57]

The medieval *Arts poétiques* are followed in fourteenth- and fifteenth-century France by the equally technical manuals of *seconde rhétorique* (what we now think of as rhetoric and poetry being designated as "first" and "second rhetoric"). Beginning with Eustache Deschamps's *Art de dictier et de fere chançons, balades, virelais et rondeaulx* of 1392, the *Arts de Seconde Rhétorique* flourish and multiply in France. The best-known, and in many respects the most authoritative and original one[58] — certainly the most complete and best organized — is Jean Molinet's *Art de Rhétorique vulgaire* of 1493. The series closes with Pierre Fabri's *Grant et vray art de pleine Rhétorique,* first published in 1521. Fabri might be called the Quintilian, or perhaps the Boileau, of the rhétoriqueur theorists, since in his work (which is called "pleine" because it comprises both a First and a Second Rhetoric) the entire tradition is comprehensively summed up at the very moment of its first waning.

---

[56] See, e.g., John of Garland's *Poetria,* pp. 38 ff.

[57] Auerbach, *LLP,* 199, maintains that in the Middle Ages "the classical conception of grand, sublime, impassioned style which rhetoric serves as a mere handmaiden was lost. All the theoretical statements of the period show that elevation of style was equated with wealth of ornament. Through the inbreeding of the schools, the lofty style degenerated irrevocably into mannerism." Not until the early fourteenth century, with the *stilus tragicus* of the *dolce stil nuovo,* was the sublime style reborn (*LLP,* 220).

[58] According to Ernest Langlois, *Recueil d'arts de seconde rhétorique* (Paris, 1902), lxv, and Pierre Champion, *Histoire poétique du XV*ᵉ *siècle* (Paris, 1923), II, 440.

These treatises — which are by no means to be confused with the far more thoroughgoing *Arts poétiques* of the later sixteenth century — are entirely taken up with metrical and rhythmical problems. It has been suggested (Langlois, vi-vii) that they were originally intended as handbooks for candidates planning to enter poems in the *puys,* or poetic contests, most of which had highly specialized local rules. Alternatively, Langlois conjectures that since poetry had by the late fourteenth century become a fashionable pastime among the nobility, it is not unreasonable to imagine (in view of the extremely complicated poetic techniques of the day) a budding amateur soliciting the aid of an established professional. He points out (p. vii) that both Eustache Deschamps and Jean Molinet claim in their prefaces to be writing at the behest of some unidentified but noble patron. However, such protestations are patently associated with the affected modesty formula, and may therefore be discounted.

As for the terminological problem — i.e., why should poetry be called "rhetoric" in the first place? — it has already been observed that distinctions between the two disciplines tended to become blurred even in classical antiquity, and that, with the triumph of style over substance, the medieval Latin poetics was committed to a rhetoricized existence. Richard McKeon tells us that "the art of poetry came to be considered after the twelfth century... a kind of argumentation or persuasion,"[59] and J. E. Spingarn quotes Petrarch's memorable definition of the poet's prime function as being: "veritatem rerum pulchris velaminibus adornare."[60] The edifying subject matter (or *doctrina*) was thus to be adorned — even "veiled" — by a beautiful style (*eloquentia*), an obvious echo of Horace's *utile* and *dulce.*

Medieval confusion over the respective roles of poetry and rhetoric was in fact more apparent in theory than in practice, as may be deduced from the quantity of beautiful poetry — particularly vernacular poetry — composed during the Middle Ages. But one

---

[59] "Rhetoric in the Middle Ages," *Speculum* 17 (1942), 1-32; this citation, p. 28. Similarly, Castor points out that as late as 1587, the Preface to Ronsard's *Franciade* was still referring to "argumens tous nouveaux," and remarks that "the twentieth-century reader might expect that it was primarily the orator's rather than the poet's business to find out persuasive arguments to convince an audience" (*Pléiade Poetics,* 21).

[60] Joel E. Spingarn, *A History of Literary Criticism in the Renaissance* (New York, 1963 [1899]), 7.

most salient feature of this theoretical vagueness is the absence of any single term to denote "poetry," or, if it comes to that, "poet." Dante, as Curtius notes (*ELLMA,* 145), calls his treatise on vernacular poetry *De vulgari eloquentia,* and Sir John Sandys credits Nicolas Oresme (d. 1382) with the introduction into French of — among other Hellenisms — "poète" and "poème."[61] However, in the early sixteenth century the terms "rimeur" and "facteur" (cf. the contemporary English "rymer" and "maker") were still flourishing — as were "dit," "dictier," etc. — and "rhétoriqueur" was a proud title.

Much of the opprobrium heaped on the Grands Rhétoriqueurs by the young polemicists of the mid-sixteenth century (aside from the quite natural desire of a rising generation to assert itself at the expense of its predecessors) was doubtless due quite as much to their professed doctrine as to their actual practice. The rhétoriqueurs did not embrace the classical genres, the ode, eclogue, epic, tragedy, etc.; they called poetry "rhetoric" and the divinely inspired poet a "rhymer." Worst of all, of the three fundamental prerequisites for success in any literary discipline — nature, art, and exercise — the rhétoriqueurs completely ignored, or at any rate to their indignant (and ungrateful) successors seemed completely to ignore,

---

[61] *History of Classical Scholarship,* II (Cambridge, England, 1908), 166-167. Littré gives instances of *poete* from the works of two thirteenth-century French authors, Gui de Cambrai and Gautier de Coincy. Johan Huizinga remarks that Christine de Pisan (d. circa 1430) calls a mythologic piece a "balade pouétique" (*The Waning of the Middle Ages* [Garden City, N.Y., 1954 (1924)], 327; cited hereafter as *WMA*). And Langlois cites Christine's contemporary Jacques Legrand (d. circa 1425) as using the term "poetrie," which is, however, by no means equivalent to the modern "poésie." In fact, Legrand explicitly defines "poetrie" as being the "science qui aprent a faindre et a fere ficcions fondées en raison et en la semblance des choses desquelles on veult parler, et est ceste science moult necessaire a ceulx qui veulent beau parler, et pour tant poetrie, a mon advis, *est subalterne de rethorique.... poetrie aussi ne monstre point la science de versifier,* car telle science appartient en partie a grammaire et en partie a rethoricque..." (Langlois, *ASR,* viii-ix). Langlois notes that a "poétrie isolée" (i.e., a work published as a separate entity) would nowadays be termed "un traité du mythologie" (*ibid.,* x). W. F. Patterson prefers "a compendium of classical and Biblical tales suitable for riming" (*Three Centuries of French Poetic Theory* [Ann Arbor, Mich., 1935], cited hereafter as *FPT*), I, 127; C. S. Baldwin, "the study of style, and specifically the study of stylistic decoration" (*MRP,* 195). Cf. also Jean Frappier's Introduction to his edition of Jean Lemaire de Belges's *La Concorde des deux langages* (Paris, 1947; cited hereafter as *Concorde*), xlii, n. 3, pointing out Lemaire's early use of "poésie."

the first, utterly indispensable one.⁶² Jean Molinet, it is true, seems for a moment to be touching on "nature" when, in the preamble to his *Art de Rhétorique,* he assures his aristocratic patron that the latter is already so richly endowed that he has no need of instruction. "Que prouffiteront dont [sic] mes rymes emprèz vostre vive eloquence?" (Langlois, 215). But this is plainly the merest conventional claptrap, the obligatory obeisance complacently expected as his due by a social superior from the (falsely) humble man of letters, well versed in the niceties of the modesty topos. (It also irresistibly reminds one of Mascarille's "Les gens de qualité savent tout sans avoir jamais rien appris" [*Les Précieuses ridicules,* ix].) Molinet's treatise is otherwise completely preoccupied with "art," which, in view of the contemporary taste for poetic virtuosity, comes as no surprise.⁶³

In striking contrast to the plethora of manuals of "second rhetoric" composed during the last quarter of the fifteenth century is the relative paucity of contemporary treatises on rhetoric proper, or "prose" rhetoric. We are obliged (and I think for good reason) to assume that the major sources for rhetorical doctrine during this period remained — as they had been for centuries — the pseudo-Ciceronian *Rhetorica ad Herennium* and Cicero's *De Inventione,* known respectively as the *Rhetorica nova* (or *secunda, posterior*) and *Rhetorica vetus* (or *prima, prior*) of Cicero (see n. 21, above). Of all the Arts of Rhetoric produced in antiquity, these are the only two to survive intact throughout the Middle Ages. Dorothy E. Grosser has plausibly demonstrated their almost universal diffusion in medieval Europe, and their incalculable usefulness to, *inter alios,* the authors of the twelfth-century *arts poétiques,* who were particularly indebted to the *Ad Herennium* for their discussion

---

⁶² *Natura, ars, exercitatio:* "nature" is natural endowment, "art" what Castor (42) defines as "the rationalisation and codification of successful practice," and "exercise" systematic and assiduous practice.

⁶³ Eustache Deschamps comes closer to "nature" when he discusses the two musics, *musique artificiele* — i.e., music as we understand it — and *musique naturele,* or poetry (*Art de dictier,* in Vol. VII of *Œuvres complètes,* ed. Gaston Reynaud [Paris, 1891], 266-292; this citation 269 ff.). As Deschamps sees it, music can be taught by the rules of art, whereas poetry is "naturele," "pour ce qu'elle ne puet estre aprinse a nul, se son propre couraige naturelment ne s'i applique."

of the *colores* (and of *elocutio* in general).⁶⁴ Similarly, Murphy remarks (*RMA*, 112-113) that only Cicero, of the ancient rhetorical authorities, was accorded the honor of being translated into the vernacular during the Middle Ages, and that mainly in the thirteenth century, for example by Brunetto Latini. "Cicero," Murphy writes, "was so assumptively, so overwhelmingly, so pervasively regarded as prime *auctor,* that on this ground alone we could conclude that his works must have had enormous circulation and use" (*RMA*, 108).

The first printed edition of both *De Inventione* and *Ad Herennium* was that of 1470 at Venice. *Ad Herennium* was the first book to be printed at Angers in 1476, and Professor Harry Caplan notes⁶⁵ that at least twenty-eight editions appeared during the next thirty years. In addition to these two treatises, Cicero's major rhetorical works, *De oratore* and *Orator,* reappeared during the fifteenth century: *De oratore,* published at Subiaco (c. 1465) was the first book ever printed in Italy. *Orator* (and *Brutus*) followed in 1469.

The same period saw the reemergence of Aristotle's *Rhetoric*. Though this work had been translated into Latin as early as the last quarter of the thirteenth century by St. Thomas Aquinas's associate William of Moerbeke (d. 1286), the first translations of reasonably wide availability were those of Francesco Filelfo (1430) and the famous version made by the Greek scholar George of Trebizond (Trapezuntius), which R. R. Bolgar⁶⁶ believes to have been published between 1447 and 1455. The first Greek edition was the Aldine of 1508 (in *Rhetores Graeci,* which includes the *Poetics*). Giorgio Valla's Latin translation of the *Poetics* appeared in 1498, although the commentary of Averroës was widely diffused before this.

---

⁶⁴ "Studies in the Influence of the *Rhetorica ad Herennium* and Cicero's *De inventione*" (unpubl. Ph.D. dissertation, Cornell, 1953), 293. Cf. Faral, *AP,* 49: "Avec le *De inventione,* à la suite duquel elle est souvent copiée dans les manuscrits, [la *Rhétorique à Herennius*] constituait le manuel fondamental de l'art d'écrire."

⁶⁵ In his edition and translation of the *Ad Herennium* (cited n. 21 above), p. xxxvii.

⁶⁶ *The Classical Heritage and Its Beneficiaries* (New York, 1964 [1954]), 434.

Quintilian, familiar to the Middle Ages only through excerpts and paraphrase, was also rejuvenated in the fifteenth century. The *De institutione oratoria,* rediscovered in unabridged form by Poggio Bracciolini in 1416, was published in 1470 and went through many editions thereafter.[67]

These texts, embodying the chief doctrines of classical rhetoric, are, then, all known to have been available during the last quarter of the century. The situation with regard to contemporary works of rhetorical theory is, unfortunately, much less clear. If there were in fact *Rhetorics* composed in the vernacular at this time, which is by no means certain, their existence and identity remain unknown. It is also problematic which basic texts were used in the teaching of rhetoric during this period, since in the present state of the history of rhetorical studies in France, the latter part of the fifteenth century seems to have been curiously neglected (although there is no dearth of scholarly works dealing with the period from the high Middle Ages through the fourteenth century, on the one hand, and with the sixteenth century, on the other).[68] Lacking detailed knowledge of university arts programs of the period, we are confronted with scattered, tantalizing fragments of information. Charles Thurot, for instance, tells us that Guillaume Fichet "enseigna la rhétorique dans le collège de Sorbonne" (c. 1470), and that his pupil and successor, Robert Gaguin, "donna des leçons de rhétorique dans son couvent, et encouragea de tout son pouvoir à l'étude des belles-

---

[67] Harold F. Harding says that from 1470 to 1600 "there were no fewer than 118 editions... issued in Italy, France, Switzerland, Belgium, Holland, and Germany" ("Quintilian's Witnesses," in *Historical Studies of Rhetoric and Rhetoricians,* ed. Raymond F. Howes [Ithaca, N.Y., 1961], 90-106; this citation, 92). Nicolas E. Lemaire's bibliography (in his edition of Quintilian's *Opera* [Paris, 1825], VII, 277 ff.), from which Harding derives his information, lists, by my count, 11 editions (mostly Italian) of the *Institutes* between the *princeps* of 1470 and the year 1506. I will not go into the complex problem of the survival in the Middle Ages of mutilated versions of the work, the transmission of the Quintilianic doctrine through the so-called *Flores Quintilianei,* the rhetorical sections of St. Isidore's *Etymologiae,* the *Speculum maius* of Vincent de Beauvais, and the *Libri III Artis Rhetoricae* of Chirius Fortunatianus. For a valuable survey of this question, see Priscilla S. Boskoff, "Quintilian in the Late Middle Ages," in *Speculum* 27 (1952), 71-78; cf. also Paul Abelson, *The Seven Liberal Arts* (New York, 1906), 54-59.

[68] For the earlier period, see, e.g., Murphy, *RMA,* 89 ff. Murphy later points out (359), apropos of the fifteenth century, that "there is as yet no reliable general history of rhetoric in Western Europe during this period."

lettres."[69] Stephen d'Irsay reminds us that this same Guillaume Fichet, with his colleague Jean Heynlin, set up the first printing press in Paris, at the Sorbonne, and, more significantly, that one of the earliest works to come from their press was a *Rhétorique* (in Latin), "livre de propagande pour le programme d'études conçu par les humanistes, abrégé d'un cours professé par Fichet à l'Université."[70] The first page of Fichet's treatise, referring to "Marcus Tullius, latini pater eloquii," supports the thesis that rhetorical instruction of the period continued to be based primarily on Cicero. On the whole, however, the assertion that the rhetorical curriculum was palpably founded upon classical models must rest on indirect evidence. As W. H. Woodward aptly observes: "The humanist reproduced Quintilian, or Cicero, or Plutarch, without concealment. Where there was no pretence there was no plagiarism. It was not necessary to mention Quintilian; he was to every humanist a free quarry, and every scholar recognised the rock from which each new building was hewn."[71] In the same way, I hope to demonstrate in the following chapters Lemaire's easy familiarity with the precepts and theory of classical rhetorical tradition as evinced in his own writings, even when it is not possible to show conclusively that he had actually read a particular rhetorical text.

---

[69] *De l'Organisation de l'enseignement de l'Université de Paris, au Moyen-Age* (Frankfurt, 1967 [1850]), 83-84.

[70] *Histoire des Universités françaises et étrangères des origines à nos jours. I. Moyen Age et Renaissance* (Paris, 1933), 259-260. Plate XVI of d'Irsay's book is a reproduction of the first and last pages of Fichet's treatise, described as the "premier livre imprimé à la Sorbonne." P. Jodogne differs with this statement (*JLBEFB*, 57) and awards the palm to Barzizza's Latin Grammar as being the first fruits of Fichet and Heynlin's printing endeavors. Barzizza's book actually consisted of a collection of model Ciceronian letters, which James Hutton believes was presumably chosen "as a model for Latin composition, supplying something of the place that Erasmus's *Copia* later filled" (private communication).

[71] *Studies in Education during the Age of the Renaissance, 1400-1600* (New York, 1967 [1906]), 73.

Chapter II

JEAN LEMAIRE: THE TYPE OF THE
RENAISSANCE ORATOR

Jean Lemaire de Belges was born in 1473 and studied, according to his own nostalgic reminiscence in the first book of *Les Illustrations de Gaule*,[1] at Paris; Jodogne calculates that he must have been enrolled there between 1488 and 1492, assuming that he completed all requirements for the master's degree, and that Robert Gaguin may very well have been one of his professors.[2] What rhetorical instruction he received there can only be conjectured. We may assume acquaintance with *Ad Herennium* and *De inventione* as part of the standard intellectual baggage of a person educated at Paris in Lemaire's time; however, these books would probably have been so taken for granted that one would not normally expect to find explicit references to them in contemporary literary productions. This is precisely the case with Lemaire, in whose entire *Œuvres* I have been able to find but two allusions (one apiece) to the treatises in question. Lemaire ends his *Épître à Charles le Clerc* (IV, 323),

---

[1] *Œuvres*, I, 106: "... la tresheureuse Parisienne cité capitale de la couronne de France: mere et maistresse souueraine des estudes de tout le monde, plus que iadis nulles Athenes, ne nulles Rommes. De laquelle iay principalement succé tout le tant (combien que peu) du laict de literature, qui viuifie mon esprit."

[2] *JLBEFB*, 79 and 250. Jodogne mentions the noteworthy fact that, in his *Couronne Margaritique* (see below, Chap. IV), Lemaire "réserve à Robert Gaguin l'honneur du premier discours" (250). Furthermore, the distinguished French humanist was the author of a History of France (*Compendium de origine et gestis Francorum*, published in 1495), which Lemaire constantly cites as a major authority, particularly in *Les Illustrations de Gaule* and *Le Traité des Schismes*. As Jodogne phrases it, "le *Compendium* ne semble pas avoir quitté sa table de travail" (483).

to whom he has been complaining about the envy of those coveting his post as Court Historiographer, with the following words: "Cicero in Rhetoricis: Virtutis, Inuidia Comes." The allusion is to a passage in *Ad Herennium* (IV.xxvi.36) which serves to illustrate the rhetorical figure *correctio* ("O virtutis comes, invidia, quae bonos sequeris plerumque atque adeo insectaris! "). The second reference — albeit an indirect one — occurs in *Les Fragments de Chroniques* (IV, 441) under the heading *Memorialia Indiciaratus,* and is apparently a quotation from Poliziano's *Miscellanea* beginning "Zeuxis heracleutes adprime nobilis helene pinxit ymaginem cretaniatibus [sic] nimisque laudatam de qua Cicero in Rhetorica contra Hermagoram luculentissime scripsit." The famous anecdote of Zeuxis and the portrait of Helen is to be found in *De inventione,* II.i.1-3.[3]

A like assumption may be made in the case of Aristotle, who is mentioned only three times by Lemaire (III, 233, 351, and IV, 109).[4] As the first reference is, gratifyingly enough, to the *Rhetoric* (III.ix.1410a), it is tempting to claim firsthand knowledge of "le Philosophe's" rhetorical teachings on Lemaire's part, though this is by no means certain. Nevertheless, as I shall demonstrate in Chapter V, there is at least one definite indication of Aristotelian influence — direct or indirect — on the author of *Les Illustrations de Gaule.*

Whatever his exposure to specific rhetorical texts, Jean Lemaire's familiarity with the French tradition of rhétorique is indisputable. He was, to begin with, nephew and godson to the foremost rhétoriqueur of the day, Jean Molinet (to whom he specifically refers as "mon *précepteur* et parent"),[5] and it is inconceivable that Lemaire,

---

[3] Jodogne is of the opinion that the sentence may have been jotted down for future citation in *Les Illustrations* (*JLBEFB,* 283-284). However, see Lemaire's reference in *La Couronne Margaritique* (IV, 152).

[4] Lemaire first invokes "lautorité du Philosophe" in connection with the figure Comparison, the contrasting of opposites. In *La Couronne Margaritique,* Boccaccio cites — in Latin — a sentence from a letter written by "le Prince des Philosophes" to Alexander the Great: Sicut conseruamentum corporis est sanitas, ita conseruamentum animae est eruditio (IV, 109).

[5] IV, 522. Cf. "...feu de bonne memoire Monsieur maistre Iean Molinet, mon predecesseur et parent..." (II, 256); "le chief et souverain de tous les orateurs et rhetoriciens de nostre langue gallicane, cest assauoir maistre Jehan Molinet chanoine de la Salle le conte, renommé par tous les quartiers deurope ou lad. langue a lieu" (IV, 521). Molinet's *Art de Rhétorique Vulgaire* (mentioned earlier) is reproduced by Langlois, 214-252.

whose literary gifts must early have been apparent to his uncle, would not have received a thorough grounding in his craft. Moreover, he was, and most emphatically regarded himself as being, a link in the chain of "oratorical" writers that begins with the great Alain Chartier and continues through Chastellain and Molinet to Lemaire.

Alain Chartier (c. 1390-c. 1440),[6] was at the peak of his career in the 1420s, the *Quadrilogue* dating from 1422. Chartier was also an orator in the specialized diplomatic connotation of the time and actually delivered formal orations *viva-voce*.[7] No precise date is known for George Chastellain's birth,[8] but he died in 1475, at which time he was still compiling his monumental *Chroniques*. He was succeeded as historiographer to the court of Burgundy by his pupil Jean Molinet (1435-1507). The latter's own disciple — Jean Lemaire de Belges himself — was in turn commissioned to continue the *Chroniques* immediately after Molinet's death in 1507. In short, then, the four writers follow in one another's footsteps both chronologically and in their literary avocation.[9]

Jean Lemaire loses few opportunities to honor his three illustrious predecessors and, as Jodogne phrases it, "... cite ou imite volontiers Alain Chartier, ... et Georges Chastellain, et tient en très haute estime ses prédécesseurs, 'précepteurs' ou amis... et surtout... Jean Molinet."[10] In his *Epitaphe en maniere de dialogue* (IV, 319-320), Lemaire not only pays equal homage to Molinet and Chastellain, but poses a rhetorical question regarding the former's "precepteur." Could it have been "Greban ou *maistre alain?*" he asks (my ital.). Needless to say, the correct response is promptly

---

[6] E. Droz's edition of *Le Quadrilogue invectif* (cited Chap. I, n. 11) states that "il naquit à Bayeux vers 1385 et mourut en 1433 au plus tard" (p. vi).

[7] P. Champion has an informative account of this, with some interesting details relative to such an official's duties (*HP15*, I, 94). Droz, *op. cit.*, viii, mentions among Chartier's productions for the year 1425 "*Trois discours latins prononcés lors de la mission en Hongrie*."

[8] *The Oxford Companion to French Literature* (Oxford, 1966 [1959]) hesitates between c. 1405 and c. 1415.

[9] Jodogne (*JLBEFB*, 250) reminds us in effect "... que Georges Chastellain fut le maître du maître (Molinet) de Lemaire." Incidentally, Jodogne's entire thesis is aimed at establishing Lemaire's debt to the Franco-Burgundian — as opposed to the *italianisant* — school.

[10] *JLBEFB*, 482. Cf. also *ibid.*, 176: "... il est imprégné avant tout des œuvres de Molinet et de Chastellain."

given: "Son maistre qui cy gist fut Georges chastelain" (IV, 320, ll. 3 and 4).

We will see that in *Le Traité des Schismes et Conciles* Lemaire could find no more appropriate conclusion to his polemic than to reproduce verbatim an entire section of Chartier's *Exil* (see below, Chap. VII, n. 15). "En même temps qu'à l'autorité de Chartier," writes Jodogne (*JLBEFB,* 379), "c'est ... à son audace idéologique et morale, et à son éloquence que Lemaire a recours.... il semble d'autre part vouloir s'inscrire dans la grande tradition française de la littérature politique qui fut précisément ranimée par l'auteur du *Quadrilogue invectif* et, notamment, de *L'exil.*" Again, in his Prologue to *La Concorde des deux langages,* Molinet's nephew is not the least intimidated by the numinous names of the Italian masters he is about to cite as fitting representatives of "le langaige toscan ou florentin." True, Italy may boast of the *tre corone,* "Dante, Petrarque et Bocace"; "la langue françoise," on the other hand, has its own doughty "garantz et deffenseurs ... tant antiques comme modernes, si comme Jehan de Meun, Froissart, *maistre Alain,* Meschinot, *les deux Grebans,* Millet, *Molinet, George Chastelain, Saint Gelais,* et aultres ..." (*Concorde,* Prologue, p. 4, ll. 25-29; my ital.). Chastellain is further distinguished by being one (the fifth) of the Ten Orators of *La Couronne Margaritique.* One could continue at length, but the facts are already sufficient to speak for themselves. Chartier, Chastellain, and Molinet are, in the eyes of Lemaire de Belges, towering and admirable figures, as worthy of imitation as they are of veneration.

We may see that the relationship was more than chronological by turning our attention to the prose itself. Chartier, as Patterson puts it (*FPT* I, 104), "aspired to a prose measured, reverberant, stately, oratorical. Therefore posterity has looked back to him as the French Seneca, the father of classical eloquence." A fair specimen of his "dignified Ciceronian periods"[11] occurs near the beginning of *Le Quadrilogue invectif* (10), where France, devastated and desolate after nearly a century of war with England, rebukes her wayward children and attempts to arouse their ancient valor. The reader cannot, I think, fail to be struck by certain remarkable

---

[11] *FPT,* I, 101. In actual fact, Seneca rather than Cicero was Chartier's "modèle et son dieu" according to Champion (*HP15,* I, 6-7).

similarities between the following sonorous passage and the opening lines of Juno's great *vituperatio* in *Les Illustrations de Gaule* (to be studied in Chapter VI, below).

> O hommes forvoiez du chemin de bonne cognoissance, feminins de couraiges et de meurs, loingtains de vertuz, forlignez de la constance de voz peres, qui pour delicieusement vivre choisissez a mourir sans honneur, quelle musardie ou chetiveté de cuer vous tient les mains ployees et les voulentez amaties que vous bastez [attendre, bailler aux corneilles] en regardant devant voz yeulx vostre commune desertion et musez comme attendans de quelle part versera le faiz de cestui vostre naturel heberge et retrait, lequel vous pourroit tous acraventer [écraser] et enclorre vostre ruyne soubz la sienne?

While neither Chastellain nor Molinet rises to the same stylistic heights as Maitre Alain and — three generations later — Jean Lemaire, both are authentic prose masters, each in his own highly individual manner.

Chastellain's role of chronicler was that of a man of *eloquence* in the service of his ducal patron, a fact well brought out by Champion, who characterizes "le grand Georges" as "un écuyer du verbe, rempli de sentences, vraiment mis au monde pour célébrer la pompe qui l'entourait" (*HP15*, II, 318-319).

The rhetorical aspects of Chastellain's prose are omnipresent in his works. He is much given, for example, to such devices as apostrophe,[12] rhetorical questions,[13] vivid dialogue,[14] and, above all,

---

[12] E.g.: "O vous humains cœurs des François, qui, par successives générations de père en fils, en temps advenir trouverez mes escripts, lorsque la main pourrie en terre reposera soubs divine mercy, si faim vous peut prendre de visiter mes œuvres, et que loisir vous puisse traire à l'advertence d'icelles, ne vueilliez doncques noter tant seulement *le son des paroles* [my ital.], mais les causes et racines qui m'ont mu à les former telles." *Chronique*, Book VI, 14-15, in *Œuvres*, ed. Kervyn de Lettenhove (Brussels, 1863-1866), IV (1864). Cf. also (p. 20): "O jugement de Dieu! ô ineffable providence droiturière! ... O benoîte soit ta gloire et ta majesté excelse, benoîte ta miséricorde et ta justice irrépréhensible et benoît ton nom et ton règne, qui toutes choses fais à poids et à mesure! Et benoît qui te bénit et qui te craint et honnore! ..." and *passim*.

[13] See *Chronique* VI, 12: "Quel exemple en est-il de Luxembourg? Quel patron aussi en avez-vous vu de la réception devers lui de Loys [Louis XI] jà roy présent? Quelle appreuve de maintes vielles et nouvelles matières ruyneuses et aigrement eslevées...?"

lengthy and exceedingly "artificial" speeches, as befits the learned encomiast of Urbanité in *La Couronne Margaritique*. Johan Huizinga, who is heavily indebted to Chastellain as a historical source for his *Waning of the Middle Ages,* nevertheless tends to deprecate his prose style, comparing it unflatteringly to the more mediocre productions of the contemporary visual arts. "In his best moments Chastellain equals [Jan] Van Eyck at his worst.... Let us recall the group of singing angels of the altar-piece of the Lamb. Those heavy dresses of red and gold brocade, loaded with precious stones, those too expressive grimaces, the somewhat puerile decoration of the lectern — all this in painting is the equivalent of the showy Burgundian prose" (*WMA,* 285). Henry Guy is, I think, more judicious when, while admitting that Chastellain's style in the *Chroniques* is "tendu, entravé, tourmenté," he declares that it is, notwithstanding, "une style 'artiste': le lecteur assiste à la lutte d'une pensée robuste contre una langue encore nouée" (*HPF16,* I, 29).

Quite typical of the elaborate and florid eloquence favored by Chastellain is the oration of the disgraced and persecuted Queen of England (Margaret of Anjou, wife of Henry VI). This section of the *Chroniques* (Book VI, chap. 9) bears the authentic and inimitable cachet of the fairy tale. The hapless queen and the young Prince of Wales, her son, are confronted, deep in a forest of evil repute ("repaire de brigans, et dont la fame par pays portoit d'estre impitéables meurdriers couppe-gorges," *Œuvres,* IV, 302), by the nightmarish figure of a brigand, "prest et addoné à faire tout mal." The desperate queen, heedless of her own safety but ready to catch at any straw to save her child, launches into an impassioned and — despite its extremely florid and ornate character — moving oration in the deliberative mode, almost three full pages in length.

---

[14] See, *inter alia,* the lively exchanges between the various protagonists in the passage dealing with the downfall of the overweening upstart Jehan Coustain (*Chronique* VI, Chaps. 76-84), who, when detected *in flagrante delicto,* far from being fearful or repentant, bursts unceremoniously into his noble employer's private chapel ("enflé comme un sanglier devant les chiens," 259) and has the supreme impudence to reply to the latter's just commands as follows: "Voire! ce dit Coustain, lors est-ce tout? Qu'est-ce que j'aurai de mon service? Par la mort! digne beau sire, j'ai bien employé mon temps. Il me vaudroit mieux avoir servi un porchier." To which "le duc, sur son si vilain parler dernier, lui respondit froidement: 'Jehan, Jehan! je t'ay nourri trop gras.'"

Like all successful orators, the queen works upon her audience's emotions and sensibilities, to such good effect that the cruel brigand not only renounces his nefarious intent, but from that moment on, a changed and reformed character, dedicates his life to the defense of the little prince! The speech as it exists is — needless to say — made up out of the whole cloth by the author of the *Chroniques*. He acknowledges as much when, in the opening words of chapter 10, he laconically states: "A tels mots, *ou auques près en substance,* la povre royne arraisonna le brigant..." (my ital.). Such a practice was, however, perfectly respectable to Chastellain's contemporaries (see p. 106, below), and was indeed to be continued by Jean Lemaire de Belges.

Let me conclude this necessarily brief overview of the highly rhetorical quality of Georges Chastellain's style by citing without comment one of his ponderous yet stately periods, taken from this same episode of the Queen and the Brigand. Having quoted with approval the Duchess of Bourbon's apt observation to the effect that the Queen's unhappy fate had earned her a place "au livre des nobles femmes malheureuses, l'outre-passe de toutes" (IV, 307), Chastellain proceeds to justify this opinion:

> Car n'a esté vu jamais, ne ouy que un tel prince et une telle princesse chrestienne, sans avoir esté de vie énorme [i.e., infâme], par quoy provocassent Dieu contre eux, et sans estre entrés en possession de leur royaume par tyrannie et forfait, aient esté si despitement choulés [foulés] aux pieds de fortune, que eux, estans roy et royne de nature [i.e., Henry VI and Margaret of Anjou], vrais hoirs et antiques possesseurs, n'aient conservé pied de terre qui leur soit maison pour eux retraire, sinon d'emprunt, denier noir, ni blanc pour entretènement de leur vie, et non obstant toute expulsion dehors de leur propre, avecques confusion de plusieurs cruelles batailles dépressives, non avoir demouré emprès eux ne foy, ne loyauté de vassal, ne serment, ne hommage, ne quelquonque révérence, ne fidélité de service; et puis, qui plus est, ceste povre royne avoir esté sur le pas de la mort, confuse entre les mains de ses serdaux [serfs], fuyr seule par les champs comme une misérable meschante, estre constrainte, par avis d'un mieux faire, de mettre et laisser son fils en la main d'un brigant meurdrier, lui réquérir sauvement de sa vie, et qui au regret l'eust mis par avant en garde du plus grand de son

sang, l'a commis maintenant e nune main desfiable, toute riche de l'aventure [heureuse de ce hasard]!

(IV, 307-308)

Of the four writers presently under discussion, Jean Molinet is — perhaps it would be fairer to say *was* — generally regarded as the lightweight, as being somehow unworthy both to follow in the footsteps of the illustrious Chastellain and to precede his own pupil and successor, Jean Lemaire. Patterson refers to him as playing "Elisha to Georges Chastellain's Elijah" (*FPT,* I, 133); Georges Doutrepont gives him credit at least for the painstaking use in his *Chroniques* of actual diplomatic documents to which he had access; [15] and Champion disparagingly holds up his "chronique domestique et locale, pleine toutefois d'intérêt et de talent" against the "vrai monument historique" erected by Chastellain, but does concede that Molinet is endowed with a talent for caricature peculiar to Northern Europe, one which he shares with Peter Breughel and Hieronymus Bosch [16] (see above, p. 58, where Chastellain and Jan Van Eyck are compared).

A more recent critic offers a less prejudiced view. Jacques Vier does not balk at discerning in Molinet a genuine precursor of Rabelais: "... même imagination débridée, même puissance de trouvailles et de répétitions, même maîtrise de l'électro-choc verbal. Le *Testament de la Guerre* annonce la geste de Picrochole." [17] Vier, like many contemporary scholars, is, happily, far less inclined to judge the Rhétoriqueurs from the truculently biased perspective of the Pléiade (which, though entirely understandable in the context of

---

[15] *Jean Lemaire de Belges et la Renaissance* (Brussels, 1934), 181.

[16] *HP15*, II, 392, 441. In the same study, Champion cannot resist pointing out what to him appears the almost indecent incongruity of Molinet's sharing Chastellain's tomb, and receiving into the bargain an equal share of adulation in Jean Lemaire's *Epitaphe de Chastelain et de Molinet:* "Ce tombeau, avec les trois noms de Georges Chastellain, de Jean Molinet, de Jean Lemaire de Belges, c'est vraiment un lieu de recueillement pour l'historien des lettres. Car Jean Lemaire, c'est tout l'avenir; et Chastellain, c'est le noble et héraldique passé. Oui, elle semble bien petite la personnalité de Molinet, entre celle du grand Georges et celle de cet homme nouveau, si curieux, Jean Lemaire, qui annonce Ronsard" (439).

[17] *Histoire de la littérature française: XVIe-XVIIe siècles* (Paris, 1959), 17-18.

the sixteenth century, is much to be deplored in critics and literary historians of the twentieth).[18]

"l'*orateur* Molinet..., l'historien qui... veut *démontrer*.... Volontiers il *prononce des discours*, il *apostrophe ses personnages*, il *exalte* ou il *flétrit* leurs actions.... La présentation d'un livre... ne saurait guère être effectuée avec un meilleur lot de phrases *déclamatoires*.... En dehors de ce long et fastueux couplet, que d'autres pages décèlent en notre auteur un tempérament *oratoire!* C'est bien là que se trouve... sa 'faculté maîtresse'" (my ital. throughout). These words are taken from the Introduction to Doutrepont and Jodogne's edition of Molinet's *Chroniques*,[19] and in my opinion most tellingly and succinctly underscore my contention that, just as in the case of Chartier, Chastellain, and Lemaire de Belges, Molinet's prose is essentially *oratorical* in character.[20]

The same is true of his conception of his work. Henry Guy, who plainly considers Molinet to be little more than an amusing hack, remarks: "La partialité lui paraissait le premier de ses devoirs, le fondement de la morale des historiens appointés" (*HPF16*, I, 161). And indeed we read in the alternate Prologue to Molinet's *Chroniques* how Georges Chastellain was dubbed a knight of the Golden Fleece by the Duke of Burgundy, "avecq tiltre de indiciaire, comme celuy qui *demonstroit* par escripture authentique les admirables gestes des chevaliers et confrères de l'Ordre" (II, 594; my ital.). *Demonstroit* is here patently akin to "demonstrative" (or epideictic) as applied to rhetoric; and one of the principal functions of this rhetorical mode is praise (and the reverse of the coin, blame). The

---

[18] Raymond Picard's informative article "Les grands rhétoriqueurs" (in *Tableau de la littérature française*, I [Paris, 1962], 186-195) makes a plausible case, with respect to Molinet's poetry, for a greatly diversified talent, reminiscent respectively of Villon, Baudelaire, and above all of "une fraîcheur à la Ronsard." He cites (192) the following lines as an example of Molinet's best Ronsardian manner:

> Souffle, Triton, en ta bucce argentine;
> Muse, en musant en ta douce musette
> Donne louange et gloire célestine
> Au dieu Phébus à la barbe roussette...

[19] Jean Molinet, *Chroniques*, ed. Georges Doutrepont and Omer Jodogne (Brussels, 1935), III, 186.

[20] See also *ibid.*, 182: "On constate que les phrases en *développements oratoires et cadencés* [my ital.] abondent dans les récits historiques de notre écrivain... C'est... de l'*écriture soigneusement rythmée*..." [my ital.].

Prologue concludes with Molinet's declaration that he will do his utmost to continue Chastellain's great work: "... je moulleray ma plume veritable en suavité de clère facond pour *collauder* les condignes, et en aigreur de bonne *invective* pour *redarguer* les coulpables ..." (II, 595; my ital.). In other words, Molinet thought of himself as a professional man of eloquence, ready to turn his hand to any honest labor. This idea, far from being discreditable, as Guy's description implies, links Molinet and the tradition which he represents with the Italian humanists who, before the general acceptance in the fifteenth century of the neologism *humanista,* were in the habit of calling themselves "orators," thereby indicating their desire to be thought of as men of eloquence, rather than as actual practitioners of oratory in the usual sense of the word. "An 'orator' could have made his career in government, in the Church, in leisured study and collecting, in teaching or writing or scholarship ... he might have composed treatises on moral or political philosophy; he might have devoted himself to translation or editing. Usually, of course, his work included a variety of these activities. The orator was, by definition and inclination, a non-specialist."[21]

This idea of a well-rounded "Renaissance man" of letters corroborates the proposition, which literary historians have during the past twenty years or so come more and more to accept, that rhetoric plays a predominant part in the development of the entire humanist cultural program.[22] Among the great men of the Quattrocento, many were in fact rhetoricians by profession. As successive chancellors to the city of Florence, both Coluccio Salutati and Leonardo Bruni fall into this category.[23] That Bruni genuinely regarded his duties as Florentine chancellor to be essentially of a rhetorical nature is evident, since his history of the city (*Historiarum florentini populi*

---

[21] Hanna H. Gray, "Renaissance Humanism: the Pursuit of Eloquence," in *Journal of the History of Ideas* 24 (1963), 497-514; this citation 500.

[22] See Paul O. Kristeller, "Humanism and Scholasticism in the Italian Renaissance," in *Renaissance Thought* (New York, 1961 [1955]), 92-119.

[23] See Jerrold R. Seigel, *Rhetoric and Philosophy in Renaissance Humanism* (Princeton, 1968); cited hereafter as *RPRH*. Salutati's duties, according to Seigel, "consisted primarily of writing letters, both for the government of the city and for important citizens. His day-to-day concern was with the production of clear and persuasive prose, with practical rhetoric" (64-65).

*libri XII*) bears the blatantly rhetorical subtitle, *Laudatio* [i.e., panegyric] *Florentinae Urbis*.[24]

A characterization of the Renaissance "orator" expressed in terms of this sort may very appropriately be applied to Jean Lemaire de Belges, who was himself "poëte, orateur, et historien" (as he so often proudly proclaimed). This concept of a triad of related avocations did not, of course, originate with him, but was already flourishing by the late fifteenth century. Robert Gaguin (d. 1501), for example, whose name Lemaire invariably cites with reverence, was in point of fact no less eminent a historian than he was a philosopher and poet.[25]

In the sixteenth century the notion became so firmly established as to be taken for granted. Vernon Hall, Jr., while discussing the importance attached by the Renaissance to the old Horatian dictum on delight and utility in poetry, declares that the "art of the muses is frankly considered an adjunct to politics."[26] He then furnishes an instructive quotation from the *Pensieri diversi* of Alessandro Tassoni (1565-1635) in which history, poetry, and oratory are treated as sister arts.

> Sotto la Politica, come dipendenti da lei, vengono tre nobili arti, l'Istoria, la Poetica, e l'Oratoria, la prima delle quali riguarda l'ammaestramento de' Principi, e de' Signori; la seconda l'ammaestramento del popolo; e la terza l'ammaestramento di coloro, che consigliano sopra le cause publiche, o difendono le private in giudizio. [End of quotation in Hall] Comincieremo noi dall' Istoria, perche se bene Aristotile nella Poetica disse, che la Poesia era cosa più ingegnosa, io stimo con tutto ciò, che l'Istoria preceda, non

---

[24] Berthold L. Ullman, "Leonardo Bruni and Humanistic Historiography," in his *Studies in the Italian Renaissance* (Rome, 1955), 321-344, shows that for Bruni, rhetoric (i.e., literary style) performs the vital function of bringing historical events vividly to life, as Cicero used style to popularize the arid writings of the school of Epicurus, which were considered to be almost aggressively unreadable (*op. cit.*, 326). (Cf. below, Chap. IV, n. 32.)

[25] The tradition was to continue — at least in truncated form — well into the seventeenth century. John Dryden, who had been named Poet Laureate of England in 1668, two years later received an additional appointment as Historiographer Royal. And it will be recalled that his famous contemporaries across the English Channel, Racine and Boileau, became joint holders of the office of "Historiographe du Roi" in 1677.

[26] *Renaissance Literary Criticism* (New York, 1945), 72. (Cited hereafter as *RLC*.)

> tanto perche ha più nobil fine, e oggetto, quanto perche tratta cose vere con gravità, e decoro, e non finzioni come fa l'altra con vanità, e leggerezza.[27]

Ever since the time of Ph. Aug. Becker (see above, Chap. I, pp. 15-16 and n. 1), and especially since the publication in 1910 of Henry Guy's volume on the school of the Rhétoriqueurs, it has been a scholarly convention to pay tribute to Lemaire as one of the earliest precursors of the French Renaissance. The celebrated figure of the Renaissance polymath is regularly — and somewhat monotonously — invoked: "Au nombre de ces 'polyphiles,' on doit compter Jean Lemaire. Il ne fut pas l'homme d'un seul métier, encore moins l'homme d'un seul penchant. Son œuvre littéraire, pourtant si diverse, ne représente que l'une des faces de son activité, [etc., etc.]."[28] Possibly the most perceptive observation to be made in this connection is one found in a now largely overlooked work by Francisque Thibaut, whose thesis on *Marguerite d'Autriche et Jean Lemaire de Belges* (having been published in 1888) has been overshadowed by the more substantial efforts of Becker, Guy, *et al.* The following passage occurs near the end of the study:

> Il y avait vraiment en [Lemaire] l'âme d'un poète qui eut le tort de dépenser au hasard le talent dont il était doué. Aucun écrivain, en effet, ne représente mieux que lui ce qu'on pourrait appeler le vagabondage de l'esprit sans suite et sans but. Successivement clerc de finances, secrétaire d'un prince, précepteur d'un gentilhomme, voyageur, entrepreneur de bâtiments, homme d'affaires, historien, pamphlétaire, théologien, vrai chevalier errant de la littérature,

---

[27] Hall's quotation is supposedly taken from the 1646 Venice edition of Tassoni, from which in fact it varies markedly. I have therefore taken the liberty of transcribing directly from this edition (pp. 392-393), which I have quoted slightly more at length (*De' Pensieri Diversi Libri Dieci,* 1646).

[28] Guy, *HPF16,* I, 176. Cf. Paul Laumonier, *Ronsard, poète lyrique:* "[Jean Lemaire] est le vrai instaurateur de la Renaissance française, non seulement par son humanisme, par le fond païen et naturiste de ses œuvres, mais par le sens artistique très développé qui éclate dans leur composition, leur style, leur vocabulaire et la forme métrique de ses pièces strophiques" (647). Similar statements may be found in Henri Chamard, *Les Origines de la Poésie française de la Renaissance* (Paris, 1961 [1939]): "C'est justice de saluer en lui le premier poète de la Renaissance" (172); and, *passim,* in other scholars interested in Lemaire and the pre-Renaissance, e.g., Abel Lefranc, Paul Spaak, Georges Doutrepont, Jean Frappier.

jamais il ne trouva le temps de se recueillir, jamais il ne s'appartint lui-même, jamais il ne put obéir à une inspiration personnelle: il fut la victime de la domesticité.[29]

There are certain indications that Jean Lemaire himself was only too well aware of these onerous demands on his time and talents. In a letter to Marguerite d'Autriche (IV, 392-396), he urgently requests permission to reside "en vostre ville de Dole," adding weight to his cause by quoting the late Comte de Ligny's promise to award him "la première prébende vacante, en sa ville de Ligny, disant que le repos m'estoit necessaire pour mieulx labourer et le bruit continuel de court contraire" (392). And in a later missive to his patroness, he complains bitterly that a benefice at Dôle has gone, despite her promise to himself, to "ung qui ne vous fit oncques seruice."[30]

His official duties as both "Indiciaire et Historiographe" (i.e., Court chronicler rather than historian) to the ducal houses of Burgundy and Brittany[31] and as orator were inextricably entwined, as

---

[29] Pp. 245-246.

[30] IV, 406. Cf. the Prologue to *La Couronne* (IV, 15-16). Here the poet's first words are full of unconcealed resentment at being distracted from his "emprise Vtile" (probably, as Stecher observes [n. 1], a reference to *Les Illustrations*) in order to write yet another commissioned *déploration:*

  O grief eschange! ô muance odieuse!
  Labeur ingrat et œuure tedieuse,
  Quand laisser faut fructueuse escriture,
  Pour expliquer triste mesauenture.
      (IV, 15, ll. 15-18)

Such bitterness of tone cannot be explained solely by Lemaire's sorrow at the death of Marguerite's beloved husband, Duke Philibert le Beau of Savoy. The usual, quite natural, concern of a court poet in such an eventuality, i.e., unemployment, had been nullified by Marguerite's retaining him in her service notwithstanding.

[31] Lemaire was appointed historiographer to the court of Burgundy on August 26, 1507, on the death of Jean Molinet, who had held the office for 32 years. He left his post less than 4 years later, during the winter of 1511-1512, going immediately to Blois, to the court of Anne, Queen of France and Duchess of Brittany, where he was apparently expected (cf. Jodogne, *JLBEFB*, 128), since he at once became "indiciaire de la royne" (see *Œuvres*, IV, 423). Anne died on January 9, 1514.
Pierre Jodogne notes the change in Lemaire's status resulting from the first of these official appointments (which would apply with equal force to the second, needless to say): "Prendre la relève de Molinet signifiait en effet s'inscrire dans une tradition... d'éloquence au service de l'histoire et de rhétorique au service de l'actualité. Ainsi, d'écrivain privé et pour ainsi dire

evidenced by his own definition of the term *Indiciaire*: "ce terme Indiciaire vault autant à dire comme demonstrateur. Et est celui office si iuste quil ne requiert, faueur, ny acception de personnes, et ne se peut donner synon au mieulx monstrant la force de son engin, et sy est de tel subiection, quil ne se peut exercer par procureur." [32] "Demonstrateur" (Lemaire goes on to speak of giving "encoires plus ample Indice et demonstration") echoes the view of a historian's obligations expressed by his predecessor, as quoted above (p. 58).

His exposition of the historiographer's role in rhetorical terms leads Lemaire to view his mission in exactly the same light as did Leonardo Bruni with respect to Florence, viz., the systematic exaltation of his imperial and royal patronesses (Marguerite d'Autriche and Anne de Bretagne) and their respective dynasties. This is the declared purpose of *Les Illustrations de Gaule,* a work which not only its author, but also his contemporaries, believed to possess supreme historical merit. In addition to *Les Illustrations,* there are, scattered throughout the *Œuvres,* numerous encomiastic allusions to such topics as the Peace of Cambrai (of 1508); the much heralded (but abortive) European coalition — under the leadership of the Emperor and the King of France — to expel the Turks from Greece and Asia Minor; the Italian campaigns of Charles VIII and Louis XII, etc. *La Chronique Annale,* an official account of Marguerite's inaugural progress as Regent through the Imperial Provinces of the Netherlands in 1507 (IV, 474-522), combines fulsome (but to my mind heartfelt) praise of the princess — and, incidentally, of Lemaire's fellow-countrymen [33] — with indignant recriminations

---

domestique, Lemaire devenait un personnage officiel, un fonctionnaire, un écrivain d'État. Il n'était plus attaché seulement à la personne de Marguerite, mais aussi et surtout à sa cause dynastique et politique" (*JLBEFB,* 97).

[32] *Épître à Charles le Clerc,* IV, 322. Pierre Jodogne cites this letter as embodying "une magnifique illustration de l'idée que l'écrivain se faisait de son rôle à la cour de Marguerite" (*JLBEFB,* 103).

[33] See in particular IV, 480-481, the charming passage describing Marguerite's reception by "ce peuple haynnier [i.e., of Hainault] franc et ouuert en ses affectuositez plus que nul autre et aussi je ne scay quel maniere de faire plus apparoissant, plus appropriée et mieulx demonstrative en langaige, termes, voix, gestes et chiere, de la beniuolence de son homaige enuers leur prince ou princesse. Et madame se delectoit en la pure simplicité non affaictée de leur bienueillance."

against Louis XII's aggressive foreign policy.[34] We also possess the tantalizingly unfulfilled promise of the continuation of *La Chronique,* the so-called "Fragments de Chronique."[35]

If we accept J. E. Seigel's definition of the great humanists as professional rhetoricians, as "orators" (with the special meaning of the term as polemicists in the service of the state), then certainly Jean Lemaire de Belges must be considered such an orator. He believes, for example, that the duty of "tous bons Indiciaires, Chroniqueurs et Historiographes, soit de monstrer par escritures et raisons apparentes, et notifier à la gent populaire, les vrayes, et non flateuses louenges et merites de leurs Princes, et les bonnes et iustes quereles diceux: Mesmement quand lestat de la guerre est scandaleux, estrange et non accoustumé,[36] et le peril eminent de dangereuse consequence, à fin que les subietz, pour la plus part rudes et ignorans nayent cause de sesbahir, murmurer et se scandaliser entre eux mesmes, mais soient enclins et ententifz à sousterir et fauoriser le iuste droit de leurs Princes" (III, 232-233).

A large proportion of Jean Lemaire's rhetorical skill, it is apparent, is devoted to the praise of his successive patrons and to the corresponding dispraise of their adversaries. On occasion, as for instance in *La Plainte du Désiré* and *La Couronne Margaritique,* these enemies are real, yet impersonal: Mort, Infortune, Envie, and so on. However, there are also adversaries of flesh and blood to be reckoned with, whether entire nations (the French, Italians, Greeks, Turks, Venetians), institutions (the papacy), or individuals (Pope

---

[34] See IV, 504-521. Ironically enough (and perhaps somewhat disconcertingly to the twentieth-century reader) the perfidious French villain of *La Chronique Annale* was shortly to become — as husband to Lemaire's future patroness, the Queen of France — the shining hero of *La Légende des Vénitiens, De la Différence des Schismes et des Conciles,* and *L'Épître du Roi à Hector de Troie.*

[35] IV, 440-473. A fair specimen of Lemaire's gift for vivid narration may, I think, be seen in the following "fragment": "Girard Coisteau de Bracynemontry fut tué qui estoit le meilleur guide dArdennes. Et comme les compaignons de ce [se] descouraigeassent, dit le viel gentilhomme: Enfans nayes peur, tout nostre malheur est passé. Ilz nont que deux traits darbelestries et IIIJ ou V autres sans plus par faulte destre armez et pour estre trop hardys" (456-457).

[36] In this particular instance, the *rex christianissimus* Louis XII was busily engaged in whipping up popular support for his bitter dispute with the Pontifex Maximus, Julius II, a scandalous conflict if there ever was one, if not exactly "estrange et non accoustumé."

Julius II, Charles VIII and Louis XII of France). All, at one time or another, come under the lash of Lemaire the polemicist.

This polemical element of his work falls into two categories. The first comprises the treatises on Venice and the papacy, namely *Le Traité nommé la Légende des Vénitiens, ou leur Chronique abrégée* (Lyons: Jehan de Vingle, 1509) and *Le Traité de la Différence des Schismes et des Conciles de l'Église* (Lyons: Estienne Baland, 1511).[37] Both are political pamphlets of a highly topical and controversial nature, designed expressly to influence such public opinion as may be said to have existed in the first decade of the sixteenth century, which presumably may be equated with the opinion of the nobility and upper bourgeoisie. The latter work is of importance as actual documentary evidence of Louis XII's determination to rally this opinion behind him in his struggle with the papacy over the Gallican question. *La Légende* deals with a much less delicate matter, a relatively uncomplicated piece of power politics ("La raison du plus fort est toujours la meilleure"), with none of the potentially explosive issues inherent in any protracted conflict between a "Roy treschrestien" and a Supreme Pontiff.[38]

---

[37] III, 361-409 and 231-359. The second-named pamphlet is subtitled *de la prééminence et vtilité des Conciles de la sainte Église Gallicane*. There exist in addition four minor works of a political nature, discovered by K. M. Munn and discussed in some detail by Jodogne in his *JLBEFB*, 386-395. These are 1) *Le Dyalogue de Vertu militaire et de Jeunesse françoise;* 2) a ballad, *A la louenge des Princes et Princesses qui ayment la Science historialle;* 3) a brief poem entitled "Histoire, que faiz tu?"; 4) *Allégorie contre Jules II.*

[38] The same prickly subject is one of the major themes of *L'Épître du Roi à Hector de Troie*, where, instead of relying on weighty historical arguments (as is the case with *Schismes et Conciles*, which cites, e.g., Lorenzo Valla's renowned *De falso credita et ementita Constantini donatione declamatio*, published in 1443 — see Jodogne, *JLBEFB*, 375-378, on the dilemma confronting Lemaire over this citation), Lemaire makes very effective use of irony to discredit the bellicose Julius II. See in particular the passage beginning: "Il fait beau voir vn ancien prestre en armes, / Crier l'assault, enhorter aux alarmes" (III, 80, ll. 11 ff.). Henry Guy, rightly, in my opinion, judges *L'Épître du Roi* to be a sample of the poet's wares expressly designed to make a good impression on Louis XII, whose favor Lemaire was seeking against the day he should lose that of Marguerite d'Autriche (*HPF16*, I, 198). In this sense, *L'Épître* might be said to be doubly deliberative, although in fact the themes of European unity and crusade receive small emphasis in comparison with the epideictic aspects of the poem, viz., the attack on the papacy personified by Julius II, and the adulation of the King and his (supposed) great forebear, Hector of Troy.

From the rhetorical perspective, the most interesting aspect of both *La Légende des Vénitiens* and *Schismes et Conciles* is surely that they represent a serious attempt to influence the course of history by the use of persuasive language, just as in the heyday of Greco-Roman oratory. Although intended to be read rather than declaimed,[39] both these documents — and especially the shorter *Légende* — are actually, in structure, manner, and intent, regular deliberative orations. For example, *La Légende* can be subdivided as follows: *exordium/narratio* — III, 361, l. 1 - 363, l. 20; *partitio* — 363, l. 21 - 364, l. 18; *confirmatio* (by historical demonstration) — 364, l. 19 - 399, l. 19; *peroratio* — 402, l. 14 - 405, l. 16.[40] (A *confutatio* would be superfluous, since the author naturally has no desire to defend the indefensible Venetian cause.)

Unlike history and chronicle therefore, whose major concern is with the past, these political broadsheets genuinely strive to mold the future. They represent a revival of Alain Chartier's earnest efforts to influence events, as in *Le Quadrilogue Invectif*, whose purpose was to galvanize a France prostrate after a long catalogue of disasters. (Needless to say, the polemicist of Lemaire's day had the immense advantage of the newly invented printing press.) Lemaire's publications are notable in that this new dimension of French literature, while destined for great things in the course of the sixteenth century, was little known, or at any rate little emphasized, in its beginnings. The tortuous statesmanship of the Italian Wars, with their constantly shifting alliances and regroupings of the powers involved, soon outdated the henceforth irrelevant *Légende,* but the advent of Luther and the Protestant Reformation gave a new lease of life to Lemaire's *Schismes et Conciles*. The tract, "intended in the first instance," as Kathleen Munn writes, "to be a weapon of Gallicanism as opposed to Ultramontanism... was used in Latin versions as an instrument of Lutheranism as well."[41] Thus its author

---

[39] Jodogne (*JLBEFB*, 324) notes that the title *Légende* is given "un sens latinisant," i.e., Lemaire employs it with its Latin gerundive force: *legenda*, "fit to be *read*."

[40] The apparent hiatus between pp. 399 and 402 is actually occupied by a *Ballade double*.

[41] *A Contribution to the Study of Jean Lemaire de Belges* (Scottdale, Pa., 1936), 26. Miss Munn informs us (*ibid.*) that in 1532 (i.e., 21 years after its first appearance and in all probability at least 7 years after its author's death) the treatise was published as *Le Promptuaire des Conciles*. Alfred Humpers

inadvertently achieved an enduring influence in a religious upheaval which far exceeded in magnitude "le futur tresgrand vingtquatrieme schisme" (III, 243) which he had originally predicted in 1511.

The second type of polemic prevalent in Lemaire's writings consists in an undercurrent of certain political and religious themes discernible throughout the *Œuvres*. Thus, the very title of what is generally considered to be Lemaire's maturest and artistically most successful piece, *La Concorde des deux langages,* reflects the author's preoccupation (one might almost say obsession) with European unity.[42] The similarly framed title *Concorde du Genre humain* requires no elaborate explanation. The work was composed in celebration of what Lemaire — in common with many others — over-optimistically believed to be the dawn of universal peace ushered in by the Treaty of Cambrai. (This was to have been a universal *European* peace only, since the Turkish question remained to be settled by force of arms.) Indefatigably he returns to the then widely held ideals of Crusade, Concord, and the Reform of established religion. One should nevertheless avoid jumping to hasty conclusions by descrying, in this authentic innovator in the literary sphere, a profound and influential religious or political theorist. Abel Lefranc, for instance, rather incautiously writes: "Certes, il est surprenant de rencontrer, à la fin du règne de Louis XII, un homme d'une telle liberté de jugement, d'une indépendance de pensée qui atteint presque celle de Rabelais." Lefranc goes on in all seriousness to dilate on Lemaire's "don de prophétie," an allusion to his having foretold (in *Schismes et Conciles,* written ten years before the Reformation), "la nécessité

---

(*Étude sur la langue de Jean Lemaire de Belges* [Liège and Paris, 1921], 7, n. 5) lists a Latin edition: *Johannis Marii Belgae, Historici quondam Christianissimi Gallorum Regis Ludovici XII, de Schismatum & Conciliorum Ecclesiae universalis differentia.* And Ph. Aug. Becker (*JL,* 381, n. 1) cites an English version of 1539 entitled: *The abbrevyacion of oll general Concellys holden in Grecia, Germania, Italia and Gallia, compyled by John Le Meyre in 1519* [sic] *and translated by John Gowgh the Printer herof.*

[42] H. Guy (*HPF16,* I, 194) believes that the term "langage" is, in this context, of far wider extension than mere "language," and implies rather "les états d'âme, le genre de culture, les opinions qui caractérisent chaque peuple." Jean Frappier (*Concorde,* Introduction, xxiv) approves of this definition. On the other hand, Hermann Gmelin considers that Guy goes too far and that "langage" signifies no more than "style" (if not quite as much as "literature"). "Das Prinzip der Imitatio in den romanischen Literaturen der Renaissance," in *Romanische Forschungen* 46 (1932), 83-359; this citation 250, and n. 1.

historique de ce grand mouvement religieux." [43] Jean Lemaire's contribution to the cause of reformation surely lies rather in his excellent and forceful popularizations of generally current ideas.

One characteristic passage of this type is the peroration of Genius's sermon, where, in tones strangely reminiscent of Urban II's appeal to the French nation at Clermont in 1095,[44] the archprelate of Venus calls upon the "Peuple de Gaule aussi blanc comme let" to liberate Asia Minor (*Concorde*, 31-32, ll. 580-606). Similar effusions are not uncommon in the *Œuvres,* especially in the third book of *Les Illustrations de Gaule,* whose thesis is the desirability of the reunion of Charlemagne's former domains in Gaul and Germania: hence the modified subtitle, "De France Orientale et Occidentale" (II, 259).[45] Also in *Les Illustrations,* Apollo (I, 266-267) predicts the glorious renascence of Troy in the form of the nation-states of modern Europe, reunited thanks to Marguerite d'Autriche (". . . une Princesse Auguste, qui sera lors nommee Dame de paix vniuerselle . . ."). P. Jodogne, who throughout his masterly study on Jean Lemaire constantly emphasizes the *political* thrust of the writer's works, observes that his magnum opus, conceived as early as the year 1500 and originally entitled *Les Singularités de Troie* (*JLBEFB,* 404), was, at the behest of Marguerite d'Autriche, vastly broadened in scope to become "œuvre de propagande en faveur de l'entente franco-bourguignonne" (*ibid.,* 405).

To generalize, then, on the credit side of the epideictic balance sheet in Lemaire's earlier (or Burgundian) period (1504-1511) appear in undisputed first place his venerated patroness Marguerite d'Autriche and her house; on the debit side, France and her perfidious policies, most disgraceful of which was Charles VIII's cynical repudiation of Marguerite (in 1491), after a betrothal dating back to her infancy.[46] *La Chronique Annale* has some fascinating insights into French *realpolitik* as conceived by Louis XII before the Treaty of Cambrai; let us mention, *inter alia,* a dastardly plot

---

[43] "Jean Lemaire de Belges," in *Rev. des Cours et Conf.* 19 (1911), 102-104.
[44] Perhaps not so strangely, after all. See below, Chap. IV, n. 10.
[45] ". . . sera veu comment lesdites deux nations d'Allemaigne et de Gaule, ont pour le plus du temps esté coniointes et alliees ensemble, comme sœurs germaines: et par ce moyen, ont dompté et suppédité toutes les autres, sans grand difficulté . . . Car elles deux ensemble, cest la plus grand force du monde" (II, 271-272).
[46] See, e.g., IV, 105-106, 132-133, and *passim.*

to seize Arras by treachery (IV, 485-489), and Louis's devious machinations against the Emperor Maximilian I and Pope Julius II (IV, 504-509). Such expressions as the following (italicized) abound in *La Chronique Annale*: "Le Roy loys fit marcher une grosse puissance par mer et par terre en Ytalie. Et lui mesmes les suiuit, *prenant couleur* de vouloir reduire à vraye obeissance... ses subgectz rebelles, *combien que le souspecon de son emprise fust autre*... [le] Roy loys pretendist de circonuenir le pape Julles... affin de finablement esleuer iceluy cardinal [d'Amboise] à la papalité et consequemment led. Roy mesmes *usurper le tiltre de lempire où il nauoit nul droit*" (IV, 504-505). There are several ironic shafts aimed at the "trafficques cauteleuses du Roy qui se dit tres chrestien," whose conduct is most detrimentally contrasted with that of "la maison Daustriche et de bourgogne" (IV, 509). And *Les Chansons de Namur* (1507), Lemaire's most overtly Francophobe work, triumphantly recounts the totally unexpected — yet from the standpoint of poetic justice eminently satisfactory— drubbing received by a column of heavily armed French troops at the hands of a few stouthearted Flemish shepherds. The poet gives free rein to his glee at the discomfiture of "ces braghars vantereaux / Fiers que lyons, farouches que toreaux, / Frecz fins francois de grand orgueil non francz" (IV, 296, ll. 11-13), and not unexpectedly alludes to the dauntlessness of David and — by implication — to the swaggering bully Goliath (IV, 303, l. 2).[47]

At a later stage in his career, now in the service of Anne de Bretagne, Queen of France, Lemaire's primary targets are Pope

---

[47] Johan Huizinga, *WMA,* believes that in *Les Chansons de Namur,* Lemaire is deliberately attempting (by way of a variation on the traditional themes of the equality of all men on the one hand, and the nature of true — as opposed to hereditary — nobility on the other) "to acquaint the nobles with the fact that those whom they treat as villeins are sometimes animated by the greatest gallantry" (66). P. Jodogne is not altogether in accord with this judgment. "Nous avons vu que Lemaire n'exalte pas les paysans vainqueurs sans en rire un peu, comme s'il était partagé entre la sympathie véritable et l'amusement moqueur" (*JLBEFB,* 305). This ambiguity is accounted for by the fact that when Lemaire is addressing Marguerite d'Autriche or the vanquished Frenchmen he makes no bones about glorifying his stalwart peasant-heroes. When, on the other hand, he is speaking to the Burgundian nobility, he tends to emphasize the burlesque aspects of the affair. Consequently, his "sympathie... pour 'le populaire' n'est... pas aussi pure qu'on pourrait le croire à première vue" (307).

Julius II (together — to a fairly high degree — with the institution of the papacy itself) and the Republic of Venice, followed closely by the Turkish presence in Constantinople and in Europe. His undisguised hostility to the Greeks is mainly restricted to the ancients and is a logical consequence of his passionate adherence to the Trojan cause.[48] The Italians receive one sharp rap over the knuckles in passing, on account of their infuriating tendency to regard all other nations — and tongues — as innately barbarous (I, 11).[49] It is noteworthy that Lemaire never once betrays his former loyalties by attacking the Austro-Burgundians, a fact which might well be thought sufficient to "repress the triumph of malignant criticism" (as Samuel Johnson tartly observes in the Preface to his *Dictionary*) with respect to the venality with which he has sometimes been charged.

---

[48] Lemaire's Hellenophobia is much in evidence in *Les Illustrations*. See, e.g., his patriotic conviction regarding Gallic primacy in the invention of writing: "Iulius Cesar au sixieme liure de ses Commentaires [dit] que les Gaulois de son temps vsoient de lettres Grecques. Mais certes ilz les auoient telles beaucoup auant que les Grecz. Tesmoing Xenophon en ses Equiuoques," etc. (I, 67. The claim is reiterated, I, 113.) On the same page: "A cause de ce tresnoble Roy Saturne, et Patriarche Samothes, surnommé Dis, nostre Gaule commence bien destre illustree et anoblie. Et ne fust ce que pour lamour des lettres et de philosophie quil enseigna premier en icelle, ne desplaise à la vanterie de Grece, qui long temps ha vsurpé ce los..." Lemaire goes to great lengths to demonstrate that these rascally Greks have also had the impudence to usurp, in the name of "le petit Hercules Grec" (I, 114), the fame due the "real" Hercules. In a passage heaping opprobrium on Greece ("Les poëtes Grecz ont beaucoup menty de cestuy Laomedon" [I, 114]; "Toutes ces menteries et fictions Grecques, sont bien aisees à mespriser et annichiler" [I, 115]), Lemaire sets the record straight, to his own satisfaction at least: "...si les Grecz pleins de mensonge et de vaniloquence, attribuent les tiltres et les gestes du grand Hercules de Libye... cest faulsement et à tort: attendu que ledit Grec [i.e., "le petit Hercules"] nestoit autre chose fors vn Pirate, larron et escumeur de mer, homme de tresmauuaise vie, et qui mourut meschamment" (*ibid.*). There follows a catalogue of the odious crimes and treacheries committed by the said Hercules, including the first fall of Troy and the abduction of Hesione.

[49] As the title of his illuminating essay would indicate, Pierre Jodogne seeks to demonstrate that Jean Lemaire's rightful place is at the very center of the Franco-Burgundian tradition. Consequently, there is revealed throughout the *Œuvres* a steady awareness of the need to defend the honor of the French language and culture against Italian arrogance and disdain. Jodogne in fact stoutly denies that Lemaire was ever in the slightest degree Italophile (as had been maintained by G. Doutrepont, in particular), and his consistent

So frequently and with such fervor does Lemaire allude to the themes of religious reform and political unity that it seems clear — although one may not legitimately credit him with being their originator — that it is too harsh and simplistic by far to accuse him outright, as does H. Guy, of selling his conscience to the highest bidder. [50] Jean Lemaire's prodigious capacity for total and unfeigned identification with the cause of the moment should alone exculpate him from so unworthy a charge. I will do no more than echo Henri Weber's disquisition on the extremely insecure tenure of a court poet in the early Renaissance [51] in order to nullify to a great extent Guy's insensitive condescension towards, e.g., Jean Molinet. [52] In my considered opinion, insincerity is not one of Lemaire's failings (except, of course, in the rhetorically orthodox and meaningless protestations of modesty which occur in his exordia and conclusions). His polemical writings are invariably distinguished by an air of impassioned — if perhaps ephemeral — convictions. [53]

---

approach to this extremely complex problem is well expressed in the book's concluding paragraph:

> Lemaire reflète donc, dans son attitude comme dans son œuvre, la complexité des sentiments "citramontains" de l'époque de Louis XII. Il est profondément enraciné dans une tradition franco-bourguignonne perméable depuis longtemps aux productions de l'humanisme italien, et, par sa situation d'écrivain de cour, il est sensible aux premières modes italianisantes. Mais, politiquement et psychologiquement, il est hostile aux Italiens. Face à l'Italie, à la langue et à la culture italiennes, il défend avec fierté la langue et la tradition françaises.
>
> (*JLBEFB*, 485)

[50] "Nous verrons Jean Lemaire haïr la France pour le compte de Marguerite d'Autriche et la chérir aux frais d'Anne de Bretagne..." *HPF16*, I, 62-63.

[51] Weber, *La Création poétique au XVI<sup>e</sup> siècle en France* (Paris, 1956), stresses the social subordination and dependence on wealthy patrons of the poets and other writers of Lemaire's day. Weber specifically refers to the excessive and unsubtle flattery characteristic of rhétoriqueur *complaintes funèbres* ("genre... essentiellement faux," 66), citing as examples Lemaire's *Temple*, *Plainte*, and *Couronne*. He reminds the reader that it is entirely possible that Lemaire, "le plus grand poète de cette génération, soit mort dans la misère" (66).

[52] "Jamais conscience ne se vendit plus honnêtement..." *HPF16*, I, 161.

[53] P. Spaak, *Jean Lemaire de Belges, sa vie, son œuvre et ses meilleures pages* (Paris, 1926), bears out my contention that Lemaire is, in the heat of composition at least, more sincere than not in his beliefs. After admitting that it is not always easy to determine the proportions of sincerity and real indignation present in Lemaire at any given moment, Spaak says: "Mais il

Such qualities are indeed enviable in a writer (or orator) engaged in propagandizing, since, as all the master rhetoricians of antiquity are agreed, the most potent of the three principal means of effecting persuasion [54] hinges upon the character (*ethos*) of the speaker himself. "The orator," Aristotle teaches, "persuades by moral character when his speech is delivered in such a manner as to render him worthy of confidence ... moral character, so to say, constitutes the most effective means of proof" (*Rhetoric,* I.ii.4). Evidently the man who believes whole-heartedly in his cause [55] has, right from the outset, an incalculable moral advantage over one whose services are quite unashamedly available to the highest bidder. Between these two extremes there is found the true professional, who performs any task assigned to him to the best of his ability, simply because it is his duty to do so. For example, Leonardo Bruni in private correspondence admits that he has grossly overpraised Florence and her policies in his *Laudatio,* but justifies himself in the name of art: the exigencies of the panegyric mode are responsible for such overstatements of the case. [56] Jean Lemaire, on the other hand, is constitutionally incapable of such Olympian detachment. Indeed, there is much evidence to support the view that his eloquent affirmations accurately reflect his personal feelings. I do not propose to belabor the point here, except to note a revealing passage from his personal correspondence (on which attention was

---

développe cependant quelques idées sur lesquelles [il] est revenu trop souvent, avec trop de ténacité et de passion, pour que nous contestions qu'elles exprimèrent sa conviction réfléchie" (p. 80). These "idées" are of course precisely the themes of political unity and crusade of which we have been speaking. And Lemaire's personal devotion to, above all, Marguerite d'Autriche, seems unassailable, notwithstanding his (apparent) defection to the court of France, which was in all likelihood motivated by the jealous intrigues of rivals.

[54] "The proofs furnished by the speech are of three kinds. The first depends upon the moral character of the speaker, the second upon putting the hearer into a certain frame of mind, the third upon the speech itself, in so far as it proves or seems to prove" (Aristotle, *Rhetoric,* I.ii.3).

[55] Cf. Cicero, *De oratore,* II.xlv.189: "I give you my word that I never tried, by means of a speech, to arouse either indignation or compassion, either ill-will or hatred, in the minds of a tribunal, without being really stirred myself, as I worked upon their minds, by the very feelings to which I was seeking to prompt them."

[56] See J. E. Seigel, *RPRH,* 253. Seigel continues: "For the humanists, eloquent affirmations of the virtue of a city-state and its citizens were not primarily expressions of personal feelings; they were the performance of a professional task."

originally focused by P. Spaak, *JLB,* 75-76), one which sheds a fascinating light on his psychological makeup. In a letter to Louis Barangier, secretary to Marguerite d'Autriche — whose service Lemaire has but recently left — the author defends himself against certain malicious charges made by his detractors, insinuating, *inter alia,* that he has "escript quelque chose contre elle, et que à Paris l'en treuve le publicquement par escript" (IV, 419). After an indignant rebuttal of these accusations, Lemaire vehemently prays that if he has in any way offended the princess he may "morir subitement et sans confession. Car se je ne l'eusse tant aymée, je n'eusse pas tant escript de bonnes choses à sa louenge. Et autant que j'en ay escript d'elle, en écriprai je de la royne [Anne de Bretagne], ma noble maistresse qui me fait tant de biens. Et en ce ne feray je nul tort à Madame; car là où je sens, mon cuer s'adonne du tout, et la raison le veult bien" (IV, 422). The concluding sentence (which Spaak justly calls "ce mot charmant") is entirely in keeping with Lemaire's unstinted loyalty, not so much to the cause as to the *person* of his current benefactor.[57]

---

[57] The tone, rather than the precise meaning of the closing words of the passage, reminds one strongly of the famous lines in *Purgatorio* (XXIV, 52-54), where Dante tells the old poet Bonagiunta da Lucca "I'mi son un che, quando / Amor mi spira, noto, e a quel modo / Ch' e' ditta dentro, vo significando." An intriguing example of the enduring problems which Lemaire's outspoken loyalty might in all innocence stir up is revealed in Jean de Tournes's salutation to the reader in the first edition of *La Couronne Margaritique,* published by himself — under the editorship of Antoine du Moulin — only in 1549, more than forty years after its composition. The snag was that *La Couronne* was written to "illustrer" Marguerite d'Autriche, and consequently it contains certain unflattering allusions to the repudiation of the princess by her betrothed, Charles VIII of France. Worse, there is also a downright impertinent (and extremely unkind) comparison of the physical charms of Marguerite and Anne de Bretagne (who had displaced Marguerite), to the great detriment of the latter. "... au tresgrand desplaisir delle et de tout le peuple de France, [Marguerite] se vid desnuer de tiltre de Royne, dont vne autre fut incontinent saisie, voire vne autre, qui touchant hautesse dextraction ne de formosité corporelle, ne de rectitude, perfection et integrité de membres [Anne is said to have been lame], nestoit en rien à elle comparable" (IV, 126-127), writes Lemaire with unfeigned outrage at his patroness's humiliation. Forty years later, therefore, Jean de Tournes, defending *La Couronne* in advance from the attacks of "plusieurs cerueaux trop delicats," sensibly points out that "quelquesfois les Autheurs escriuent par commandement, ou comme affectionnés à leurs superieurs, ou comme passionnés, et ignorans autrement les importances des choses, quilz escriuent," which is why, he tells the reader, "ie me suis long temps abstenu de te mettre en auant ceste Couronne: pource que ie y uoyois

Thus far I have attempted to put into perspective for the reader of our own day the concepts of an earlier age regarding the responsibilities, duties, and functions of an "orator," here exemplified by Jean Lemaire. In the next chapter, we shall examine to what extent Jean Lemaire's concept of the writer and his function is permeated by rhetorical doctrine, as revealed by his terminology. That this issue is no negligible one is self-evident in the light of rhetoric's role as perhaps *the* prime mover of the Renaissance. Ever since the publication in 1927 of Charles Homer Haskin's illuminating study on *The Renaissance of the Twelfth Century,* literary critics and historians alike have become progressively more persuaded that periods whose writers are intensively preoccupied with questions of form soon begin to assume characteristics which we generally associate with "the" Renaissance, whose evolution seems to spring directly from the humanistic activities of Petrarch and his circle. Thus we have the Carolingian renaissance of the ninth century, and that of the twelfth, which saw the flowering of the *roman courtois* in the vernacular and could produce a humanist of the stature of John of Salisbury (to name but one outstanding figure). But each of the lesser renaissances quickly proved abortive: the Carolingian hegemony was followed by a period of political, economic, and social chaos; the brilliant promise of the twelfth-century classical revival was eclipsed by the rise of scholasticism, with its emphasis on Aristotelian dialectic and concomitant neglect of literary form. However, the ensuing period was far more propitious to humanistic tendencies, which were at last able to develop relatively unchecked. These tendencies were, in origin at least, largely rhetorical in nature. Such, essentially, is the thesis propounded succinctly by Walter J. Ong, S. J., in the following passage:

> The principal domestic struggle of Western culture has been between a philosophically centered and a rhetorically centered regimen. The forces engaged have been the champions of the speculative intellect versus the champions of the practical intellect. On this basis was waged the struggle between Socrates and the sophists, the struggle which led to John of Salisbury's *Metalogicus,* and the struggle which

---

Lautheur trop abandonnément parlant en faueur de sa Maistresse, et au desauantage dautruy." Nevertheless, de Tournes justifies his author in the name of his "louable et equitable intention" (IV, 8-9).

was echoed in Swift's *The Battle of the Books*. The victory has gone first to one side and then to another. Under the Roman Empire and until the eleventh century the rhetoricians were in the ascendency, but by the thirteenth century philosophy seemed destined to win out, only to receive a sharp set-back when rhetoric triumphed and made the Renaissance.[58]

---

[58] "The Province of Rhetoric and Poetic," in *PR*, 53-54. Humanism's debt to rhetoric was earlier recognized by Giuseppe Toffanin in his *Storia dell' umanesimo*. Jean Cousin, Paul Oskar Kristeller, and Hanna Gray express similar opinions. Cousin sees French classicism "comme un effort vers la clarté rationnelle; à son origine, cet effort a l'enseignement de la grammaire et de la rhétorique latines ... nous espérons montrer que cette rhétorique latine ... a imposé à ceux qui suivaient ses conseils une façon de voir, de sentir, de penser uniforme" ("Rhétorique latine et le classicisme français," in *Rev. de Cours et Conf.* 34 [1933], I, 503 and *passim*). Kristeller maintains that the humanists were "professional rhetoricians ... who developed the belief, then new and modern, that the best way to achieve eloquence was to imitate classical models, and who were thus driven to study the classics and to found classical philology" ("Humanism and Scholasticism in the Italian Renaissance," 98-99). Cf. Hanna Gray's contention that "The bond which united humanists, no matter how far separated in outlook or in time, was a conception of eloquence and its uses. Through it, they shared a common intellectual method and a broad agreement on the value of that method. Classical rhetoric ... constituted the main source for both" ("Renaissance Humanism," 498).

CHAPTER III

JEAN LEMAIRE'S CONCEPTION
OF THE WRITER AND HIS CRAFT

The strongly rhetorical cast of Lemaire's thinking is immediately apparent in his constant recourse to certain key words or phrases. He brings into play, for example, an entire battery of near-synonymous terms denoting "speech" or "discourse." *Collation, collocution, devises, dire, harengue, oraison, propos, sermocination, traditive* are all met with in *La Couronne Margaritique* alone,[1] not to mention cognate words like *deduction, explication,* and *exposition,* which are used by speakers to characterize the didactic nature of their utterances. Lemaire also employs the term *peroration* in its specialized Late Middle French interpretation, "discours" (cf. Huguet), as in "Peroration de lactevr avx nobles lecteurs et auditeurs de ce liure."[2]

---

[1] *Collation*: IV, 78; *collocution* and *devises* (Lemaire is at this point distinguishing between formal public address and private conversation) IV, 105; *dire*: IV, 140; *harengue* and *oraison,* as the normal words designating "speech," "oration," are extremely widespread in the *Œuvres; propos*: IV, 77; *sermocination*: IV, 96. *Sermocinatio* is the Latin equivalent for "dialogue," which Quintilian includes under the general heading of *prosopopoeia* (IX.ii.31). (Cf. *Ad Herenn.,* IV.liii.65.) Lemaire, however, employs the term to signify "oration" in the general sense. St. Isidore, the fourth of the Ten Orators of *La Couronne Margaritique,* bringing his speech to an end, says "ie imposeray silence à ma longue sermocination" (IV, 96). *Traditive* (an unusual word): IV, 109. Stecher's note is interesting: "*Traditive* semble ici analogue à *collation* (allocution, sermon). De *tradere memoriae,* livrer à la mémoire, on est arrivé à faire *traditive,* chose apprise par tradition, comme on lit encore dans Corneille et dans Furetière." *Deduction*: IV, 108; *explication*: IV, 121; *exposition*: IV, 120.

[2] II, 468. Munn, *A Contribution,* 18, rightly conceives that such expressions (cf. II, 260, and IV, 507) denote the author's intent that his prose, as

The cumulative effect of this type of language is to create a distinct and coherent impression of the figure of the writer and his role in society as conceived by Jean Lemaire de Belges. In order to illustrate the extent to which this conception has been molded by the rhetorical tradition, I propose, first, to examine Lemaire's use of the word *rhétorique* and his terminology relative to the writer and his art; then to study two interrelated topics — *pronuntiatio,* or delivery, and *urbanité* — whose rhetorical origins are particularly worthy of note (and on the subject of which Lemaire has some very interesting comments to make); and, finally, to touch briefly upon his concept of style and eloquence.

### Section 1: "Rhétorique"

According to Edmond Huguet's monumental *Dictionnaire de la langue française du XVIᵉ siècle, rhétorique* can mean either "rhetorical" in the strict sense, as in "encores en pourra il maudire les rhetoriques couleurs..." (I, 249), or "conforme aux lois de la rhétorique, éloquent, élégant." [3] Jean Frappier's glossary to *La Concorde des deux langages* gives "Poésie ou art de s'exprimer, soit en prose, soit en vers," a definition which fits the bill exactly so far as Lemaire's customary use of the word is concerned. The poet Guillaume Cretin in *Le Temple d'Honneur* is styled "chief et monarque de la rhetoricque françoise," [4] while Marguerite d'Autriche is praised for her skill in vocal and instrumental music, painting, and "rhetorique, tant en langue Françoise comme Castillane" (IV, 110-111). The same lady expresses her appreciation of *La Première Épître de l'Amant Vert* — written to divert her after the death of her beloved husband — in the following graceful (and encouraging) quatrain:

---

well as his verse, be read aloud. *Peroration* appears in its strictly rhetorical acceptation, i.e., conclusion of an oration (or piece of sustained prose) in "Fin et peroration, là où l'acteur parle à son euvre," *La Concorde du genre humain,* ed. Pierre Jodogne (Brussels, 1964), 79 (cited hereafter as *Genre humain*).

[3] Huguet also gives "praticquant la rhétorique, habile à parler," and a substantival version, "rhéteur, homme habile à parler," neither of which, to my knowledge, occurs in Lemaire.

[4] *Le Temple d'Honneur et de Vertus,* ed. Henri Hornik (Geneva, 1957), 45, l. 21 (cited hereafter as *Temple*).

> Ton escriptoire a si bonne praticque
> Que, si m'en crois, sera bien estimée.
> Parquoy concludz: Ensuyz sa Rhetoricque,
> Car tu scez bien que par moy est aymée.[5]

The figure of Rhetoricque personified appears in *La Plainte du Désiré* (to be discussed at greater length in Chapter VII): in *that* instance, as we shall see, the concept of rhetoric is primarily the medieval one of embellishment, ornamentation, aureate language.

An interesting juxtaposition of *rhétorique* and *oraison* occurs when the Archpriest Genius lyrically describes the language of young lovers as pure poetry: "Leur oraison est pure rhetoricque."[6] Nor must we omit the oft-quoted (and much-glossed) statement made by Lemaire, in a letter to François le Rouge, to the effect that "Rhetorique, et Musique sont vne mesme chose" (III, 197). My intent here is simply to point out Lemaire's interest in the extremely close kinship between poetry and music[7] (which is of course scarcely an original notion on his part). He insists on the fact that the young Molinet was "adonné au seruice de musicque et rhetoricque" (IV, 521-522), and that Bardus, legendary ruler of Gaul and eponymous founder of the "secte de Poëtes et rhetoriciens... nommez Bardes," was the "inuenteur de rhythmes, cestadire de Rhetorique et de musique" (I, 70), a fairly reliable indication that, as rhythm and rhyme

---

[5] *Les Épîtres de l'Amant Vert*, ed. Jean Frappier (Geneva, 1948), 51, n. 43 (cited hereafter as *Amant*).

[6] *Concorde*, 31, l. 574. Another example of Lemaire's use of the term *rhétorique* as "poetry" occurs in *Amant* II, ll. 69-71, where the martyred parrot (v. *Première Épître*, l. 268) confesses the inability of *rhétorique* to express the horror of the inferno reserved for evil beasts, an intriguing illustration of what Curtius (*ELLMA*, 159-162) calls the "inexpressibility topos": "Droit là voit on ung grant trou tartaricque / Si treshideux que nulle rhetoricque / Ne sçauroit bien sa laideur exprimer."

[7] It need hardly be said that the relationship between the two disciplines is a vast and complex subject of great antiquity. Almost all students of Lemaire have a contribution to make regarding his attitude to the problem. W. F. Patterson, for example, interprets Lemaire's remark in the light of Deschamps's "musique naturelle" (see Chap. I, n. 64 above), as an allusion to "alliterations, rare words and difficult rimes," without reference to harmony (*FPT*, I, 192). Henri Chamard, in *Histoire de la Pléiade* (Paris, 1961 [1939]), on the other hand, credits the poet with precisely the attempt to "faire de l'harmonie la vertu maîtresse du vers" (I, 136-137), while J. Frappier (*Concorde*, xxii-xxiii) notes the analogies between rhétoriqueur poetic technique and contemporary polyphony (not to mention flamboyant gothic architecture).

are cognate terms, so music and poetry are regarded as closely related arts. John of Garland's late thirteenth-century *Poetria de arte Prosaica, Metrica et Rithmica,* one of the most influential of the *Arts poétiques,* is often credited with being the main medieval transmitter of the ancient doctrine, which the author himself ascribes to Boethius.[8] Molinet's *Art de Rhétorique* of 1493 — obviously Lemaire's immediate source — defines poetry in much the same way as the *Poetria*: "Rethorique vulgaire est une espece de musique appellée richmique" (Langlois, 216). The earliest reference to the equating of poetry with music that I personally have come across is in Quintilian, where, in a long development setting forth the prerequisites of the ideal orator, occurs the following passage: "I should like for the benefit of the uninstructed, those 'creatures of the heavier Muse,' as the saying is, to remove all doubts as to the value of music. They will at any rate admit that the poets should be read by our future orator. But can they be read without some knowledge of music? Or if any of my critics be so blind as to have some doubts about other forms of poetry, can the lyric poets at any rate be read without such knowledge?" (I.x.28-29). What Quintilian is getting at here is precisely the affective impact of music on the listener (cf. Wallace Stevens in "Peter Quince at the Clavier": "Music is feeling, then, not sound"), with its obviously invaluable potentialities for the orator. "Give me the knowledge of the principles of music," he writes, "which have power to excite or assuage the emotions of mankind."[9] Accordingly, this notion of an alliance between the two arts has as one indispensable source a work of rhetorical instruction: indeed, the very work in which the theory of classical rhetoric at its peak is crystallized.

---

[8] "Sed notandum quod rithmica species est musice, ut ait Boetius in Arte musica..." *Poetria* (cited Chap. I, n. 50 above), 6. Cf. *ibid.,* 158.

[9] I.x.31. Curtius has a revealing paragraph on the impact of rhetoric on music, where, among other things, he tells us that the "system of teaching music was adapted from that of teaching rhetoric," and that there existed a musical *ars inveniendi,* and even a musical topics (*ELLMA,* 78). (Cf. Chap. I, n. 45 above on the influence of rhetoric on painting.)

## Section 2: The Writer

### A. Acteur

Although the synonyms *escripteur* and *escrivain* both appear a few times (e.g., I, 3, 4, 287, 325, etc.), by far the most common general term Lemaire uses for "writer" or "author" is *acteur,* found on innumerable occasions throughout the *Œuvres*. Frequently, it appears in phrases indicative of the scrupulous care with which Lemaire has assembled weighty authorities to support his historical judgments (this is, as might be expected, especially conspicuous in what he fondly believed to be a compilation of authentic historical worth, *viz.*, *Les Illustrations de Gaule,* as also in the polemical pamphlets *La Légende des Vénitiens* and *De la Différence des Schismes et des Conciles*). Thus, the reader constantly meets with expressions like "plusieurs autres acteurs tressuffisans, lesquelz seront mes guides et mes garans en ceste oeuure" (II, 47); "ces choses sont approuuees et autorisees par Dictis de Crete" (I, 130), etc. Lemaire's especial favor goes to the phrase "les (vrays) acteurs autentiques."[10] Not only are there "acteurs autentiques," but also "liures autentiques" (I, 90) and "escrits autentiques" (II, 242).[11]

*Acteur* and *auctoriser* are obvious cognates, and the latter term is particularly revelatory of Lemaire's notion of the writer's role when we find it in such a sentence as "l'une desdictes parties s'efforçoit d'exaulcer [rehausser], auctoriser et honnourer nostre langue françoise et gallicane" (*Concorde,* 4, ll. 40-42), where it is practically synonymous with *illustrer.*[12] In the concept of *illustration*

---

[10] E.g., "auecques ample probation comment Lacteur ha suiuy en ceste histoire les vrays acteurs autentiques" (II, 236, title); "les anciens acteurs autentiques" (II, 59); "nous nous rapportons au iugement des nobles lecteurs beniuoles, combien il y ha peu auoir de peine, et dindustrie, dauoir recueilli et assorty tant de matieres diuerses, et de tant d'Acteurs autentiques pour les faire seruir tout à vn propos" (I, 342).

[11] Huguet renders *autentique* as "bon, excellent, louable"; Frappier (*Concorde,* glossary) as "connu, célèbre, noble par son antiquité."

[12] Munn (*A Contribution,* 20) notes "the insistent recurrence of the word 'illustrer' in the literature of the whole century." As might be expected, sixteenth-century critics writing on Lemaire almost to a man praise him for his "illustration" of the French vernacular. Thus, Du Bellay, defending and illustrating French in his turn, singles out Lemaire from among the generation of despised "rymeurs" as one who has "premier illustré & les Gaules & la

(as in his title, *Les Illustrations de Gaule*), we see Lemaire preoccupied at once with defending and glorifying his language and his nation. "La signification du tiltre de ce volume," he tells us (I, 11) is to "esclarcir en ce langage François, que les Italiens par leur mesprisance acoustumee appellent Barbare (mais non est) la tresvenerable antiquité du sang de nosdits Princes de Gaule tant Belgique, comme Celtique: Et au surplus mettre en lumiere les choses arcanes et non vulgaires de lhistoire Troyenne [i.e., Les *Singularités de Troie*] non touchees si à plein par autre quelconque qui par cy deuant en ayt escrit, en cestedite langue."

Lemaire establishes the credibility of his historical account by citing ancient authorities "pour mieux autoriser les Illustrations de Gaule" (I, 104); he is most insistent that "ces choses ne sont point feintes par maniere poëtique: mais sont autorisees historialement par vn tresnoble escripteur" (I, 325). By relentlessly producing his authorities — not unlike the modern graduate student — Lemaire is merely following standard medieval dialectical practice, or rather utilizing one of the three kinds of proof customarily invoked in the Middle Ages: proof from Reason, from Authority, and from Experience.[13] "Si ay en ce cas pensé satisfaire à ceux qui desirent congnoitre, que non seulement par opinion vulgaire et commune renommee, mais par viues raisons et vrayes autoritez, la nation Galli-

---

Langue Francoyse" (*Deffence* II.ii). Etienne Pasquier's *Recherches de la France* (in *Œuvres choisies,* ed. Léon Feugère [Paris, 1849]) speaks of the "infinité de beaux traits dont il a illustré notre langue, dedans ses *Illustrations de la Gaule*" (I, 242). Antoine du Moulin, editor of the collective edition of 1549, uses the same term of Lemaire, whom he desires in recompense to "reillustrer" (IV, 6), while the humanist printer Jean de Tournes writes warmly of "nostre Iean le Maire, illustrateur de nostre France" (IV, 8). Of the numerous appearances of the word (and its derivatives) in Lemaire, I will merely cite three of the most characteristic examples: "La figure [a genealogy] deuant mise au Prologue... sert de beaucoup à singulariser Troye, et illustrer Gaule" (I, 16); "nostre Gaule commence bien destre illustree et anoblie" (I, 67); "ce iardin [= *les Illustrations*] remply et illustré de singularitez" (I, 8). Apropos of *singularitez,* Cousin's essay, "Rhétorique latine et classicisme français" explains the reason for the word's prominence in Lemaire's title by the sixteenth century's unbridled enthusiasm for a special kind of indiscriminate erudition, "entretenue par l'amour des anecdotes rares, des curiosités, des 'singularités' et 'cas estranges'" (503-505), practically anything being grist to the mill provided only it was derived from the ancients.

[13] "We establish a geometrical truth by Reason; a historical truth, by Authority, by *auctours*. We learn by experience that oysters do or do not agree with us." C. S. Lewis, *The Discarded Image,* 189.

cane et Françoise, tant Orientale comme Occidentale, est de extraction toute pure Herculienne et Troyenne," triumphantly proclaims the author of *Les Illustrations de Gaule* (II, 468-469), arguing simultaneously from Reason and from Authority. A historian must perforce confirm his statements wherever possible; when authorities are lacking, reason will often step into the breach with a conjectural explanation of the facts — which method, based as it is on probability and the plausible, is nothing if not rhetorical.

B. *Poëte*

There would seem to be little doubt that much of the credit for elevating the status of the poet and his art to the quasi-divine level accorded them in the mid-sixteenth century really belongs to Jean Lemaire and to the Grands Rhétoriqueurs rather than to the Pléiade poets. The latter merely confirm and consolidate — gloriously, it is true — a tendency which had first shown itself in France forty years before their time. Although the terms *poëte, poëme,* and *poëtique* were already established by the mid-fifteenth century, they do not seem to have been much in use before the turn of the fifteenth and sixteenth centuries (see above, Chap. I, p. 40 and n. 61). Their appearance in Lemaire's *Œuvres* is therefore very early, a fact often noted by modern commentators. (His employment of the time-honored *rymeur, facteur,* is minimal; I cannot now recall any instances outside the single line in *La Concorde des deux langages* in which both appear: "Facteurs, rymeurs maint beau dictier recordent" [19, l. 286]. The old *dictier* found in the same verse, on the other hand, is relatively common, occurring, e.g., in *Le Temple,* 76, l. 727; IV, 279; I, 162, 220; II, 233, etc. The cognate *ditter,* "to compose verse," is seen, e.g., in I, 172, 202; and *dictz [dits, ditz]* is also fairly widespread [v. IV, 154, 319, etc.].) To my knowledge, however, no one has as yet remarked upon Lemaire's unremitting insistence on the *nobility* of poetry and the poet (and indeed of the writer as such).

Lemaire's consistent association of *poëte, poësie* with such adjectives as *noble, tresnoble, tresgrand, cler, trescler, souverain, renommé, tresrenommé* is a distinctly Renaissance phenomenon. In the high Middle Ages there was not even a special word for poetry, as we have noted, nor was the art eulogized as a matter of course.

On the contrary, Boccaccio, in the fourteenth and fifteenth books of his *Genealogiae,* feels constrained, not to praise poetry (or, more strictly, literature as a whole), but rather to defend it.[14] Yet the apotheosis of the poet had already begun, thanks to the determined efforts of Petrarch, who made it perfectly clear that the mighty deeds of the heroes would long since have been forgotten but for the poets.[15]

With no great effort on my part, I have accumulated some sixty specimens of the "noble Poëte" type in the *Œuvres* of Jean Lemaire. *Les Illustrations de Gaule* is especially rich in this regard, and might well be subtitled *Les Illustrations des Poètes.* I will not overwhelm the reader with such a mass of material, but a few characteristic phrases may be of interest. Thus, "ce noble Poëte et Orateur, maistre Alain Charretier" (III, 355); "princes orateurs et monarques poetes [Georges Chastellain and Jean Molinet] de nostre langue gallicane" (IV, 321); "plusieurs nobles acteurs Grecz et Latins" (I, 350); "Cicero, prince deloquence" (II, 304). It is no exaggeration to say that terms designating members of the literary profession are almost invariably accompanied by flattering epithets in these works. Furthermore, quite in accordance with the Petrarchan tradition, Lemaire rarely misses an opportunity to ennoble poets as a class by associating them with the aristocracy, and particularly with royalty.[16] In *La Couronne Margaritique,* for instance, of the ten famous *hommes de lettres* who each deliver an oration in honor of Marguerite d'Autriche, three are specifically named as having been in the service, and indeed in the confidence, of the mighty of this world. "Maistre Iean Robertet iadis secretaire de trois Roys de France, et de trois Ducz de Bourbon" (IV, 77-78); "messire George Chastelain Indiciaire et Historiographe souuerain, anciennement nourry et esleué en la maison de Bourgongne" (IV, 96); "maistre Martin Franc... iadis Secretaire du premier Duc de

---

[14] See Curtius, *ELLMA,* 549.

[15] On the "poets and princes" topos, see Alice W. Sperduti's unpublished dissertation "Petrarch on Poetry" (Cornell, 1947), 113-114. Cf. Curtius, *ELLMA,* Excursus IX: "Poetry as Perpetuation," 476-477. And in Jean Molinet's *Chroniques* for the years 1474-1506, the alternate prologue contains an eloquent passage (592-594) on this very theme.

[16] Hall, declares, not unreasonably, that in addition to demonstrating the importance of the poetic art by stressing this relationship, sixteenth-century French writers were bent on justifying royal patronage (*RLC,* 143).

Sauoye" (IV, 127). Dame Rhetoricque in *La Plainte du Désiré* urges her disciples to serve as wise counsellors to great men ("Mes orateurs, par voz dicts prouffitables, / Persuadez aux grans princes notables," etc.),[17] and in *Le Temple d'Honneur* the distinguished company of some twenty illustrious personnages "tant antiques que recentz" does not fail to summon, "comme ministres et secrétaires d'Honneur et de Vertu," a corresponding group of eminent men of letters, from the ancients, Josephus and Livy, through the Middle Ages to the most recently departed of the Rhétoriqueurs, Octovien de Saint-Gelais (*Temple*, ll. 1102-1121).

Two other matters also deserve mention in relation to the systematic praise of poetry. I refer in the first instance to the Neoplatonist doctrine of *furor poeticus*, elaborated by Marsilio Ficino as an offshoot of his commentary on the Socratic dialogue *Ion*, wherein the poet is depicted as a divinely inspired being. *Furor poeticus*, a tenet of cardinal importance to the literary theorists of mid-sixteenth-century France, is first mentioned in a French critical work at the very beginning of the century (*L'Instructif de la seconde rethoricque* of 1501, attributed to Regnaud le Queux). What can thus be claimed as one of the first allusions to the doctrine in French poetry appears, I believe, in Lemaire's *La Plainte du Désiré* (1503), in the line "Les motz dorez que les haulx dieux luy baillent" (76, l. 245). There is a yet more specific reference in *La Concorde des deux langages*:

> Les neuf beaux cieulx que Dieu tourne et tempere
> Rendent tel bruit en leurs spheres diffuses
> Que le son vient jusqu'en nostre hemispere.
>
> Et de là sont toutes graces infuses
> Aux clers engins, et le don celestin
> De la liqueur et fontaine des Muses.[18]

The actual expression *fureur poeticque* does occur once, in a relatively minor yet most interesting work, *La Concorde du Genre Humain* (long thought to be lost, but happily rediscovered by P. Jodogne), composed in honor of the Peace of Cambrai (1508). Writing of the near-impossibility of ever doing justice to the lofty

---

[17] *La Plainte du Désiré*, ed. Dora Yabsley (Paris, 1932), 85, ll. 309-310.
[18] *Concorde*, 18, ll. 262-267. See also Frappier's notes 77-79, on pp. 63-64.

themes treated in this work (which is a perfectly conventional use of the affected modesty topos, or rather of its near relative, called by Curtius the "inexpressibility topos"),[19] Lemaire, likening his subject to a "champaigne large et patente," exclaims in despair that to cover it in even a summary fashion "souffiroit à paines ung autre Pegasus volant, combien qu'il fut abuvré de la fontaine des Muses et eust prins escueil [i.e., "élan"] de fureur poeticque" (59, ll. 330-332).

The second point I wish to raise here concerns the ancient belief — revived with much fanfare in sixteenth-century France — that eloquence, wisdom, and erudition go hand in hand.[20] "Les dieux puissans ont gens cytharisans / Auctorisans leur loz par grans estudes," sings the poet,[21] thereby informing lesser mortals with equal conviction and concision of his own peculiarly privileged status. And, as we are told in *La Couronne Margaritique*, "Vertu... prisa l'eloquence et sauoir" of the Ten Orators.[22] There is almost certainly an echo here of what Spingarn calls the "ethical" theory of the origins of poetry.[23]

---

[19] *ELLMA*, 159. Whereas the affected modesty topos is used to proclaim a particular individual's incapacity, ineptitude, unworthiness, etc., the inexpressibility topos is a flat denial that *anyone* could handle the matter adequately. Shakespeare's Chorus may be said to combine both conventions in the Prologue to *Henry V*:

>But pardon, gentles all,
>The flat unraised spirits that hath dar'd
>On this unworthy scaffold to bring forth
>So great an object: can this cockpit hold
>The vasty fields of France? or may we cram
>Within this wooden O the very casques
>That did affright the air at Agincourt?
>                                    [etc.]

[20] Cf. Cicero's remark to this effect, Chap. I, p. 22 above.
[21] *Temple*, 54, ll. 120-121.
[22] IV, 154. "The critics are almost unanimous in demanding that the poet be learned," writes Hall (*RLC*, 67), citing Scaliger, Castiglione, and Lionardi as corroborative witnesses. Cf. Du Bellay's "l'amplification de nostre Langue... ne se peut faire sans doctrine & sans erudition" (*Deffence*, II.iii), and his insistence upon not only natural endowment, — the ancient *natura* — but also "doctrine" (*ars*). "Qu'on ne m'allegue point aussi que les poëtes naissent, car cela s'entend de ceste ardeur & allegresse d'esprit qui naturellement excite les poëtes, & sans la quele toute doctrine leur seroit manque & inutile" (*ibid.*).
[23] *Op. cit.*, 117; i.e., that anti-Platonic conception expressed in Horace's *Ars poetica* in the famous passage where it is claimed that earliest poets were divine prophets and lawgivers and, in a word, the founders of civilization (*Ars poetica*, ll. 391-407).

Yet the eulogizing of poets is not *per se* rhetorical, although the encomiastic mode itself undoubtedly is. But for Jean Lemaire all literary disciplines are so closely interrelated that — without blurring the distinctions between them — what he has to say of the poet applies in like measure to the writer of prose, the historian, the orator. This is why it is next to impossible to consider his view of any one facet of the writer's craft in isolation from the others.

## C. *Poëte, orateur, historien*

Lemaire's lofty conception of the poet applies with equal force to other branches of literature, above all to those which he himself practiced, namely history, and what he calls "oratory." *Orateur* is a term requiring special attention, since in Lemaire's parlance it can mean either "writer" or "orator" (in the usual acceptation), or even "poet." [24] Thus when we read "maistre Jehan de Meun, orateur françois" (*Concorde*, 44, 1. 264), the word is fairly evidently a synonym of either "poëte" or "escrivain," whereas plain "escrivain" is the most likely interpretation of *orateur* in the sonorous phrase "messire Marsille Ficin de Florence, philosophe Platonique, prestre, medecin, et orateur tresrenommé" (IV, 120). There is also a specialized technical connotation, designating the member of a diplomatic mission charged with the actual delivery of a communication from one head of state to another: "Hermolaus Barbarus, homme de grands lettres et vertus, lequel les [ = the Venetians] auoit seruis d'Orateur presque enuers tous les Princes Chrestiens. Et comme il fust sur ses vieux iours en ambassade pour eux deuers le Pape," etc. (III, 384-385). As we noted in Chapter II, above, the father of French eloquence, the great Alain Chartier (d. circa 1440), himself served France in an official capacity as Orator.

As often as not, the word *orateur* is coupled in Lemaire's writings with such related (in the professional sense) words as *historien, philosophe, poëte*: e.g., "maistre Martin Franc..., poëte, philosophe et historien" (IV, 127); "messire Robert Gaguin..., philo-

---

[24] Pierre Jodogne states that since *orateur* is generally contrasted with *poète* (with reference to men of letters), the term in all likelihood signifies "prose-writers." He admits, however, that the distinction is not always clear (*JLBEFB*, 82; and 82, n. 2). *Rhetoricien* is also found in the *Œuvres*, but comparatively rarely. See, e.g., "une secte de Poëtes et rhetoriciens" (I, 70), where the term appears to have much the same meaning as *orateur*.

sophe theologien, poëte, orateur et historien" (IV, 62). But the juxtapositions in which Lemaire unabashedly takes the greatest delight are "poëtes et historiens" and "poëtes, orateurs et historiens," as in "aucuns poëtes, orateurs et historiens de la langue françoise" (*Concorde,* 4, ll. 25-26). It seems fairly clear that in such a context *orateur* does not signify "poet," especially when the formula refers to such famous orators as, e.g., Ulysses, Paris (II, *passim*), and Cicero (*Temple,* 89, ll. 1113-1115).[25]

Although synonymy was a recognized rhetorical technique, the frequent, resounding repetition of "poëtes, orateurs et historiens" and its variants cannot be solely accounted for by the sheer joy of piling up near-synonyms (as in the case of *orateur* and *poëte* especially) for the sake of it, or again for the numinous, formulaic effect thus obtained, although this is doubtless not without influence on Lemaire. Nor can one dismiss entirely the possibility that the exigencies of prose rhythm and the instinct for fine cadences play a part in the author's marked predilection for such phrases.[26] But such considerations, concerned exclusively with form, neglect entirely the question of content; and content is extremely significant, because — as we noted in Chapter II, above — Lemaire's concept of the writer's exalted vocation — particularly that of the poet and historian — is here contained in essence.

### E. *Imitateur*

In the dedication (to the painter Jean Perréal) of the 1510 edition of *Les Épîtres de l'Amant Vert,* the poet styles himself "Jan Le Maire de Belges, treshumble disciple et loingtain imitateur des

---

[25] We should also take note of *Œuvres,* II, 234, where one might easily be misled into reading "orator," were it not for the clue "escriuit": "vn grand orateur de Grece, nommé Isocrates..., sachant que cest trop dangereuse chose de mesdire des dames, ainçois escriuit plusieurs louenges de ladite Heleine." Isocrates, though a famous rhetorician, was not in fact an orator; his speeches were not delivered orally at all, but instead appeared in published form. Lemaire may have known this.

[26] Among others, Alex. L. Gordon, in *Ronsard et la Rhétorique* (Geneva, 1970), notes the extreme fondness of sixteenth-century poets for the practice of what might perhaps strike the modern reader as needless repetition (p. 109), a good deal of which is undoubtedly due to unrestrained verbal exuberance (cf. e.g. Rabelais, *passim*). Moreover, "poëtes, orateurs et historiens" can be read as a line of decasyllabic verse.

meilleurs indiciaires et historiographes" (*Amant*, 3), an appellation which shows him to have been at the very least aware of what was shortly to become in France (as it had long been in Italy) one of the fundamental articles of faith of the Renaissance literary credo, viz., *imitatio*.[27] One must, however, be on one's guard against making excessive claims of originality in Lemaire's behalf, since the very wording he uses in the above quotation is itself an imitation of that employed by two of his most admired predecessors.[28] (M. Jodogne is of the considered opinion that Lemaire's imitation is not a matter of theoretical principle at all, but exists rather "au niveau pratique et souvent inconscient de la création poétique" [*JLBEFB*, 39]). But he is incontestably the first French writer consciously and methodically to imitate Homer (see below, Chap. IV, 101). Furthermore, *imitatio* is a rhetorical doctrine of impeccable ancestry. This is confirmed by Quintilian's *De institutione oratoria*, which categorically states: "... there can be no doubt that in art no small portion of our task lies in imitation, since, although invention came first and is all-important, it is expedient to imitate whatever has been invented with success" (X.ii.1). From Quintilian derived the strong emphasis laid upon imitation by Joachim Du Bellay in his *Deffence et Illustration de la Langue Françoyse*,[29] published almost forty years after Lemaire's own *Illustrations*.

SECTION 3: THE FUNCTION OF LITERATURE

There is a notable proliferation in Lemaire's works of such cognates as *loer, louenges, loz, laudation, collaudation, laudatoire*

---

[27] The systematic imitation of ancient exemplars, that is, rather than *imitatio naturae* (mimesis), which was a later development, bound up with the resurgence of Aristotelianism.

[28] "... je, Jehan Molinet, loingtain immitateur des historiographes" (*Chroniques*, I, 28); and "... Alain Charretier ... lointaing immitateur des orateurs" (*Quadrilogue*, Prologue, 1. 6). It is noteworthy that here Lemaire uses "imitateur" with reference to recent vernacular authors. For a comprehensive survey of imitation as practiced by Jean Lemaire (which comprises, besides Homer, Virgil, Ovid, Lucretius, and other ancients, that of medieval writers like Dante and Petrarch), see Gmelin, "Imitatio" (pp. 248-280 are devoted to Lemaire).

[29] Chapter VIII of the first book is entitled "D'amplifier la Langue Francoyse par l'immitation des anciens Aucteurs Grecz & Romains."

(together with their negative counterparts, *blasmer, reprehension, vituperation, invective,* etc.). The "secte de Poëtes et rhetoriciens" founded by Bardus of Gaul illustrates exactly the moralizing function of medieval poetry (and indeed of medieval literature *in toto* — witness Molinet's concept of the role of history). We are told that they "chantoient melodieusement leurs rhythmes . . . en louant les vns et en blasmant les autres."[30] "Melodieusement" instantly calls to mind the second element of literature's two-fold office, namely, delightful *eloquentia* to counterbalance utilitarian *doctrina*. The famous Horatian formula ("Aut prodesse volunt aut delectare poetae / aut simul et iucunda et idonea dicere vitae")[31] represents the best-known statement of the ancient theme, long adduced as poetry's first line of defence in the face of Plato's fulminations against the art and its practitioners in his *Republic*. Hence it is quite in the order of things for Jean Lemaire to harp constantly on the *utile-dulce* of his own writings. For example, the Prologue to *La Couronne Margaritique* (IV, 15) speaks the poet's mingled sorrow and exasperation at being compelled by unhappy circumstance to leave his "emprise *vtile*" (l. 4) and "*fructueuse* escriture" (l. 17; unless otherwise noted, all italics in Lemaire's text are mine). Similarly, the Prologue of *Le Traité des Pompes funèbres* concludes with a brief apologia of history, which "est necessaire *prouffitable et delectant* et digne de recommandacion" (IV, 273). We may also note Rhetoricque's injunction to her followers regarding their "dicts prouffitables" (*Plainte,* 85, l. 309).

Now the medieval notion of poetry's utility — its most celebrated exponent in the Trecento being Boccaccio (in his *Genealogiae*) — can be in large measure attributed to the confusion and intermingling of the theory of that discipline with the ancient precepts of rhetoric, whose avowed purpose is essentially *persuasion*. This, for example, is the explicit goal of Rhetoricque in *La Plainte du Désiré*: to persuade the mourners to grieve no longer for the dear departed nobleman de Ligny, and to convince them by demonstration (i.e., by means of epideictic oratory) of his surpassing worth.

---

[30] I, 70. Cf., e.g., "Pour collauder la divine clemence" (*Genre humain,* 51, l. 82); "De la laudation ou vituperation des Roys degypte, apres la mort" (IV, 290); ". . . vne inuectiue exclamatoire" (III, 403).

[31] *Ars poetica,* 333-334. Cf. *ibid.,* 343-344, "omne tulit punctum qui miscuit utile dulci, / lectorem delectando pariterque monendo."

This also accounts for the presence in Lemaire's works of a group of key words associated with the most basic of rhetorical functions. "Persuadez aux grans princes notables / Que desormais ne prestent nul escout / Aux envieux..." is the directive received by the "orateurs" in *La Plainte du Désiré* (85, ll. 310-312), and in *La Couronne Margaritique* the emerald is specifically acclaimed for its marvelous power of bestowing "eloquence et paroles persuasiues" on its happy possessor (IV, 114). Lemaire is notably fond of expressions like "persuadee par paroles" and "persuadee par douces requestes" (I, 128 and 169).

The success or failure of rhetoric, then, is measured in terms of its persuasive efficiency. By this criterion, Rhetoricque's oration in *La Plainte du Désiré* is not quite up to the mark, because the audience seems to be only "presque demy persuadez, mais non encores du tout esbranlez de leur doleance: car *l'efficace* du parler rhetorical n'avoit pas esté assez vifve a l'equipolent du dueil."[32] The word *efficace,* which in the early sixteenth century is equivalent to "efficacy," "effectiveness," "effect" (sometimes "power"), is almost invariably used by Jean Lemaire in conjunction with *persuasion, eloquence, parler, oraison,* and similar terms. The historic *harengue* delivered by Pope Urban II at the Council of Clermont in 1095 is praised for its "merueilleuse efficace," as well it might be, seeing that it launched the First Crusade (III, 287. Cf. the crushing "response verbale et effectiue" made by the Emperor Maximilian I to a Venetian embassy [III, 238].) Similar phrases indicative of Lemaire's sensitivity to linguistic effectiveness are not hard to find, especially in *Les Illustrations de Gaule,* where, for instance, the innocent Pegasis Oenone discovers that the seductive eloquence of Paris is "de telle efficace, quelle pourroit tirer en sa sentence mesme vn cœur adamantin" (I, 179). Nor should we forget that the destruction of Troy results directly from the impact of Venus's all-too-persuasive rhetoric on the impressionable Paris, when she makes by far the most effective speech of all those contained in *Les Illustrations.*[33]

---

[32] *Plainte,* 90 (l'Acteur), ll. 4-7.
[33] "Leloquence artificielle de dame Venus, ses paroles delicates, et sa douce persuasion causerent telle efficace et telle emotion au cœur du ieune... Paris," etc. (I, 249).

Section 4: The Question of Rhetorical Delivery
— "Pronuntiatio" and "Urbanité"

Perhaps the most overtly rhetorical pages in Lemaire's entire *Œuvres* are those recounting the Judgment of Paris (I, 230-260), which consists basically in a contest of oratorical skill, mingled with some of the author's most memorable descriptive passages. The manner in which the participants in this scene speak — the *pronuntiatio* or *actio* — is very minutely observed. Venus, every inch the *femme fatale*, cajoles the naïf Paris "dune voix doucement organisee procedant du creux de sa poitrine amiable" (I, 243). The reluctant judge presiding over the celestial beauty pageant, only too conscious of his awesome responsibility and of the dire consequences likely to ensue, no matter what his decision, delivers his final opinion "dune voix tremulente et casse, et pleine de crainte, ayant le visage honteux" (I, 257). The mortally offended Juno, on the other hand, displaying as hellish a fury as was ever observed in woman (let alone goddess) scorned,[34] lets fly at Paris in a truly superb piece of vituperation: "Mais Iuno Saturnienne (embrasee de grand ire et impatience) ne se peut onques abstenir de desgorger la fumee de son despit: ainçois dun visage palissant, et duns yeux allumez par grand fureur, dune voix aigre, sonoreuse et abrupte, et dune oraison Satyrique et pleine de mordacité, increpa son Iuge Paris, en ceste maniere..." (I, 258).

Further examples abound of Jean Lemaire's unremitting search for the *mot juste,* for the uniquely individual note which will convey his characters' *pronuntiatio* to the life. The very verb *pronuncer* (i.e., *réciter, déclamer*) is often used when Lemaire is describing a speaker's delivery, where some other, less specific term might have served; the Muse Melpomene, for example, "prononça en graue accent, ses autentiques tragedies" (I, 220). Almost identical phrasing is used of Juno, who "prononça son oraison de graue accent."[35]

The emphasis in the above passages is laid principally on the first part of *pronuntiatio* (which, as we saw in Chapter I, the *Rhe-*

---

[34] "Car il nest point de plus grief desdain à vne noble femme, que de se voir vaincue et surmontee en question de beauté corporelle" (I, 257).
[35] I, 232. See also II, 19, 36, 120, and *passim*; and cf. *Plainte,* 68 (l'Acteur), l. 5: "Les verbes que Paincture pronunça sont cy apres recitez."

*torica ad Herennium* considers under two headings): namely, voice quality. The second part, physical movement, includes both gesture and facial expression (v. *Ad Herenn.*, III.xv.26), which latter is indeed evoked in such terms as *contenance, visage honteux* (and especially in Juno's "visage palissant" and "yeux allumez par grand fureur"). That effective gesture and facial expression are indispensable to a telling delivery is also explicitly recognized in the eye-witness account of the future Emperor Charles V, then only eight years old, holding forth in a brief oration to the Three Estates of the Netherlands: "Et lors mons$^r$ larchiduc representant bien son prince en si jeune aaige les en pria par une petite harengue plus entendue par les gestes de son visaige que par la sonorité de sa voix puerille, mais toutesuoyes en telle sorte quil debvoit bien souffrir au peuple" (IV, 516-517). But on the whole, gesture in the strict sense, which is described with such a wealth of detail in the ancient treatises, is virtually ignored by Lemaire. It is *verbal* delivery which fascinates him.

An interesting by-product of Lemaire's attention to correct rhetorical practice may be observed in the encomium of *urbanité* which is pronounced by the great Georges Chastellain (d. 1475) in *La Couronne Margaritique*. *Urbanité*[36] is most meticulously defined as follows: "La propre diffinition de ceste vertu est telle: Vrbanité, est vne elegance, vne courtoisie ou vne gaillardise de deuiser plaisamment en resiouissant les assistans, sans les facher: et est Vrbanité moyenneresse de deux extremes, cestasauoir, de dicacité et rusticité: par dicacité, on peult entendre irrision, bauerie, moquerie, ou braguerie en paroles: et par rusticité, vilenie, rudesse, ineptitude et malplaisance en langage" (IV, 104). *Urbanitas* is the subject of an exhaustive discussion by Quintilian (VI.iii.8, 17, 45, 103 ff., 107; VI.iv.10), who specifically notes that it represents "the total absence of all that is incongruous, coarse, unpolished and exotic whether in thought, language, voice or gesture" (VI.iii.107). The resemblance between the ancient and the modern definition is close: both call to mind, in their ideal of unaffected elegance, good manners, and above all easy flow of language, the admirable figure of the seventeenth-century *honnête homme* — not to mention the Cor-

---

[36] Spaak hints that the French word may well be a neologism coined by Lemaire himself. *JLB*, 47, n. 7.

tegiano of Baldassare Castiglione, himself an exact contemporary (1478-1529) of Lemaire de Belges.

Marguerite d'Autriche is depicted by Chastellain as the very embodiment of *Urbanité*: "... elle est tenue pour le vray parangon de courtoisie et d'Vrbanité, comme celle, dont la bouche mellifluente est toute arrosee de pure eloquence naïue et tressouefue faconde. Laquelle chose elle ha fait maintesfois apparoir ... tant en receuant les nobles hommes estrangers, qui viennent souuent deuers elle de par les Roys et Princes..., desquelz ilz ont charge de legation et ambassade, ou autrement, comme en les entretenant de gracieuses collocutions, et leur faisant response condecente à leurs belles harengues et graues propositions, tellement que iamais ne partent delle sans admiration, et pareillement en ses deuises familieres et domestiques" (IV, 105).

*Urbanité*, then, may be displayed to equal advantage on grand ceremonial occasions and in private, whether a princess is engaged in making a formal response to an ambassador or simply unbending among her intimates. As *exempla* of *urbanité*, Lemaire cites two "plaisants contes" in which Marguerite's ready wit and agreeable sense of humor are shown in a most flattering light (IV, 105-107). In brief, *urbanité* is that sureness of taste which instinctively matches the style of address to the occasion: the grand and stately manner ("gracieuses collocutions") and the effortless wit are but two sides to the same coin, "pure eloquence naïue et tressouefue faconde." A rhetorical source, in this instance, furnishes what amounts in practice to a whole ideal of behavior.


### Section 5: Style (Eloquence and Elegance)

Thus far we have discussed Lemaire's concept of what literature is and what it should do. He is just as attentive to matters of style. Various nuances of the word itself appear in his works: e.g., *La Plainte du Désiré* (84, ll. 246-247) praises the Comte de Ligny as "Celuy qui sceut de guerre autant le stille / Que Marius .." (Huguet cites these lines as an illustration of *style* meaning "manière d'agir," "procédé," "méthode.") In *Le Temple d'Honneur* we find the term employed in its modern connotation; [37] in similar vein, Lemaire commends the fifteenth-century historian of the Papacy, Platina, for having written "en beau style elegant" (III, 245-246). On another occasion, while excoriating Dion of Prusa for having dared to suggest that Troy never really fell — a most disconcerting thesis which, if correct, would utterly invalidate his own *Illustrations* — Lemaire takes pains to remark that it is only Dion's subject matter which is "vaine, plate, ridicule et adulatoire." His style (*parler*), on the contrary, "est tout pur oratoire" (II, 244). The distinction between *fond* and *forme* is made quite explicit in the author's introduction to *La Légende des Vénitiens*: "Plaise aux Lecteurs supporter benignement *la grosse tornure du langage peu elegant*: car iay plus eu de regard à ce que la narration historiale soit garnie de verité, que coulouree de fleurs de rhetorique... la Legende des Venitiens... est digne de lire: *non pour sa forme mais pour sa matiere*" (III, 364). Lemaire's anxiety that this point be constantly borne in mind by the reader is underscored by its repetition in abbreviated form at the end of the treatise, where he states that *La Légende*'s merit consists more in its being "veritable que enrichie daucunes couleurs dart oratoire" (III, 402). His phraseology discloses a palpably medieval outlook on style as being the colors of rhetoric whose function it is to brighten and enrich a work after its original composition.

An attentive reader can hardly fail to be impressed by the continual recurrence of the adjective *elegant* in Lemaire's *Œuvres*. It is in fact one of his favorite laudatory words. On occasion he gives it in its customary acceptation, as when he describes how the shepherd Paris fits into court life as to the manner born, because "en tout estoit si propre, si elegant, et si bien luy seoit" (I, 330). Similarly, Mercure, in the Prologue of Book II, addresses himself to the "treselegante et tresdelicate noblesse Royale et Ducale" (II, 3); the future St. Helena is lauded as being "la plus belle, et la plus elegante du monde" (III, 256). But Lemaire especially favors *elegant* used in association with matters of stylistic excellence. The French language, for instance, "est maintenant la plus elegante,

---

[37] "... pource que son parlement / Peut servir à maint & à mainte, / Par legier stille & rude emprainte / En escript l'ay cuydé reduyre" (*Temple*, 100, ll. 1404-1407. Cf. *Concorde*: "Maint noble dit, cantilennes et odes, / Dont le stille est subtil et mirificque," 19, ll. 296-297).

congnue et vsitee es nobles courts de nosdits Princes" (I, 10). Apuleius is hailed as "ce treselegant acteur" (I, 272), and the peerless Marguerite d'Autriche — as one might expect — composes not only prose, but also poetry "treselegamment" (IV, 111).

Eloquence and elegance are always intimately allied in Lemaire's conception of style. So far as medieval poetry is concerned, *eloquentia* is interpreted as the beautiful language, the veils of fiction, in which some edifying and instructive *doctrina* is to be arrayed; but for Jean Lemaire *eloquence* also — and much more significantly — signifies precisely what it had to classical antiquity: i.e., fluent, forceful, and persuasive speech. It is not for nothing that each of the Prologues to the three books of *Les Illustrations de Gaule* is supposedly written by Mercure, in his capacity as "Diev d'eloqvence, ingeniosité et bonne invention" (I, 3). This device humorously grants the author licence to address his princely patrons, for once at least, as an equal,[38] or even as a superior. On his numerous appearances in *Les Illustrations,* the witty Mercure is rarely bereft of his "Dieu d'éloquence" tag,[39] but in spite of this proud title the only time his vaunted eloquence is actually deployed to good effect (aside from in the Prologues) is when he relays to the three goddesses their judge's humble petition to view them naked (I, 251-252).

Jean Lemaire, then, restores to "eloquence" its primal connotation of potent, effective speech, while the tenacious medieval misinterpretation which equated eloquence with literary style is, as we see in his works, in the process of being displaced by the term *style* itself. Eloquence is regarded as admirable *per se,* as is elegance. Lemaire dedicates *La Concorde du genre humain* to "deux nobles Lyonnois" who are described glowingly as "sourjons et receptacles d'Honneur, d'Humanité, d'Eloquence, et de toute Gaillardise

---

[38] Cf. George Bernard Shaw's provocative use of the same trick in the Prologue to *Caesar and Cleopatra,* where the Philistine audience is subjected to a long and disdainful harangue by the god Ra.

[39] J. Frappier notes indulgently that Jean Lemaire does not altogether respect the traditional hierarchy of gods who are the "guides et inspirateurs des poètes. En bon rhétoriqueur, il semble accorder une sorte de primauté à Mercure 'le Dieu d'éloquence,' et par conséquent de 'rhétorique.' Pourtant le rôle d'Apollon et des Muses ne lui a pas échappé... il décrit dans son récit des noces de Thétis et de Pélée un Apollon musagète." "L'Humanisme dans la poésie de Lemaire de Belges," in *Romance Philology* 17 (1963-64), 272-284; this citation 274-275.

mercurienne" (79, ll. 888-890). His revered patroness Marguerite d'Autriche is renowned, he maintains, for "la bouche mellifluente... toute arrosee de pure eloquence naïue" (IV, 104-105); the simple shepherd lad Paris is as much awed by the "merueilleuse eloquence" of Oenone as he is by her "souueraine beauté" (I, 165-166); and undeniably, "lhomme eloquent est armé de deffence et de diligence, contre tous ennemis" (I, 204).

Yet Lemaire's enthusiastic approval of eloquence does not blind him to its potential abuse at the hands of an unscrupulous person (or deity) — which inherent flaw was, as we recall, largely at the root of Plato's misgivings with respect to rhetoric. In the Judgment scene, neither Juno, Pallas, nor Venus is any too fastidious when it is a matter of scoring off the competition, but Venus is the least inhibited of all in her use of eloquence as a means to an end. So flagrantly indeed does she exploit her oratorical cunning that the author of *Les Illustrations* feels obliged to stigmatize her eloquence as "artificielle" (I, 249). The epithet may naturally be construed as a commendation of her skill and artistry, but is, I feel sure, to be taken in this particular context as signifying "sly," "crafty," "artful,"[40] especially since Lemaire later upbraids Paris at some length for being gullible enough to award the prize to Venus at the cost of earning the undying enmity of Juno and Pallas.

Broadly speaking, it can be argued that Jean Lemaire's concept of eloquence, though still distinctly medieval in some respects, is perceptibly classical in others. Such an outlook would necessarily presuppose an overriding concern with actual speech, a subject that will be examined in the next two chapters of this essay.

---

[40] Cf. Huguet's "artificieux," "rusé."

Chapter IV

THE DISTRIBUTION AND FUNCTION OF ORATIONS
IN THE WORKS OF JEAN LEMAIRE

Even a cursory reading of Lemaire's *Œuvres* reveals that they are highly oratorical in the primary as well as the extended sense of the term. This fact is most graphically illustrated by the sheer mass of actual orations contained in all the major works and — almost without exception — at crucial points in the narrative. For our present purposes, "oration" is taken to mean any speech, whether in prose or verse, formal and dignified in manner, and of at least a certain minimal length. What is commonly accepted as dialogue does not fall within this category, and is in any event not much practiced by Lemaire. To my recollection, passages of sustained dialogue occur only two or three times, notably in a tart exchange between Juno and Venus (I, 252) and in the episode where Oenone reveals to Paris's foster-parents the august lineage of her husband and persuades them to let him take part in the Trojan Games (I, 290-294).

In order to demonstrate this striking omnipresence of orations, I propose to begin by cataloguing them briefly. Short pieces of verse — *chansons, virelais,* and the like — although oratorical in manner and intent,[1] are not included in this enumeration, nor is another

---

[1] E.g., *Les XXIIII Couplets de la valitude et conualescence de la Royne* (III, 87-97); *Les Regretz de la Dame infortunee* (III, 187-193), and the encomiastic songs of the seven shepherds and shepherdesses in the first part of *Le Temple d'Honneur,* 50-64, ll. 1-390. (For an informative analysis of the pastoral elements of this *déploration,* see Alice Hulubei, *L'Églogue en France au XVIe siècle* [Paris, 1938], 156-162.)

highly rhetorical form to which Jean Lemaire is much given, namely apostrophe (or, more accurately, *exclamatio*),[2] which I shall discuss later. Here then is the survey, work by work.

In *Le Temple d'Honneur et de Vertus*, the personified "paranimphe et garde des Vertus," Entendement, delivers a formal address to the widowed Anne de France.[3] This is tripartite in nature and consists of an exhortation to be of good heart, a panegyric of the deceased Pierre de Bourbon and his widow, and a description of the Temple d'Honneur itself.

The encomiastic *Plainte du Désiré* would have no artistic *raison d'être* at all were it not for the speeches of Paincture and Rhetoricque which make up the bulk of the piece.

As for *La Couronne Margaritique*, we have Infortune's harangue to Atropos (IV, 21-25) in 120 lines of octosyllabic verse, inciting her to destroy Duke Philibert le Beau; another (rather conventional) verse oration, delivered by "Hebe Deesse de Ieunesse" (IV, 33-40), lamenting Philibert's untimely end and describing the heartrending sorrow of his young widow, Marguerite d'Autriche; and Vertu's address to the Ten Orators (IV, 57-62). This last is an extremely curious piece indeed. Vertu informs her favored disciples of their duties in the precise, no-nonsense manner of a judge instructing the jury; transmits these instructions with a wealth of erudite detail more commonly associated with the present-day graduate seminar; and, as if this were not sufficient, somehow contrives to imbue the whole thing with the authentic evangelical fervor of a coach's pregame peptalk. Finally, there are the Ten Orations themselves,[4] which alone take up more than half of this long work (62-153).

---

[2] Faral (*AP*, 70-71) distinguishes the classical apostrophe, "le procédé qui consiste à se détourner du juge pour s'adresser directement à l'adversaire" from the connotation given the word by medieval poetic theorists, viz., "la figure que les anciens nommaient *exclamatio* et qui consiste simplement à interpeller une personne ou un objet quelconque."

[3] Pp. 79-81, ll. 817-866, and 82-93, ll. 887-1220. Entendement's oration is briefly interrupted by the author, 81-82, ll. 867-886.

[4] The Orators, in speaking order, are: Robert Gaguin; Albertus Magnus; Jean Robertet, rhétoriqueur; St. Isidore of Seville; Georges Chastellain; Boccaccio; Arnauld de Villeneuve, thirteenth-century alchemist, whose collected writings were published at Lyons in 1504; Marsilio Ficino; Martin [Le] Franc, rhétoriqueur; and Vincent de Beauvais, author of the encyclopedic *Speculum maius*.

*La Concorde des deux langages* contains (in the "Temple de Vénus" section, ll. 367-616) the justly lauded "sermon" preached by Genïus, "prelat venerïen," "premier primat haultain / De toute Gaule..."[5] (Lemaire's own charmingly whimsical variation on the ancient *carpe diem* theme), which ends with a spirited encomium of the French nation. Significantly enough, Genïus, who — like Erasmus's Folly — is not above eulogizing himself (ll. 526-564), proudly boasts of his descent from the eloquent Mercure (l. 539).

In the exultant piece on the Treaty of Cambrai, the eponymous (and rather cumbersomely named) Nymph, "Concorde du genre humain," regales Maximilian I with a formal prose oration in the epideictic mode (pp. 65-69), eulogizing the guiding spirit behind the Treaty (the Emperor's own daughter, Marguerite d'Autriche) and urging that she be rewarded with the well-earned title of "Augusta."

One of the most graceful passages of *La Première Épître de l'Amant Vert* is the elegant little account of the life, unrequited love, and tragic death of Marguerite's pet parrot, which the Amant puts into the mouth of a "gente pucelle." As he foretells, she will ensure that no "pelerins passans" will leave his tomb ignorant of his sad story (ll. 221-256). If Concorde's oration to Caesar is in the grand Ciceronian manner so much admired by French humanists of the generation following Lemaire's,[6] the eulogy of the Amant Vert is by comparison simple, small-scale, unaffected, and genuinely moving.

The latest in date of Jean Lemaire's published works are *Les Trois Contes de Cupido et d'Atropos* (Paris, Galliot du Pré, 1526), which recount the appalling consequences arising from the drunken mix-up by Love and Death of their respective bows and arrows. In other words, this is an allegorical account of the origins of "la Verole grosse" (III, 54), a theme which fascinated sixteenth-century

---

[5] Ll. 206 and 199-200. The latter denomination is a nice satiric touch, seeing that the Archbishop of Lyons — formerly, as Lugdunum, chief city of Roman Gaul, and consequently ranked above the upstart Paris in the French diocesan hierarchy — to this day rejoices in the title "primat des Gaules." And the Temple of Venus is of course in Lyons, as ll. 133-145 make abundantly clear.

[6] Cf., e.g., Ulrich Gallet's stately periods in the "harangue faicte... à Picrochole," *Gargantua*, chap. XXXI.

writers.⁷ The second *conte* comprises some 98 lines of direct speech (out of a total of 402), largely of a comic character: Venus berates her son for his disgraceful misconduct, Atropos jeers at Venus, and Cupido and Atropos engage in a vulgar slanging-match. *Conte* III contains an amusing courtroom scene with Volupté as counsel for Venus, and Megere representing Atropos, complete with formal judicial procedure and legal jargon; but as Lemaire's authorship of this — and the first — piece is disputed, I shall do no more than mention it in passing.⁸

As polemical tracts in the deliberative mode of rhetoric, *La Légende des Vénitiens* and *La Différence des Schismes et des Conciles de l'Église* have already received our attention in the preceding chapter. At this point, we may note the author's preoccupation in the latter work with formal discourse. On two occasions, he provides his own vernacular rendering of what purport to be historic speeches, given respectively by Pope Urban II (see above, p. 85) and the Emperor Maximilian I. The second of these is preceded by the original Latin text (III, 236-238) and is apparently cited by Lemaire on account of his admiration for the Emperor's proficiency in extemporizing in Latin.⁹ Urban II's mighty crusading oration (280-287) is of much greater interest, not only because of its intrinsic

---

⁷ Cf., *inter alia*, a Neo-Latin didactic poem uncompromisingly entitled *Syphilis*, composed by the distinguished Italian humanist and physician Girolamo Fracastoro (d. 1553), and the dedication, by an even more celebrated medical man, of his book (*Gargantua*) to two special segments of his public: "Beuveurs très illustres, et vous, véroléz très précieux..."

⁸ For an exhaustive discussion of the attribution of the *Contes* either to Lemaire or to some other person or persons unknown, I refer the reader to P. Jodogne (*JLBEFB*, 463-474). The distinguished Belgian scholar, basing his arguments mainly on stylistic grounds, concludes that only in the second *Conte* can one easily recognize "la griffe de Lemaire" (474), "la même plume heureuse" (*ibid.*) to which we owe *Les Épîtres de l'Amant vert*.

⁹ "Lempereur... respondit de sa viue voix, tout presentement, sans delay ou organe dautruy, en langue Latine..." (III, 235). The Latin text is headed: "*Responsio extemporanea Caesaris Maximiliani, ad oratorem Venetum.*" Curiously, Pierre Daru (*Histoire de la République de Venise* [Paris, 1821]), who describes — as does the gleeful Lemaire — Maximilian's blunt rejection of the Venetian peace overtures (Daru, III, 466-470), words the title of the oration in such a way as to imply that the ambassador's supplication, and not the Emperor's response, was extemporaneous: "*Domini Maximiliani imperatoris augusti ad Antonii Justiniani oratoris veneti supplicationem extemporaneam responsio*" (*ibid.*, 471, n. 1).

elegance and power, but because the version printed in *Schismes et Conciles* was long believed to be the only one still extant.[10]

As we might expect, Lemaire's longest work exhibits the greatest number of orations — more than thirty, in fact. *Les Illustrations de Gaule* comprises three parts,[11] of which the finest, beyond a doubt, is enshrined in the second half of Book I, beginning with chapter XX. This is the celebrated idyll of Paris and Oenone. It is in this section of the work, and in the narration of the Trojan War in Book II, that the oratory (including such notably rhetorical devices as apostrophe) is concentrated. Herewith follows a list of the principal speeches — in chronological order — found in *Les Illustrations*.

The "pere putatif" of the youthful Paris benevolently instructs the young shepherds in a graceful encomium of the pastoral life (I, 147-151). A large part of Book I, chapter XXV, is taken up by Paris's protestations of love for Pegasis Oenone (I, 176-178) and her encouraging response (179-181). Passing over Oenone's tale of

---

[10] In his *Histoire des Conciles d'après les documents originaux*, trans. and ed. Dom H. Leclercq, O.S.B. (Paris, 1907-1913), Mgr. Karl-Joseph von Hefele conjectures that the official text may no longer exist because the Pope must have spoken to the crowd in Romance, whereas the chroniclers would have recorded his words in Latin (V, 421, n. 1). The fate of these hypothetical Latin versions long remained a mystery. Hefele gives the gist of the oration in a scant 36 lines (*ibid.*, 420-421), as compared with the six and one-half pages of Lemaire's translation. The general thrust is manifestly identical in both versions, but there was until recently no way of telling whether or not, as Georges Doutrepont wonders (*Jean Lemaire de Belges et la Renaissance* [Brussels, 1934], 118), Jean Lemaire could have had an actual copy of the integral text in his possession. However, thanks to Pierre Jodogne (*JLBEFB*, 374), we now know that Lemaire translated the speech word for word from the *Historiarum ab inclinatione romanorum Imperii decades* of the Italian humanist Blondus Flavius Forliviensis (published at Venice in 1483).

[11] Francisque Thibaut's résumé (*MAJLB*, 164-165) is neat, succinct, and worth quoting:

> Les *Illustrations* sont formées de trois livres de valeur inégale. Le premier commence avec le déluge, et déroule dans 18 chapitres la suite des anciens rois, depuis Noé... jusqu'à... Pâris.
> Le deuxième est consacré à la guerre de Troie: l'enlèvement d'Hélène, son arrivée au palais de Priam, l'ambassade des Grecs pour réclamer la princesse, les combats livrés autour d'Ilion, la mort de Sarpédon, de Patrocle, d'Hector, et d'Achille, voilà quels en sont les principaux épisodes.
> Le troisième raconte les diverses migrations de la noblesse troyenne, jusqu'à Austrasius duc de Brabant, et retrace l'origine des maisons de France, de Bourgogne et d'Autriche.

Adonis (I, 194-195), we come to the centerpiece of the entire work — the archetypal Beauty Contest — the Judgment of Paris, with its trilogy of orations delivered by Juno, Pallas, and Venus (I, 233-249). The episode ends with Juno's splenetic vituperation of Paris (I, 258-259); but before the fateful decision is made, there is a brief interlude. At this point, the reluctant and embarrassed judge diffidently puts it to Mercure that a fair verdict is scarcely possible while, as he discreetly phrases it, the goddesses' "benoites corpulences seront couuertes et voilees de ces precieux aornemens" (I, 251). The god of eloquence duly relays the message in what can only be described as a miniature masterpiece of deliberative rhetoric, or persuasion in the précieux manner (seasoned with a barely discernible touch of malice).[12]

The enraged and disappointed runners-up having gone off in high dudgeon, Juno to Samos and Pallas to Athens, Venus returns alone in triumph to Mount Pelion, gloatingly "faisant monstre et ostentation de sa pomme doree à tous les autres Dieux et Deesses" (I, 261), to the extreme annoyance of Apollo. He proceeds to hold forth in a lengthy tirade (I, 262-267) directed against the impious conduct of the Trojans. Exactly at the midpoint, Apollo's historical narrative changes into prophecy, as he presages the destruction of Troy. But *Les Illustrations* is after all a work dedicated to the glorification of the supposedly Trojan-descended rulers of Christendom (whose Trojan genealogy amounted practically to an article of faith in Lemaire's day).[13] Consequently, Apollo softens the blow by de-

---

[12] Here is the full text of Mercure's speech:

> Certainement, mes treshonnorees dames, sa raison est droituriere-ment bonne, et bien fondee: Car si la pierre precieuse estant exposee en estimation de sa propre bonté et value, nest veüe à descouuert, sans vmbrage et sans fueille, il nest au monde si bon lapidaire ne si sage congnoisseur, qui sceust au vray iuger de sa nobilité. Voz precieux habillemens pourroient deceuoir son œil. Car ilz occupent la perfection de vostre belle facture, et mussent lintegrité de voz perfections. Si vostre different gisoit sans plus en lestimation de la resplendeur des bagues et ioyaux dont vous vous parez, ou en la louenge des façons de voz riches habits, et achesmes, armes, ioyaux et autres accoustremens, ie diroye que ne prinssiez pas la peine de mettre ius voz nobles vestemens: Mais non, ains tend à plus haute chose: Cestasauoir, en lequiparation de la formosité de voz propres diuines corpulences, et en discerner prudentement le choix et lequipolence de voz membres illustres.

[13] This was particularly true in aristocratic circles, but, as P. Jodogne observes, contemporary scholars (e.g., the eminent Robert Gaguin [d. 1501])

claring that eventually the Destinies will bring forth from the survivors of Priam's stock "plusieurs tresgrans et tresglorieux Princes, tant de la nation Germanique, Gallique, Françoise, Belgique, Bourguignonne, Espaignole et Britannique, comme aussi de la gent Italienne." [14]

Hecuba's supplication that her long-lost son Paris be reinstated (I, 326-327) is as brief as it is effective. (Lemaire himself calls it "persuasion de grande efficace.") Of still slighter content are two equally portentous utterances, namely the actual judgment handed down by Paris (I, 257) and Oenone's well-meant but disastrous proposal (I, 289) that her husband attend the Trojan Games as a means of getting himself "reintegré en la maison paternelle." These three short orations are all alike in that they contribute to the ultimate fulfillment of Troy's tragic destiny.

Book II of *Les Illustrations* begins with Antenor's return to Troy from an unsuccessful diplomatic mission whose object had been to secure the return of Priam's sister, "madame Hesione detenue en seruage par Telamon Roy de lisle de Salamis" (I, 339). His "relation" (reported in indirect speech) is a sorry catalogue of Greek "refus, opprobres et menasses" (II, 11). The council of the Trojan princes which is then convened is dominated by an outburst from Paris (II, 11-13), whose tone is stridently and uniformly Hellenophobic. The opinion of the others is summarily dispatched in a scant three lines by a Jean Lemaire who obviously intends keeping Paris in undisputed possession of the limelight. Priam allows his better judgment to be clouded by his son's accomplished

---

were considerably more skeptical (*JLBEFB*, 408). However, Lemaire's intention, though he had undoubtedly convinced himself of the solid historical foundations of his work, was (in part, at least) to gratify his noble, royal, and imperial readers and patrons.

[14] The careful reader will not have missed the hierarchical enumeration (a standard rhetorical device) — in descending order of importance from Jean Lemaire's point of view — of the ruling dynasties of sixteenth-century Europe, beginning with the Holy Roman Empire. The distinction between "Gallique" and "Françoise" was surely even then a rather fine one, after more than a millennium of ethnic intermingling between Gaul and Frank, and today the separate category "Bourguignonne" is utterly meaningless (to the non-Burgundian, that is). The deliberate relegation of "la gent Italienne" to the last — and apparently least — place may reflect not only the dismal political condition of that disunited land, but perhaps also the author's own patriotic pride, injured by the admittedly provoking Italian trick of dismissing all outlanders as uncouth barbarians (see above, Chap. II, p. 65).

rhetoric, and unwisely consents to let Paris seize "aucune des plus nobles femmes de Grece, pour prisonniere" as a rather unsubtle means of putting counter-pressure on the Greeks.

Curiously enough, that same Helen who is destined to be the ruin of Paris and his entire nation first appears to the reader (*Illustrations* Book II, chap. III) in a dilemma similar to that previously experienced by the artless judge of the ill-fated celestial beauty contest on Mount Ida. Her father King Tyndareus, embarrassed by the necessity of making an impossible choice (among a turbulent multitude of royal suitors all equally prepared to repay rejection by war), gets himself out of difficulties thanks to a "bon expedient" (II, 33), whereby the princes must swear in advance to abide by Helen's decision. She then picks Menelaus, in a graceful and modest oration as befits a young girl, displaying throughout a nice coolness which puts the callow and feckless Paris to shame (II, 36).[15]

The point in Lemaire's narrative which marks the traditional beginning of Paris's downfall — his arrival in Lacedaemon as leader of Priam's legation to Menelaus — is highlighted by a cluster of six speeches: an exchange of exquisitely urbane and flattering compliments (II, 48-52 and 54-57) between the ambassador and the king, followed by a secret council of war summoned by a Paris bent on justifying the abduction of his host's wife. His own speech (II, 62-63) is crassly opportunistic ("Quelle opportunité voudriez vous

---

[15] It is tempting to see Jean Lemaire against the background of the age-old "Querelle des Femmes" in the role of the staunch feminist. Confining the matter for argument's sake to *Les Illustrations de Gaule,* it is easy to find numerous displays of feminine resourcefulness and courage (the adolescent Helen coolly choosing among her bellicose suitors, II, 36); determination (Hecuba persuading Priam to reinstate Paris, I, 326-327); fidelity unto death (Pegasis Oenone dying of grief at her faithless husband's obsequies, II, 204-207). Opposed to such admirable virtues, the male characters of *Les Illustrations* frequently appear in a most unflattering light. The vaunted judicious powers of the youthful Paris utterly desert him just when he has most need of them (I, 257); his father Priam is fatally indecisive at crucial moments (I, 327; II, 13, etc.); King Tyndareus, who lacks the firm resolve and presence of mind of his own daughter Helen (II, 32) is at least excusable on the grounds that Jupiter himself cuts an equally sorry figure in a rather similar situation (I, 223). However, it must be remembered that Lemaire is following traditional accounts in *Les Illustrations*; furthermore (as a cynic might point out), his two greatest patrons were both women, and royal ones to boot. Nevertheless, Lemaire undeniably seems to go out of his way to emphasize the sterling qualities of his female characters in contrast to the deplorable shortcomings of the males.

plus grande que ceste cy? ne quel meilleur loisir?"). Aeneas speaks next (II, 63-65), an Aeneas whom the reader of Virgil might well fail to recognize. His main preoccupation is with the feasibility of the scheme ("et si atant vient que la chose se doiue executer, aumoins quon donne bon ordre à tout. Car ceste cité est fort puissante et bien peuplee de gens courageux et hautains"). The third opinion is expressed by the impetuous Deïphobus (II, 66-69), who exemplifies a sure grasp of audience psychology (that most necessary prerequisite of the orator) by appealing to his brother's vanity. He also inflames Paris — and, incidentally, himself [16] — by reminding him of countless unavenged atrocities perpetrated by "ces Gregois icy." (In effect, then, Deïphobus is condoning an outrageously dishonorable act in the very name of honor.) [17] The crowning touch is given by the "capitaine des gens de guerre et nauires de Paris" (II, 69-70). With the characteristic overconfidence of his profession ("... la difficulté y est bien petite... Laissez moy seulement manier laffaire quant à cest endroit... ne ten soucie autrement"), he convinces the inexperienced Paris to go ahead with his plans, thereby assuring the destruction of Troy.

The next speech in *Les Illustrations,* Book II, is Cassandra's narration of the events which led up to her being cursed with total non-credibility (II, 90-91). Then comes the lament of Pegasis Oenone, abandoned by her faithless husband, Paris (II, 120-126). This soliloquy is a fairly close rendering of the fifth epistle of Ovid's *Heroides* (*Oenone Paridi*). The next piece of discourse is Aeneas's disdainful reply (II, 145-146) to the threats of the infuriated Menelaus during a particular crisis of the Trojan war.

---

[16] Students of rhetoric have long been aware of the insidiously autohypnotic power of speech. George Kennedy, *The Art of Persuasion in Greece* (Princeton, 1965), 24, cites Disraeli's memorable quip at the expense of Gladstone, "inebriated with the exuberance of his own verbosity," and adduces a historic instance of the sort of catastrophe that can result from an orator's going beyond his original intentions. Kennedy shows how Aeschines, instead of merely rebutting certain charges leveled against Athens, quite unexpectedly (to himself as much as to his audience) called for war against the offending Amphissians. Philip of Macedon intervened, and Athens suffered a disastrous blow from which she never fully recovered (*ibid.,* 240).

[17] Expediency is, with feasibility and honor, one of the three so-called topics of deliberative rhetoric. In other words, the deliberative oration is concerned with whether the action recommended is feasible, expedient, and honorable (or the reverse). For an informative exposition of this aspect of rhetoric, see Clark, *RGRE,* 138-140 and 218-219.

The subsequent episode of the inconclusive duel between Menelaus and Paris (II, 152-160) is taken over "presques mot à mot" by Jean Lemaire from *Iliad,* II (1-177), speeches and all. The reason he gives for this is the straightforward, excellent, and unanswerable one that he considers Homer's account of the affair to be "beau et delectable" (II, 152), and eminently worth reproducing just as it stands.[18] The speeches in this section include 1) Hector's vituperation of Paris; 2) the latter's reply; 3) and 4) Hector's and Menelaus's speeches to the opposing armies; 5) Iris's message to Helen; 6) the Trojan elders' comments on Helen's fatal beauty; 7) Priam's request that Helen point out the Greek leaders to him; 8) Helen's reply; and 9) Agamemnon's prayer to Jupiter.[19] Oenone's lamentation over Paris's corpse (II, 205-206) is the last oration in Book II. As for Book III, this baldly unadorned and anticlimactic chronicle of pseudohistorical events, by far the least successful section of the work, is to all intents and purposes devoid of direct speech in any form.

Having thus surveyed the wide distribution of formal orations exhibited in the works — and especially in *Les Illustrations de Gaule* — we now come to the important question of their function therein.

---

[18] "It is expedient to imitate whatever has been invented with success," says Quintilian (X.ii.1). Lemaire has frequently been acclaimed as the first writer deliberately to imitate Homer in the French language, even at one remove (i.e., by way of Lorenzo Valla's Latin translation). Cf., e.g., Thibaut, *MAJLB,* 199; Lefranc, "JLB," 775; Spaak, *JLB,* 126. Hermann Gmelin ("Imitatio," 255-256) really goes much too far, I think, when cautioning against the excessive enthusiasm displayed by, among others, Clément Marot (who writes, in his *Épître* LV *[A madame de Soubise, partant de Ferrare pour s'en venir en France],* of "Jean Le Maire Belgeois, / Qui l'ame avoit d'Homere le Gregeois"). In his anxiety to tone down what he clearly regards as extravagantly laudatory statements, Gmelin evokes the dichotomy existing between the "anschmiegsamen, lebendig-bewegten und plastischen Stil" of Lemaire's translation from the *Iliad,* and his own "schwerfälligen Einleitung." To me, on the contrary, it is a striking tribute to Lemaire's creative powers that his own narrative is not, in actual fact, completely overshadowed by Homer's.

[19] Here follow the page references for Lemaire's versions of the speeches, with the corresponding passages of the *Iliad* in parentheses: 1) II, 154-155 (III, 39-57); 2) II, 155-156 (III, 59-75); 3) II, 157 (III, 86-94); 4) II, 157-158 (III, 97-110); 5) II, 159 (III, 130-138); 6) II, 160 (III, 156-160); 7) II, 160 (III, 162-170); 8) II, 160 (III, 172-177); 9) II, 162-163 (III, 276-291). It will have been noted that Lemaire omits ("à cause de brieueté" [II, 160]) the passage where Helen identifies the Achaean leaders to Priam (*Iliad,* III, 178-242).

Some of the speeches exist, certainly, for their own sake. The old shepherd's pleasantly relaxed expatiation on the delights of the bucolic life, Oenone's tale of Adonis, and Cassandra's story are all traditional themes on which the sixteenth-century author takes a manifest pleasure in embroidering and displaying his narrative gifts to best advantage. In other cases, particularly in the *déplorations* and the two *Concordes*, the eulogizing intent itself dictates, to a writer of Lemaire's patently rhetorical cast of mind, an oratorical form. Indeed, as we have already seen, without the speeches *La Couronne Margaritique* would shrink to less than half its actual length, and *La Plainte du Désiré* would practically cease to exist. Then there are the translations, comprising the group taken from the *Iliad*, Oenone's lament, and those included in the polemical writings of Lemaire. Insofar as *Les Illustrations de Gaule* is concerned, however, the majority of the speeches are — *grosso modo* — of the author's own invention.[20]

Even a casual reading of this book, then, shows us a writer who rarely misses an opportunity to emphasize that *Les Illustrations* is a work of the profoundest historical pretensions. His spokesman, Mercure (in an intriguing appearance as both author's publicist and literary critic) excoriates previous attempts to do justice to the illustrious origins of Europe's reigning houses (I, 3-4) as altogether devoid of respectable weight and credibility.[21] In fact, he has no qualms about damning their authors as "mauuais escriuains" who have irresponsibly allowed the glorious history of Europe's Trojan ancestors to fall "en decadence, et deprauation ruïneuse, comme si elle fust destime friuole, et pleine de fabulosité..." (*ibid.*). This alone, he maintains, justifies the composition of a new, solidly based

---

[20] A statement that can be made with confidence thanks to G. Doutrepont's painstaking researches into the matter of Lemaire's sources. See his *Jean Lemaire de Belges et la Renaissance* (cited hereafter as *JLBR*), 403-416, Annexe I: "Tableau détaillé des emprunts de Lemaire dans les *Illustrations*."

[21] "...comme si [ladite tresnoble histoire] fust destime friuole, et pleine de fabulosité" (I, 4). In this same passage, Mercure, addressing Marguerite d'Autriche, makes a significant allusion to the rebirth of learning in terms distinctly reminiscent — before the event — of Gargantua's superb letter to his son in the eighth chapter of *Pantagruel*: "...en ce temps heureux et prospere de la monarchie de ton geniteur, Empereur des Chrestiens, *que toutes sciences sont plus esclarcies que iamais,* ie stimulay et enhardis lentendement du tien tresadonné seruiteur voluntaire, Secretaire, Indiciaire et Historiographe Iean le Maire de Belges... à ce quil osast entreprendre ce labeur..."

history which will set the record straight once and for all,[22] a work founded on "la verité historiale"[23] of "les vrays acteurs autentiques," to whom "la fabulosité des poëtes"[24] is anathema. Naturally, this polarization of poetic "fabulosité" and historical "verité" puts Lemaire in something of a quandary. He is himself, after all, wearing two hats, the poet's as well as the historian's. Which in a word is the nobler, or at any rate the worthier, of the two disciplines in question?

In *Les Illustrations,* he is usually typical of the age in his uncritical acceptance of, e.g., the *Aeneid* and the *Metamorphoses* as bona fide historical sources. Yet even the great and sincere reverence he bears for "[le] prince des poëtes Virgile" (I, 325) does not inhibit him in the least when he considers it his duty to point out the Latin poet's shortcomings as a historian.[25] Lemaire is always most careful to clear himself in advance of any potential charges of *fabulosité.*[26] Thus, when writing on the subject of giants, he is momentarily afraid lest "parauenture aucun scrupuleux pourroit

---

[22] "Mon intention principale," he writes in the second book of *Les Illustrations* (II, 59-60), "... est de mettre en auant, ce que les autres ont obmis, et de rassembler tout en vn corps, le plus curieusement et veritablement que ie pourray, ce que les anciens acteurs autentiques ont couché des gestes de Paris, Heleine, et Oenone, en escrits diuers, et menues particularitez, pour en forger *vne histoire totale.*" He adds, with the understandable pride of the groundbreaker: "Laquelle chose nha esté encores attentee de nul autre, que ie sache, ny en François ny en Latin."
[23] See, e.g., II, 199: "... nostre acteur Dictys de Crete qui suit la verité historiale, met que [etc.]."
[24] See, e.g., II, 233: "... Castor et Pollux ... translatez au ciel par la fabulosité des poëtes ..."
[25] "Tout ainsi comme Virgile faillit bien lourdement, en escriuant, que Dido fut onques amoureuse d'Eneas," he writes (in *Schismes,* III, 254), with an acerbic comment touching the ineptitude of certain "autres aussi mauuais historiens." And cf., with respect to the same matter, "la fiction menteresse du Poëte Virgile" (IV, 148). The simple truth is, of course, that Jean Lemaire is highly eclectic when it comes to authorities. If Virgil, or any other source, provides corroborative material for *Les Illustrations,* he is hailed as an "acteur autentique"; if the contrary is true (and so great a name as Virgil cannot simply be ignored; logic demands that he be refuted when in direct conflict with Lemaire's thesis), it is usually a case of "les poëtes feignent que..." (see, e.g., I, 108, 270; II, 40, and *passim* for the use of this and similar expressions).
[26] Cf. "Les rvines de Troye la grand, comme vne treslamentable et trespiteuse Tragedie assez esclarcies, nettoyees et purgees de tout erreur fabuleux, par le second liure precedent de noz Illustrations" (II, 247-248).

cuyder que ce sont fables" (I, 51), and so with a flourish produces Holy Writ as his authority.

It is plain to see that Jean Lemaire is intensely aware of the dignity of history and of the responsibility of the historian to his readers. Accordingly, in the "Excvse de lactevr" (I, 347-349), while apologizing to the "seigneurs vertueux, et dames honorees, qui lisez ce liure" because the promised sequel to his history remains as yet unpublished, he explains that the annoying delay is due in part to the fact that Book I requires "aucune reueüe, correction et ampliation, à cause de sa grand importance...." The difference between the attitude expressed here and that regarding his *ad hoc* political writings is immediately apparent. History is a major genre, which demands not only careful verification of the facts at issue, but endless stylistic polishing into the bargain; the value of a pamphlet like *La Légende des Vénitiens,* on the other hand, lies exclusively in its content, and rhetorical colors can safely be dispensed with (see above, Chap. III, 103-104). Furthermore, it is obvious that in the production of a political broadsheet, speed is of the essence. This is not to say that *La Légende* is not well written; quite the reverse — it is as tightly organized and cogent a piece of prose as could be desired in a work intended above all to *persuade.* [27] But it is definitely not what Jean Lemaire would regard as befitting so exalted a theme as that of *Les Illustrations.* The classical doctrine (which survived throughout the Middle Ages) of the appropriate levels of style is thus rigidly adhered to: unlike the grand style, which is for moving, and the middle, which is for delighting, the plain is for *proving.*

That Jean Lemaire views history as very serious business indeed is therefore not disputed. This being so, how is one to explain (let alone justify) the presence in a self-styled historical work of so many speeches which are, in the very nature of things, pure fiction? For example, Lemaire's source for the sequence of events prior to Paris's

---

[27] P. Jodogne bears me out in this, when he states, apropos of *La Légende*: "On remarque toutefois quelques phrases très soignées du point de vue formel... ou des invectives non dépourvues d'effets de rhétorique" (*JLBEFB*, 322, n. 3). As a general rule, Jodogne — quite legitimately in the context in which he is writing — equates "rhétorique" with the art of the rhétoriqueurs, but in this instance he is speaking of rhetorical effects in the usual acceptation of the term. (The passages which he cites by way of illustration [*Œuvres*, III, 372 and 398-399] are both apostrophes.)

departure for Lacedaemon is Dares of Phrygia's *De excidio Troiae historia* (chapters V-X). Now Dares's narrative is extremely laconic — not to say downright meagre — in both style and content. The entire history of the ten years' war, including its causes, is related in some thirty pages (in the Bonn edition of 1837). Chapters VI and VII treat of Priam's council, at which the fateful decision to send Paris to Menelaus (and Helen) is made. Paris (under his cognomen, Alexander) urges his father to assemble a fleet, and tells how Venus has promised him the fairest woman in all of Greece for his bride. Dares allots him a scant eleven lines of reported speech. Even allowing for the increase in verbiage which must be expected when translating from Latin into French or any other modern European language, Lemaire's more than fifty lines of direct speech obviously represent a considerable augmentation of the original material.

Strange though it may seem to the twentieth-century reader, the criterion of the sixteenth in such matters was primarily one of verisimilitude.[28] Not that poetic fiction was consistently viewed in a purely negative light as frivolous *fabulosité,* something to be shunned by the grave moralist (or historian). On the contrary, the term was often employed with its medieval connotation of the veil of beautiful fiction which serves to conceal truth. Hence, Mercure's denunciation of those who have ignorantly degraded the noble history of Troy [29] continues to the effect that this history "est veritable et fertile, et toute riche de grans mysteres et intelligences poëtiques et philosophales, contenant fructueuse substance souz lescorce des fables artificielles." A similar use of "fiction" (or rather "feindre") as something inherently praiseworthy occurs in the passage "A bon droit feint le poëte Homere que le beau Paris fut soustrait de la bataille par la Deesse Venus: cestadire par sa mollesse, lascheté et peuvaloir.... Aussi y peult auoir cause historiale pourquoy ledit poëte feint que Paris fut soustrait de la bataille par Venus."[30] Actually, this type of rationalizing interpretation of the

---

[28] Cf. e.g., Jean Lemaire's attitude when faced with equally respectable (but diametrically opposed) authorities: "Mais comme iay desia dit autrefois, ie vueil principalement ensuiuir lopinion de Dictys de Crete: car elle est plus vraysemblable" (II, 61).

[29] See above, p. 102.

[30] II, 168-169. In the same passage, Lemaire speaks warmly of "plusieurs autres nobles fantasies dudit poëte..." Cf. Cretin's liminary lines to *Le Temple*

ancient legends and myths is quite characteristic of Lemaire in his role as historian.

Nevertheless, his abiding preference is for the "vraysemblable," as when he earnestly seeks to demonstrate that despite caviling opinions to the contrary, there is nothing improbable about the contention that the shepherd boy Paris "sceust iouer de la lyre ou violle" (I, 228). Was not "le Roy Dauid encores exerçant estat de bergerie" a skilled musician? This ever-present insistence on the plausibility of a given argument is patently bound up with the basic *persuasive* function of rhetoric, and so the devising of such arguments constitutes legitimate rhetorical invention (see Chap. I, p. 25). Therefore, when Lemaire fleshes out the bare bones of Paris's oration as reported in Dares's outline, supplying not only the living words, but the impassioned accents in which they were delivered, we may be sure that nothing could be further from his intent than *fabulosité*. Quite the reverse: the composition of orations to be put into the mouths of historical figures is a practice which can lay claim to the most respectable antecedents, going back at least as far as Herodotus and Thucydides.[31] Also (a point which is all too often overlooked nowadays) a discourse composed in due form is just as much a bona fide literary genre as is, say, a sonnet or a novella, and may thus be used to enliven an otherwise possibly arid stretch of narrative. Leonardo Bruni appears to have been among the first moderns to reintroduce the set-piece oration into historical

---

(46, ll. 20-24), where Lemaire's own "fictions poeticques" are highly praised as "Plaines de sens non tant soit pou ethicques."

[31] G. Kennedy (*APG*, 48) theorizes that Herodotus "had apparently constructed many of his speeches on the basis of what he thought ought to have been said. Thucydides has elaborated this into a major principle of historical composition. He claims ... to reconstruct what the speaker ought to have said.... 'Ought,' that is, in the rhetorical sense, the right topics and techniques for the occasion, not in the sense of politically or morally right..." There is an obvious affinity here to Aristotle's famous dictum on ideal imitation, in which he postulates the superiority of poetry to history on the grounds of a higher reality: "The real difference [between the historian and the poet] is this, that one tells what happened and the other what might happen. For this reason poetry is something more scientific and serious than history, because poetry tends to give general truths while history gives particular facts" (*Poetics*, ed. and trans. W. Hamilton Fyfe [Cambridge, Mass., and London, 1965 (1927)], Loeb Classical Library, ix.2-3). The later Renaissance tended to reverse this distinction, as witness, e.g., Alessandro Tassoni's remarks quoted above, Chap. II, 55.

writing. B. L. Ullman justifies the adoption by Bruni (and Renaissance historians in general) of the fictional speech for reasons that are — in part, at least — soundly Aristotelian: "We must think of these speeches as a convention that served a useful purpose. With this medium a vivid picture could be painted that might be *psychologically more true* [my ital.] than a mere description. After all, a characterization of an individual in accepted historical form can be quite incorrect. Moreover, the speeches enabled the author to express some of his own ideas more forcefully. As this fact was well known, no one was deceived." [32] The council of war scene discussed above (p. 98) bears out Ullman's argument. The speeches of the four protagonists — especially that of the fire-eating young Deïphobus — excellently illustrate the psychological truth in question, portraying the respective characters of the orators a good deal more convincingly (and economically), perhaps, than would be possible in a "mere description."

For Jean Lemaire the historian, it is the pedagogic aspects of the genre which prevail, rather than any methodical attempts to study and re-create a past epoch for the contemporary reader.

---

[32] Ullman, *op. cit.* (in Chap. II, n. 24, above q.v.), 331-332. Cf. Quintilian's comment (VIII.iii.62) on displaying facts "in their living truth to the eyes of the mind." The pressing need for an alliance between wisdom and eloquence was fully recognized by at least one medieval theorist, the great John of Salisbury, whose powerful apologia for the Trivium, the *Metalogicon* (ed. and trans. by Daniel D. McGarry [Berkeley and Los Angeles, 1962]), contains (I,i) the following lines: "Reason would remain utterly barren, or at least would fail to yield a plenteous harvest, if the faculty of speech did not bring to light its feeble conceptions, and communicate the perceptions of the prudent exercise of the human mind. Indeed, it is this delightful and fruitful copulation of reason and speech which has given birth to so many outstanding cities... One who would eliminate the teaching of eloquence from philosophical studies, begrudges Mercury [Eloquence] his possession of Philology, and wrests from Philology's arms her beloved Mercury." And a contemporary critic, also writing of the Trivium (Robert Griffin, *Coronation of the Poet* [Berkeley and Los Angeles, 1969], 21-22), shows that whereas the differentiation between logic on the one hand and rhetoric and poetry on the other consists theoretically in the opposition between a primarily *intellectual* and a primarily emotional, *imaginative* movement, in actual practice, "in prose composition and in poetry alike, the distinction was often radically blurred or simply dismissed." Thus Lemaire's argument that if David was a harpist, then why not Paris also (see above, p. 106) is grounded as much on a logical deduction — a piece of reasoning by analogy — as on his fertile imagination's informing him of the poetic *rightness* of Paris's musicianship. (See also Chap. V below, p. 127 and n. 29).

Throughout the Middle Ages, history (and, above all, ancient history) was universally regarded as *"figura rerum* or phenomenal prophecy," as Erich Auerbach puts it in his seminal essay "Figura." [33] The earlier generations of Italian humanists still tend to stress history's pedagogic utility. [34] It is hardly to be wondered at, then, if this particular approach to the subject is preponderant in Lemaire. Machiavelli (1469-1527) and Guicciardini (1483-1540) produced their historical masterpieces only during his maturity — i.e., too late to influence him to any significant degree — whereas the Italian humanists with whom he *was* familiar invariably (and inevitably) belonged to the preceding period, like Marsilio Ficino (1433-1499), Francesco Filelfo (1398-1481) and Cristoforo Landino (1424-1498). This is why it is at least arguable that *Les Illustrations de Gaule* was partly conceived (though certainly not consistently executed) as a kind of *Institutio principis Christiani*, [35] being dedicated as it was to the guardian of the future Emperor Charles V, his aunt Marguerite d'Autriche. [36]

---

[33] In his *Scenes from the Drama of European Literature,* trans. Ralph Manheim (New York, 1959), 11-76; this citation p. 53. Lemaire's predisposition to a moralizing and rationalizing interpretation of history, or rather mythology, is a reflection of what Auerbach calls the "analogism that reaches into every sphere of medieval thought" (61-62). See, e.g., the "Explication tant morale comme philosophale ... du iugement de Paris," which explains that the golden apple awarded to Venus by Paris signifies "son noble chef qui estoit de rondeur spherique, et de splendeur aureine comme la pomme: et consequemment son entendement enclos dedens, il laddonna du tout à vie voluptueuse, et venerique, et mesprisa la vie actiue de Iuno, et la vie contemplatiue de Pallas" (I, 272).

[34] See Myron P. Gilmore, *The World of Humanism* (New York, 1969 [1952]), 201-202, who refers to the time-honored belief that "the record of the past was in reality philosophy teaching by example."

[35] J. Stecher (*Notice,* li) sees *Les Illustrations* as a "panégyrique de l'honneur conjugal," "une sorte de *Télémaque* allégorique, à l'usage du futur Charles-Quint." P. Spaak (*JLB,* 115-116) speaks of Lemaire's attempt to "extraire de son roman poétique une pédagogie à l'usage ... de ses maîtres et protecteurs." A. Lefranc ("JLB," 777) comments in much the same vein. Since *Illustrations* I was published in 1511, Lemaire's supposed attempt to influence the young Archduke's education antedates that of Erasmus — whose *Institutio* appeared only in 1516 — by several years.

[36] See the Prologue to Book I (6): "Dont il appert, que qui veult tirer ceste matiere à sens moral, on la peult appliquer à linstruction et doctrine dunchacun ieune Prince de maison Royalle, comme estoit Paris Alexandre. Or ne scay ie nulle Princesse viuant auiourdhuy sur terre (sauue la bonne paix des autres) qui puist en ce premier liure plus conuenablement tenir le lieu de dame Pallas, que ta personne, Princesse illustre: Ne aussi ne scay ie, qui mieux

THE DISTRIBUTION AND FUNCTION OF ORATIONS    109

Yet another utilitarian feature of Lemaire's orations is that they more often than not serve to motivate his narrative at crucial points. When, for example, Hecuba by her persuasive eloquence induces Priam to restore Paris to his royal estate (I, 326-327), she adds impetus to the train of events originally set in motion by Paris's own decision to award the Apple of Discord to Venus. His doom is then conclusively sealed by the effectiveness of his own oration at Priam's council (at the beginning of Book II), by the speeches of his counselors (and himself) in Sparta, and so on. This is the very stuff of deliberative [37] rhetoric, and with remarkably few exceptions formal oratory in *Les Illustrations de Gaule* is of the deliberative kind. Even such decorative orations as the old shepherd's discourse (I, 147-151) and the tale of Adonis (I, 194-195) can by no means be classified purely as art for art's sake. The former — despite its agreeably light tone — is a solemn exhortation to the young shepherds to be happy in their lot, and unceasingly underscores the utility, dignity, and general excellence of "ce tresnoble mestier," "en les encourageant à ce noble labeur" (I, 147 and 151). ("Et encores du temps present, cest la maniere de plusieurs nations prochaines et loingtaines, quelles eslisent leurs Roys et leurs gouuerneurs de telz gens que vous estes: Pource quil leur semble quil nest point de plus liberale entremise, de plus iuste acquest, ne de plus parfaite generosité, que de pastourerie" [147].) And if Oenone tells Paris the sad story of Adonis, it is to be taken as a most urgent admonition against recklessness while hunting, or, in other words, as an *exemplum* ("... des autres bestes cruelles et furieuses elle admonnestoit tousiours Paris de fuyr les duyeres [i.e., retraites], en luy racontant lhistoire du malheureux iouuenceau Adonis" [I, 194]) — itself a rhetorical figure, which we shall examine in Chapter VI. The orations of the three goddesses during the Judgment scene are all expressly designed to influence the judge's decision, and it is noteworthy that Venus, the most flamboyantly effective oratrix of the trio, owes her victory in part to a device traditionally

---

puist figurer le personnage du tresbel enfant Royal, Paris Alexandre, que le tien trescher neueu Larchiduc Charles d'Austriche et de Bourgongne, Prince des Espaignes, etc."

[37] The very term is echoed in, e.g., "Quand donques lesdits Princes sceurent la venue du Roy Menelaus, ilz conuindrent trestous ensemble en son palais, pour prendre *deliberation* sur laffaire, qui tant leur touchoit au cœur" (II, 95-96).

recommended by classical rhetoricians, viz., that of the appeal, not to her one-man audience's reason, but to his emotions.[38]

Thus far we have concentrated on the *utility* of history. To this there corresponds, as any student of medieval literature would expect, an element of *delight*. *Les Illustrations de Gaule,* unfortunately for its author's lofty pretensions, has not the slightest value as serious historical instruction (whatever its merits as a moral fable). But taken purely as a work of artistic creation, distinguished by virtue of its sumptuous and harmoniously cadenced prose, it is of high significance. In such a context, the orations may be considered as a perfectly legitimate form of *ornatus,* or rhetorical embellishment. Given the occasional arid source — Dares of Phrygia, for one — the spontaneous reaction of the author of *Les Illustrations* is to adorn and enliven his work with passages of amplification, throughout the Middle Ages the single most important rhetorical device prescribed by the treatises.[39]

Lemaire's prose style in *Les Illustrations* is conspicuously poetic, which is interesting not only in itself, but because no less eminent an authority than Quintilian warns against confusing two such fundamentally different disciplines as history and oratory. He grants that historical knowledge may be useful to the orator as a "nutriment which we may compare to some rich and pleasant juice," then continues: "For history has a certain affinity to poetry and may be regarded as *a kind of prose poem [quodammodo carmen solutum],* while it is written for the purpose of narrative, not of proof, and designed from beginning to end not for immediate effect or the instant necessities of forensic strife, but to record events for the benefit of posterity and to win glory for its author."[40] This definition of history is of particular import in that it seems to describe a genre somewhere between epic and history as we understand it today. This is precisely the position of *Les Illustrations,* and, for that matter — *mutatis mutandis* — very nearly that of such twelfth-

---

[38] See Martin L. Clarke, *Rhetoric at Rome* (London, 1953), 78 ff., on Cicero's extraordinary emotional power. And cf. Quintilian, VI.i.51-52.

[39] See Auerbach, *LLP,* 208.

[40] X.i.31; my ital. Nothing could more succinctly describe the widely divergent aims of Jean Lemaire de Belges in composing, on the one hand, the utilitarian *Légende des Vęnitiens;* on the other, the highly poetic *Illustrations de Gaule.*

century *romans antiques* as Benoît de Sainte-Maure's *Roman de Troie*.[41] The latter work, incidentally, comprises numerous orations, and, notably, in the first volume,[42] those delivered at Priam's council which directly result in the rape of Helen.

Many of the foregoing remarks on history apply with equal force to other genres as well, but above all, insofar as Jean Lemaire is concerned, to the *déplorations*. The underlying organizing principle of *La Couronne Margaritique*, for instance, consists in the series of ten encomiastic orations sponsored by Vertu. It may well be that the author (despite an apparently unfeigned admiration for his patroness) divided his plethora of hyperbolic praise among ten eminent "orateurs" as a useful expedient thanks to which he himself might appear not quite so blatantly sycophantic or tediously repetitious. In other words, it is a "distancing" device whereby the author, by interposing what amount to mere lay figures between himself and the reader, places himself at one remove from that reader. Even a court poet — one might almost say, *especially* a court poet — cannot seriously be expected to maintain an unflagging level of adoring enthusiasm throughout one hundred and fifty pages. By spreading the load among ten confrères, the author not only sets up what Ph. Aug. Becker calls a *Redeturnier*,[43] but also creates a far more plausible effect into the bargain, since it is much more likely that ten speakers might each sustain a suitably high pitch of excitement for, say, the compass of ten pages, than that a single one might continue unaided for a full hundred. Finally, the series

---

[41] Benoît does not appear to have been known directly to Jean Lemaire. F. Thibaut (*MAJLB*, 181-183) believes that such knowledge as he may have had of *Le Roman de Troie* came by way of a medieval Italian intermediary, Guido delle Colonne, author of a condensed Latin translation (which appeared in 1287) of Benoît's poem.

[42] *Le Roman de Troie*, ed. Léopold Constans (Paris, 1904), I, ll. 3651-4166. (Paris's oration, which comprises an account of the Judgment episode, extends from l. 3845 to 3928. Benoît's sources for this section of the work, like Jean Lemaire's, include Dares of Phrygia and Dictys of Crete.) See above, Chap. II, 69-70, for a discussion of the correlation between such cultural phenomena as the twelfth-century renaissance and formal rhetorical studies.

[43] Becker, *JL*, 62. In actual fact, the oratorical contest is a cooperative venture, with the Ten all vying in a fraternal spirit to outdo one another in praise of Marguerite. There is no real competitive edge, in striking contrast to the Judgment of Paris orations, which Becker rightly calls "ein Wettkampf der Reden" (*op cit.*, 146).

of orations, all variations on a single theme, displays the author's own virtuosity to distinct advantage.

It seems clear, therefore, that oratory, whose omnipresence in Lemaire's *Œuvres* is so readily visible, has a crucial role to play. Having mentioned earlier (above, p. 106) that the oration is in fact a distinct literary genre, we will in the next chapter attempt to see how Jean Lemaire copes with this form, by analyzing some of the most significant specimens from a strictly rhetorical viewpoint.

Chapter V

A STUDY OF SOME SELECTED ORATIONS

Forensic oratory, which as a general rule predominates in the treatises of ancient rhetoricians, is virtually nonexistent in the works of Jean Lemaire, unless — which seems unlikely — the third *Conte de Cupido et d'Atropos* is his composition (see above, Chap. IV, n. 8). Although the judgment speech delivered by Paris (I, 257) does contain some scraps of legal phraseology ("sans faueur, fraude, ou corruption quelconques: Ie dis et pronunce par sentence diffinitiue" etc.), it is hardly to be considered in the forensic category, being, first, extremely short (twenty lines in all), and, second, a judgment, not a speech for the defense or the prosecution. The nearest approach to a judicial oration in Lemaire would seem to be the one pronounced by the nymph Concorde du Genre Humain (*Genre humain,* 65-69), when she petitions the Emperor Maximilian I to reward his daughter's successful diplomacy with the title "Auguste." However, a more accurate definition of this speech would be deliberative with epideictic overtones, and it is thus that we shall consider it. The would-be analyzer of Lemaire's orations begins fully to comprehend what is meant by the expression *embarras de richesses,* particularly with regard to the two modes of rhetoric exemplified by Concorde's harangue. As it is scarcely feasible to study them all, we must content ourselves with a few specimens of each type.

To illustrate the epideictic mode, we will examine Georges Chastellain's encomium of Urbanité in *La Couronne Margaritique* (IV, 102-107); the old shepherd's discourse in praise of his calling (I, 147-151); and Juno's *vituperatio* of Paris (I, 258-259). As for deliberative rhetoric, I have on grounds of general excellence selected — in addition to Concorde's speech — the orations of the three goddesses (I, 233-249).

Jean Lemaire's theme of themes was the exaltation of his patroness, Marguerite d'Autriche, in whose honor he composed what is in many respects his most curious work, *La Couronne Margaritique*. Quite a good case could be made for linking *La Couronne* with the "art of memory" tradition — wholly rhetorical in origin — which was so vastly elaborated in the Middle Ages and the Renaissance. Dr. Frances Yates has demonstrated the capital role played in the medieval development of the mnemotechnical tradition by Cicero's *De inventione* and the anonymous *Rhetorica ad Herennium*. The former treatise is important because in it Cicero subdivides his definition of the virtue Prudence into "memory, intelligence, and foresight" (II.liii.160); and the latter because the prototypical *ars memorativa* is embodied in III.xvi-xxiv. The Middle Ages piously believed both works to be by "Tullius" and consequently, since "Tullius in his First Rhetoric states that memory is a part of Prudence [and] Tullius in his Second Rhetoric says that there is an artificial memory by which natural memory can be improved . . . the practice of the artificial memory is a part of the virtue of Prudence."[1] According to Dr. Yates, what medieval man was concerned with remembering invariably turned out to be matters of faith and doctrine, hence, in particular, the virtues and vices.[2] Now the *Ad Herennium* specifically recommends as a most valuable mnemonic device the mental association of the concepts to be memorized with a series of strikingly beautiful (or ugly) human figures, figures which are actually engaged in *doing* something (*agentes imagines*, III.xxii.37), and which are moreover dressed in distinctive fashion.[3] The background is to be a house or other architectural unit,[4] which the Middle Ages took to mean "some 'solemn' building" (*Yates, AM*, 77).

---

[1] Yates, *Art of Memory* (cited hereafter as *AM*), 20-21.
[2] *AM*, 55.
[3] "Crowns or purple cloaks" are recommended for the beautiful images; the ugly ones may be disfigured with bloodstains, mud, red paint, etc. (*ibid.*). Miss Yates suggests that Martianus Capella's allegorical figures of Rhetoric and the other liberal arts enjoyed such high favor in the Middle Ages because they "conform remarkably well to the rules" for the *imagines agentes* (*AM*, 52).
[4] ". . . an intercolumnar space, a recess, an arch, or the like" (III.xvi.29).

Viewed in the light of the memory tradition, Jean Lemaire's *déplorations* take on an added dimension. One thinks, for example, of the six living statues ("ymages exquises") which spell out the name PIERRE in *Le Temple d'Honneur et de Vertus* (74-75, ll. 684-702).[5] The ten lovely damsels of *La Couronne Margaritique* (IV, 55-57) would appear to be an even more graphic illustration of the tradition. They are, as in the previous case, personified Virtues (the Orators name them for us: Moderation, Animosité [courage], Rectitude de conseil, Grace, Vrbanité, Erudition, Regnatiue Prudence, Innocence, Tolerance, and Experience — "toutes relucentes de forme angelique, et speciosité celeste"). Vertu herself adorns their foreheads ("selon la mode Italique, qui bien leur seoit"), each with a precious stone: Margarite [pearl], Adamas [diamond], Rubis, Gorgonie [coral], Veneris gemma [amethyst], Esmeraude, Radiane ["vne pierre precieuse de noire couleur, et neantmoins translucente," I, 116], Iaspe, Topace, Escarboucle (again, we are indebted to the Orators for this information). Then, "en vne grand salle clere et bien enluminee, dor et de peinture," she arranges them "à maniere dun cercle, en sentretenant par les bras entrelassez lun dedens lautre, ayans leurs cheres ioyeuses tournees deuers les gens," and thus forming "le vif patron dune belle et riche couronne: car chacune delles particulierement tient le lieu dun flouron." This striking symbolism is to my mind a perfect example of the *imagines agentes* conceived by the author of the *Ad Herennium* and discussed at length by Dr. Yates. Seeming to clinch the matter, the Ten Orators, in their admiration at the wondrous sight (and even before Vertu has explained what it signifies), speculate that the ten Virtues stand for the "neuf Muses auec leur mere *Memoire*."[6]

When the Orators have been duly enlightened, Vertu informs them in most precise and explicit terms what it is she expects them to accomplish in their successive encomia of Marguerite:

> ... nous mettrons en auant vne chose que vous ferez, presupposant premierement et auant toute œuure, que sans

---

[5] The initial letters P·I·E·R·R·E are represented by the virtues Prudence, Justice, Esperance, Raison, Religion, and Equité (*Temple,* 76-78).

[6] IV, 57. While Mnemosyne is frequently associated with her daughters in such phrases as this (cf., e.g., *Genre humain,* 60, l. 352; *Illustrations,* I, 209 and 220), the very mention of Memory in this context cannot fail to strike a responsive chord in the reader of Miss Yates's fascinating book.

nulle doute toutes ces belles Vertus noz filles vous sont congnues nommeement et distinctement. Prenez donc toutes les lettres capitales de leurs noms, en commençant par celle qui porte vne M. en chef. Et voyez si iceux dix caracteres indiuidus de lalphabet, sauroient former le nom de la plus vertueuse et plus fortunee Princesse qui soit auiourdhuy viuant sur terre. Et dabondant, donnez vous garde de ces dix pierres precieuses qui sont es fronts de ces dix pucelles, et vous trouuerez, par la composition de leurs premieres lettres semblable signifiance.... Mais quant aux qualitez et aux alliances des Vertus et des gemmes, nous voulons que vous nous sachiez à dire, si linuention comprinse en nostre imaginatiue, est bien conduite et mise à effect selon la raison, et sil y ha point de discrepance quant à lobiect pretendu. Cestadire si les excellences de ces dix Vertus, et les proprietez des dix gemmes, ont concordance si mutuelle, que delles puist resulter, comme en vn miroir trescertain, le vif exemplaire de la dame dessus mentionnee. (IV, 58)

Vertu's address may well be partly inspired by the extremely complicated rules established for the *puys* of late medieval France and Burgundy (see above, Chap. I, 39), a hypothesis which is supported by the fact that she is in effect setting up a kind of oratorical contest. At any rate, Vertu's entire approach is distinctly medieval, rather than classical, in both outlook and expression.

The fifth speaker in this venture is the illustrious Burgundian rhétoriqueur and historiographer, Georges Chastellain, and consequently his thematic letter is "U."[7] Like the other nine orations, Chastellain's is a tripartite encomium, the appropriate gem, virtue, and lady being lauded each in turn. (It should be noted that the order of exposition changes from orator to orator: virtue, gem, lady; lady, virtue, gem, and so on.) Every speaker has many sage and apposite comparisons to make with the modern paragon, Marguerite d'Autriche.[8] The most interesting part of Chastellain's dis-

---

[7] "Pour enrichir ce noble diademe, / George produit icy dame Vesta, / Vrbanité, qui tresbon effect ha, / Et de Venus la gracieuse gemme" (IV, 97).

[8] In "The Moral Thought of Renaissance Humanism" (in *Rennaissance Thought* II [New York, 1965], 20-68), P. O. Kristeller devotes a section (53-56) to the study of comparison (or *paragone*) as a "typically humanist fashion in which the various forms of human life were discussed.... Ancient rhetoric had insisted that it was the task of the orator to praise and to blame, and the praise of some virtue or quality was often combined with the blame of its contrary... In humanistic literature, the rhetorical contest between two

course is the very agreeable encomium of Urbanité (IV, 102-107) which we have already had occasion to mention in Chapter II above.

Encomium as a subdivision of epideictic oratory is the most stylized of all ancient rhetorical genres. The *Rhetorica ad Herennium* (III.vi.10) enumerates the general topics for praise (not forgetting to point out that the contraries of these same topics may serve as the bases for censure) as follows: "External Circumstances, Physical Attributes, and Qualities of Character," continuing more specifically, "To External Circumstances belong such as can happen by chance, or by fortune, favourable or adverse: descent, education, wealth, kinds of power, titles to fame, citizenship, friendships, and the like, and their contraries." After similar elaboration as regards Physical Attributes and Qualities of Character, *Ad Herennium* states that the development of these topics provides the proof and refutation in an epideictic cause.[9] By the fourth century A.D., a rhetorician such as Aphthonius would have a more or less immutable formula worked out for all types of encomia (i.e., of a race, a city, a family, an individual, etc.). The encomium of a person comprises the following sections: a prologue, discussion of the subject's race (broken down into nationality, native city, ancestors, parents); education (subdivided into pursuits, art, laws); achievements (of soul, of body, of fortune, each further subdivided), which are the main topic; finally, comparison and epilogue.[10]

Chastellain-Lemaire may or may not have been directly acquainted with Hermogenes and Aphthonius (see Chap. I above), but in any event displays a fair knowledge of the encomiastic tradi-

---

contrasts or rivals was a favorite sport... the comparison between Scipio and Caesar, between republic and monarchy, [etc.]" (53-54). Hermogenes of Tarsus (second century A.D.) appends a brief section on comparison to his discussion of encomium in the *Progymnasmata* (reproduced in translation in Baldwin, *MRP*, 23-38), mentioning the fact that "some [authors] of no small reputation have made it an exercise by itself" (33).

[9] H. Caplan defines (*Ad Herenn.*, 172-173, n. b) the essential distinction between deliberative and forensic oratory on the one hand and epideictic on the other: "Whereas in both deliberative and judicial causes the speaker seeks to persuade his hearers to a course of action, in epideictic his primary purpose is by means of his art to impress his ideas upon them, without action as a goal." C. S. Baldwin (*MRP*, chap. I, "The Sophistic Trend in Ancient Rhetoric") shows how in Imperial times oratory became more and more an occasion for dazzling virtuoso performances (cf. particularly p. 9 ff.) as its power and influence over the course of events steadily waned.

[10] See Aphthonius, *Progymnasmata*, 273.

tion when speaking of Urbanité. The prologue to his encomium consists of a mere half-dozen lines (IV, 102, ll. 20-25) of transition leading from the preceding account of Vesta, and proclaiming the seemliness (and indeed the indispensability) of Urbanité "à toutes Princesses et grands Dames." Then, in strict accordance with the rhetorical canons, Chastellain exhibits the distinguished genealogy of Urbanité: "Vrbanité... est de la famille de dame Temperance,... et est fille de Moderation... sœur de Clemence, de Studiosité, d'Humilité, de bonne Contenance, de Simplicité et de Suffisance," etc. (IV, 102). Next comes a traditionally rhetorical procedure for which the early sixteenth century shows a perhaps excessive fondness, namely a study of the derivation of the subject's name,[11] starting with the Greek "Eutrapelia qui vaut autant à dire comme bonne idoneïté à toutes choses" (IV, 103), followed by the Latinism "Vrbanité, pource quelle est toute ciuile, compaignable et humaine," and finally in good French, "gentillesse ou courtoisie." So much for External Circumstances. Physical Attributes are passed over in silence, but Qualities of Character are dealt with at some length in a charming *portrait moral* (103-104), which depicts the virtue as a gracious lady, full of natural dignity, considerate of the feelings of others, elegant, courtly, and eminently amiable (see Chap. II, above). The princess Marguerite, "nostre seconde Vesta," is then held up as the exemplar, "le vray parangon de courtoisie et d'Vrbanité" (IV, 105), and the apparently genuine readiness of her wit is displayed to advantage in a couple of brief but singular anecdotes (a form, incidentally, for which the author's marked

---

[11] For Lemaire's constant recourse to etymological (and toponymical) interpretation intended to prove a point, see G. Doutrepont's *JLBR*, 204-206. Jean Frappier ("L'Humanisme de Lemaire de Belges," in *Bibliothèque d'Humanisme et Renaissance* 25 [1963], 289-306) also has some interesting comments on Lemaire's "senefiances" (297, n. 6). Quintilian has much to say regarding the utility of etymology (see especially I.vi.28 ff.), though he cautions against the ludicrous consequences which may ensue from an excessive "passion for derivations" (I.vi.34-38). Etymology had from classical times been considered a *locus* of invention; in the Middle Ages, much emphasis was laid on its usefulness in praising and blaming. For example, John of Garland (*Poetria*, 18) writes: "In ethimologiis locum habemus inueniendi: ut, si aliquis intendat laudare Dominum Papam, dicat: 'Vere dominus papa piissimus pater; dicitur "pater patrum," quod ipsius nominis ethimologica exposicio manifestat, et dicitur a "pape" grece, quod est "admirabile" latine. Vnde "papa" "sacerdos admirabilis," quod in eo ex prerogatiua uite et scientie declaratur'"

predilection is equalled only by his very real talent as a raconteur).[12] By a process of deductive reasoning,[13] these anecdotes enable Chastellain to state unequivocally that, as Marguerite is demonstrably possessed of a high degree of Urbanité, so does she the more resemble Vesta (107). This concludes the praises of Urbanité, and with a few additional reasons "pour corroborer ma comparation" (i.e., of Marguerite with the amethyst and Vesta), the speaker winds up the encomium of the princess who is its true embodiment.

Very different in character is the old shepherd's oration in the first book of *Les Illustrations de Gaule*. This is only to be expected, after all, for whereas the formidably erudite Burgundian chronicler is addressing a veritable academy of poets, historians, orators, philosophers, and theologians in appropriately awe-inspiring surroundings,[14] Paris's foster-father holds forth in an equally suitable (*mutatis mutandis*) setting.[15] He faces an audience of simple shepherd lads to whom, "comme le bon precepteur en vne escole enseigne ses disciples, il leur lisoit debonnairement vne leçon de sa science Ruralle" (I, 147).

With regard to the respective subject matters of the rhétoriqueur and the shepherd, the distinction is, on the face of it, crystal clear: the former's theme is the typically "artificial" one of a great lady and her superhuman merits; the latter occupies himself with the natural, salubrious pleasures of the countryside. In Chastellain's oration we find precisely those elements we should expect to find, i.e., learned comments on genealogy backed up by the combined authority of Pliny's "histoire Naturelle," "les Astrologues," and the Apocalypse; an equal knowledge of ancient mythology and of modern history, as evinced by the genealogies of the goddess Vesta and

---

[12] See below, Chap. VI, 150-151, for Lemaire's use of the anecdote as *exemplum*.

[13] This type of argument is characteristic of the *enthymeme*, the typical mode of rhetorical proof, as the syllogism is the type in logic. In rhetoric, as G. Kennedy points out (*APG*, 316), the "premises and conclusions are probable rather than certain" (as in logic).

[14] In the "haut palais crystallin du Roy honneur" (IV, 41), to be precise.

[15] "...en lombre dun tilleul ou dun ormel bien large et bien fueillu..." (I, 146). One might justifiably deduce from this that Jean Lemaire was acquainted with the medieval doctrine of the *Rota Virgilii* (see Chap. I, 38, above). It is worthy of note that after his dramatic change of fortune, Paris speaks only in such places as befit his princely estate, i.e., in royal palaces or on the field of battle, rather than in those appropriate to the *humilis stilus*.

of the princess Marguerite; instances of Greek and Latin etymological exegesis; a talent for the lapidary definition (of Urbanité); the artfully nonchalant use of Latin quotations. However, the shepherd is frankly no more representative of his calling than is Virgil's Tityrus. Since he is himself a figure of classical mythology, it is small wonder if his discourse is sprinkled from end to end with mythological allusions. His intent is undeniably didactic, as he exhorts the younger generation, by praising the wholesome pastoral life, to follow in his footsteps; but then Chastellain's intent is plainly no less so. Even the extravagant comparisons of *La Couronne Margaritique* are exactly paralleled, as we shall see shortly. What *is* strikingly different is the impression, skillfully created by Lemaire, of the ease and artlessness with which the wise old man speaks. All of the Ten Orations in honor of Marguerite d'Autriche, though the author has visibly taken considerable pains to differentiate between them, to add a touch of individuality,[16] are unmistakably redolent of midnight oil. They are, one might say, papers read before a learned society. The shepherd, on the other hand, is not striving to impress a gathering of fellow-scholars, but benignly bequeathing the fruits of his experience to a group of eager and respectful children — all, moreover, save Paris, his own flesh and blood. The

---

[16] Jean Stecher notes with reference to the alchemist Arnauld de Villeneuve that "La dissertation que lui prête Lemaire est bien digne d'un chercheur de la pierre philosophale" (IV, 115, n. 1). And can it be purely coincidental, or, as I am inclined to suspect, a mildly satirical note that by far the longest of the ten orations is the one delivered by a bishop, St. Isidore? (The runner-up is a fellow ecclesiastic, the learned Dominican friar Vincent de Beauvais.) If the intent is indeed humorous, the pleasantry is doubtless traditional. In Chartier's far from amusing *Quadrilogue invectif*, for example, whereas Peuple's two harangues occupy a total of some eight pages, Clergé holds forth for no less than eighteen. P. Jodogne notes (*JLBEFB*, 251), with respect to the Ten Orators, that although in his opinion there is rarely any discernible connection between the speaker and his subject matter, it is perhaps not without significance that Robertet, who was a high official at the court of the Duke of Bourbon, expatiates on Upright Counsel; the polished Burgundian chronicler Chastellain presents Urbanity; Boccaccio (who, as Jodogne emphasizes here and elsewhere — cf. p. 64 and *passim* — meant to the French humanists of Jean Lemaire's day not so much the author of the *Decameron* as the compiler of encyclopedic Latin works such as the *Genealogiae Deorum, De casibus virorum illustrium,* and *De claris mulieribus*) delivers an encomium of Erudition. Finally, it is left to Vincent de Beauvais, another "puissant encyclopédiste," to draw the appropriate conclusions, after himself discussing Experience.

lack of pomp and circumstance is enhanced by the use of such expressions as "Mes chers enfans, ma douce nourriture" (147); "Or donques mes chers et bien aymez enfans" (149); "Certes mon filz Paris, quand ie te voy aller aux champs" (149). And the entire discourse is given in the everyday second person, aimed directly at the children sitting at his feet, whereas Chastellain and his colleagues, being very conscious of their dignity as humanists and of the solemnity of the occasion, are relentlessly impersonal in their phraseology.

The principal difference between these two orations is a formal one. We have seen how the encomium of Urbanité is in many respects modeled on classical rhetorical precepts as expounded in, e.g., the *Ad Herennium*. In sharp contrast, the bucolic encomium is much freer in organization.[17] In effect, the speaker exhorts his audience to be content — indeed, to bless their good fortune — with the station in life to which Providence has assigned them, and this he achieves by depicting the pastoral life in the most glowing and attractive colors. Needless to say, this is a very old theme indeed, going back to Virgil's *Eclogues* and beyond to the *Idylls* of Theocritus.[18]

---

[17] I am not referring here to the traditional organization of a speech according to *exordium, narratio, petitio*, etc. This we shall briefly examine in the context of a later oration (Concorde's). I have in mind rather the topics of encomium discussed earlier in this chapter. In any case, *Ad Herennium* gives the widest possible latitude to the orator by stating that: "The kinds of Arrangement are two: one arising from the principles of rhetoric, the other accomodated to particular circumstances" (III.ix.16). The author explains that in the first case one follows the usual order of *exordium, narratio*, and so on, whereas in the second the arrangement is "in accordance with the speaker's judgement." Cf. Quintilian, II.xiii.2: "... most rules are liable to be altered by the nature of the case, circumstances of time and place, and by hard necessity itself. Consequently the all-important gift for an orator is a wise adaptability since he is called upon to meet the most varied emergencies." M. L. Clarke (*RR*, 66-67), confirming that in practice orators did not hesitate to avail themselves of this licence, observes that in Cicero's mature speeches the orthodox scheme of *dispositio* is more often ignored than not, the only constants remaining the exordium and the peroration.

[18] The brilliant career of the pastoral genre in Renaissance Europe needs no comment. It suffices to point out with, *inter alios*, Abel Lefranc ("JLB," 775) and Alice Hulubei (*EF16*, 174) that here, as in other innovative aspects of sixteenth-century literature, one yet again finds Jean Lemaire at the very fountainhead. It is peculiarly apt that the earliest French translator of Homer should also be the first to evoke the Golden Age with such freshness and youthful grace. "Qui a décrit avec plus de bonheur que Lemaire le charme

The good man, then, begins (I, 147, ll. 6-28) by earnestly stressing the dignity of "ceste vocation pastorale," which is "vne occupation deïfique." He cites Apollo and Anchises (who, though himself mortal, was beloved of Venus) as corroborative examples. The remainder of the speech comprises three sections. The first (147, l. 29 - 149, l. 15) is a homily on the utility of the shepherd's calling, in which there is much emphasis on "proufit," [19] though not in any crassly commercial sense. The gain in question is regarded as a moral as well as a utilitarian one, for "nostre estat de bergerie ... est totallement fondé sur honneur et sur proufit" (149). The flocks provide the gods with pleasing sacrifices, furnish "la fine draperie" for royal and priestly vestments, [20] "somptueuses tapisseries" for the walls of palace and temple, and "alimentation necessaire" for all the citizens of Troy, including the happy shepherds themselves, who also dress in wool and sleep beneath woolen covers. "Et consequutiuement toutes autres choses partans de voz bestes à laine, sont pleines de bien, de proufit et de remede ..." (148). Nor does the speaker forget to pay due reverence to the Golden Fleece, "qui resplend maintenant au ciel, faisant lun des douze signes du Zodiaque" (149). Since the Ordre de la Toison d'Or (founded in 1429 by Philippe le Bon, Duke of Burgundy) was in the days of Jean Lemaire and Marguerite d'Autriche the highest order of chivalry in the gift of the Imperial house, the allusion is without question a discreetly adroit piece of flattery.

The second part of the encomium (149, l. 15 - 150, l. 23) is an extended metaphor founded on the following conceit: "Et imaginez que vostre maniere de viure, nest autre chose fors le vray exemplaire dun Royaume, et vne espece de regime politique dune chose publique." The departure of Paris and his companions for the fields is likened to that of "Prince Hector enuironné de ses freres et de sa baronnie"; their "chiens loyaux et bien abayans" are "voz gardes, voz descoureurs, et auantcoureurs"; their flocks represent "le nom-

---

éternel de la nature?" writes F. Thibaut (*MAJLB*, 198-199). "Qui nous a mieux fait sentir la beauté de ces paysages dont rien ne trouble la solitude? ... Cette partie des *Illustrations* n'a point vieilli; c'est elle qui assure à Lemaire la gloire d'avoir créé en France, avant Amyot, le roman pastoral ..."

[19] The word occurs six times (including one verbal use: "proufitera") in the two pages of the development. Reinforcing the notion of profit, we find "reuenue et utilité" (148) and "grand vtilité et reuenu" (149).

[20] Silk is dismissed, by comparison, as mere "fiente de vermine"! (I, 148).

bre innumerable de vostre grosse armee," while predatory wolves, lynxes, leopards, lions, bears, and "larrons nocturnes" are the ever-present enemy.

The third and concluding section of the shepherd's oration (150, l. 23 - 151, l. 23) follows quite naturally from the second, just as the second, which treats of the conduct of the state and its defence — the princely occupations *par excellence* — is inspired by the concluding words of the first (with their insistence on the *honor* of the "estat de bergerie"). There are no forced transitions or awkward hiatuses, as is sometimes the case with the Ten Orators, who, in their determination to exploit every resource of their immense erudition and considerable rhetorical skill, are occasionally guilty of precisely these lapses. This is only to be expected: the entire procedure of the elaborate triple comparisons, of ten variations on an identical theme, reeks of contrivance (as it is plainly intended to) and the mannered, ceremonious ambience of the palace of Honneur is utterly remote from the unconstrained ease of the little group relaxing comfortably beneath some venerable tree.

The rustic orator's military metaphor then reminds him that, like a prudent general consulting the oracles before committing himself to battle, the wise shepherd has his own "deuins et augures familiers" to assure him that the season is propitious. There follows a charming passage of country lore, as these mysterious and numinous matters prove to consist in cunning in the songs and movements of divers birds [21] and an intimate knowledge of the ways of the obliging bellwether, "nommé sonnaillier, ou clocheman, lequel vous deuez

---

[21] The use of the term "augures" is therefore fully warranted in this context. Lemaire takes a manifest delight, in his enumerations, in selecting the *mot juste*. Thus in I, 151: "le *sifflement* du Huas, quon dit Mylan ou Escouffle, le *tonnement* du Butor, le *iargon* du Pyuert, le *caquet* de la Pie, le *cry* de la Corneille, et le *maintien* de la Verdiere." Cf. *Amant* II, ll. 205 ff.:

> Maintz animaulx estranges et divers,
> Comme lyons *orgueilleux et pervers*,
> Ours *trescruelz*, tygres, loupz *ravissans*,
> Chiens *envïeux* par raige finissans,
> Boucz *trespuans*, chievres *luxurieuses*,
> Corbeaux *vilains*, piës *injurieuses*,
> ... ... ... ... ... ... ... ...
> Renardz *trop fins*, chauvettes *larronnesses*,
> Pourceaux *gourmans* et grives *grandz yvresses*,
> Voultours *tresordz* et huppes *sepulchrales*,
> Letz chatzhuans *portans nouvelles males*, [etc., etc.]

assoter par mignotise, et souuent luy offrir du pain. Car au moyen de sa bonne nature, il vous donra tousiours certaines enseignes du beau temps ou de la pluye aduenir" (151). Thus equipped for his calling, all that remains for the novice shepherd is to possess a little "philosophie naturelle" (or practical meteorology), in the words of the patriarchal mentor, whose discourse concludes as effortlessly as it had begun. Actually, we are given to understand that the pleasant talk flows on in the shade of the tree,[22] the absence of a formal peroration serving to point up the lack of any scholastic formality (which would be quite out of place in these circumstances).[23] This speech, in short, is a very pretty illustration of that art whose function it is to conceal art.

So far we have observed the working out in actual practice of some of the rhetorical precepts relative to panegyric. There is also, let it be remembered, a negative aspect to this genre (based on the contraries of the topics for praise), known as invective or *vituperatio*. When Paris, after subjecting the three ranking goddesses of the Olympian hierarchy to the indignity of a strip-tease, has the sacrilegious temerity not to award the golden apple to Juno, or even to the maidenly Pallas, "pleine de verecunde virginale" (I, 254), the queen of heaven "ne se peut onques abstenir de desgorger la fumee de son despit" (258), but vents her spleen on the trembling youth in a magnificent verbal onslaught (258-259).

The tirade in which Juno fulminates against Paris, "dun visage palissant, et duns yeux allumez par grand fureur, dune voix aigre, sonoreuse et abrupte," is worthy of a Phèdre, a Roxane, an Agrippine or a Hermione, and convinces this reader at least that Jean Lemaire should have been born, not a mere thirty years later, as Henry Guy would have it (see above, Chap. I, 7), but a full one hundred and fifty years, for he here gives evidence that he is a tragic playwright who unluckily missed his century. The text is extremely rich stylistically, and will therefore be studied from that point of view in the next chapter (where it is incorporated *in ex-*

---

[22] "Ainsi sermonnoit au ieune Paris et à ses autres enfans, le bon vieillard plein daffection beniuole, en les encourageant à ce noble labeur: et oultre ce leur enseignoit les signes et les remedes de diuerses maladies," etc. (151).

[23] This is wholly in accord with Horace's advocacy of literary propriety or *decorum* (see *Ars Poetica*, 153-178).

*tenso*). For the present, I would like to consider in what ways this *vituperatio* is a model of epideictic rhetoric.

It is difficult to analyze so short (44 lines) a piece in the conventional rhetorical manner. There is, for example, no exordium to speak of, as Juno begins immediately to upbraid Paris at a very high level of opprobrium without, as it were, building up to it by degrees: "O homme brutal, beste transformee, creature destinee à toute infelicité, Idole fantastique qui sembles ce que tu nes pas, vaisseau corrompu de lubricité vilaine, et sac à fiens et pourriture...." There are two major subdivisions: the first (258, ll. 8-29) is devoted to the invective of the guilty party who was so lately a judge; the second (258, l. 29 - 259, l. 14) to Juno's enumeration of grievances against the royal house which has produced such a monster, and its long history of high crimes and misdemeanors. The peroration (259, ll. 14-22) is typically Junonian (and Aristotelian) [24] in its abruptness, and is composed of dire threats of vengeance and destruction shortly to be visited upon the Trojans.

Stylistic considerations apart, the most interesting feature of the invective consists in its illustration of how the commonplaces of the epideictic mode may be reversed. Thus, with respect to Paris's External Circumstances, we have — recounted with cold and savage fury — the (very) concise history (259, ll. 1-14) of the damnable arrogance which infects the entire Trojan dynasty ("Ie congnois ores que ceux de ta maison ne sont nez, fors pour me faire iniure").[25] As for the topic of Physical Attributes, the very beauty of Paris itself serves an article of his indictment: "... mal est employee beauté corporelle en si lasche courage: mal sont assignez les biens de Dieu et de Nature en chose si desnaturee...." The *Rhetorica ad Herennium* defines the Qualities of Character (III.vi.10-11) as "wisdom, justice, courage, temperance, and their contraries." It need hardly be said that what obsesses Juno in this tirade is "the contraries." The divinely handsome youth is "brutal" and a "beste

---

[24] The *Rhetoric* itself ends with an injunction to keep the peroration short. Aristotle's own conclusion is a famous model of pithy brevity: "I have spoken; you have heard; you know the facts; now give your decision."

[25] Juno's legendary vindictiveness and elephant-like memory for slights, real and imaginary, are deftly called to mind by such indications as "Il me souuient du rauissement de Ganymedes, ton proayeul, qui fut fait et perpetré au desauantage de moy et de ma fille Hebé. Et nay pas oublié la rudesse que ton ayeul Laomedon feit à mon frere Neptune..."

transformee"; he has made his lack of the aforementioned virtues only too conspicuous by preferring "la vie voluptueuse et inutile, à la vie actiue et contemplatiue." "Nas tu eu vergongne de ... mespriser la vraye viuacité des images celestes, pour le fard couloure et teint sophistique, dune statue plate et vuide?"[26] If there remain any lingering doubts as to Paris's outstanding negation of each and every virtue, Juno at once dispels them with a withering volley of insults: "Iuge ridicule et syluestre, plus leger que nest la plume au vent, prodigue de ton honneur, courage de meretrice, pollu dun leger promettre, tout vermolu dinconstance, mal sainement deliberant, aueugle choisisseur, [etc.]." So much then — for the time being — for the epideictic mode.

Coming now to the second part of our study of Lemaire's orations, let us begin our discussion of his approach to deliberative oratory with a brief analysis of Concorde's speech to the Emperor Maximilian I (*Genre humain*, 65-69).

From the structural standpoint it is abundantly evident that the nymph's address has been influenced by the rhetorical canons of both antiquity and the Middle Ages. Her brief exordium (ll. 517-528) consists of hyperbolic praise of Maximilian's heroic qualities. This follows standard medieval epistolary practice laid down by the *ars dictaminis,* which places particular emphasis on the necessity of winning the good will of the audience.[27] The concluding section of the exordium is a discreet reminder to the Emperor that "la tendre jeunesse femelline de ceste ta tres chiere et tres digne fille unicque ne fait à comparer à ta durté robuste et virille."

This leads into the *narratio,* or exposition of the facts (ll. 529-566). The princess Marguerite, declares Concorde, has labored unceasingly, zealously, and cheerfully to further the cause of the Imperial house, in the teeth of "Infortune, son tres injurieux et tres infeste ennemy" (ll. 547-548). It is thus only fitting that she be

---

[26] This passage could be considered an interesting combination of a Neoplatonic reference and the contrast — again Platonic — between truth ("la vraye viuacité") and empty, deceptive rhetoric ("le fard couloure et teint sophistique," etc.).

[27] In other words, *captatio benevolentiae* (or *benivolentiae*) as in "le parler du ieune adolescent Paris Alexandre fut recueilli en saueur et beniuolence" (II, 13), or again in the phrase "pour capter la beniuolence du peuple" (II, 213). Cf. Cicero's *De inventione,* I.xv.21: "... *si non omnino infesti auditores erunt, principio benivolentiam comparare licebit.*"

accorded a little repose and, moreover, some seemly recompense ("[un] guerdon convenable pour la remunerer immortellement," [ll. 540-541]); for now, the nymph continues, by the grace of God and the efforts of Caesar and his daughter, I, Concorde du Genre Humain, have at last returned — this time in perpetuity — among mankind. There follows what in a forensic oration would be called the *partitio* (or *divisio,* in which the speaker announces the principal points he is about to make; ll. 567-600), but which is here actually a petition[28] in two parts. The first reiterates the claim that the princess be granted the right to "se ... reposer en oisifveté paisible et estre repeue du doulx fruict de ses travaulx passéz" (573-575); the second (578-600) that Caesar bestow upon her the "tres heureux et bien fortuné nom d'Auguste" (599-600). The supporting proofs, or argumentation (*argumentatio, confirmatio, probatio*; 600-653), are made up to begin with of historical precedents, to be followed "à l'exemple de plusieurs empereurs rommains" (600-601) who had awarded the imperial title to ladies whose merits in no wise equal those of Marguerite. A second proof is based on the etymology of "Augusta" (609-620), and once again the principle of historical precedent is invoked. Since there are no opposing arguments, no refutation is required (as would be the case in a forensic oration). Concorde's peroration (654-667) is triumphantly logical in character:[29] "Doncques, Cesar, il appert que de tout ce resulte une

---

[28] The *ars dictaminis* taught that the *petitio* was the very core of the letter, one of the three absolutely indispensable parts, the other two (according to the famous thirteenth-century *dictator,* Boncompagno of Bologna) being the *salutatio* and *narratio* (see Louis J. Paetow, *The Arts Course at Medieval Universities* [Champaign, Ill., 1910], 77-78). Charles Homer Haskins (*R12C,* 143-144) says that "the petition ... was likely to take the form of a logical deduction from the major and minor premises already laid down in the exordium and narration ..."

[29] The relationship between rhetoric and dialectic has a long, complex, and often troubled history. For Plato, the two disciplines are scarcely to be reconciled, since in his view, whereas dialectic's aim is to reveal truth by the processes of reason, rhetoric deals only in plausibility and opinion. Aristotle's *Rhetoric,* on the other hand, begins: "Rhetoric is a counterpart of Dialectic; for both have to do with matters that are in a manner within the cognizance of all men and not confined to any special science." W. S. Howell ("Renaissance Rhetoric and Modern Rhetoric: a Study in Change" [in *PR,* 292-308), sums up the ancient attitude to the respective functions of rhetoric and dialectic in these words: "... eloquence stands for the open, popular speech to political meetings, juries, and gatherings at public ceremonies and celebrations ... logic in the ancient scheme taught the young expert to communicate

clere consequence," etc., and Maximilian is practically commanded to grant the desired boon: "Ta haulte sapience ... doibt ores estre assez persuadée à ce que tu confermes en elle ceste glorieuse et bien decente appellation de 'Marguerite Auguste' " etc. (655-659).

The last of the deliberative orations to be discussed here are those belonging to the Judgment of Paris episode, which forms (whether by design or by accident, though I incline to the latter view) almost the exact core of the Idyll of Paris and Oenone [30] (I, chapters XX-XLIV). In fact, the Judgment is to my mind the focal point of the whole of *Les Illustrations de Gaule,* which without a doubt contributes to the bathos of Books II and — more especially — III. I would argue that it is no mean testimony to the author's talent that he succeeds not only in sustaining the reader's pleasurable interest during the ten remaining chapters of Book I, but indeed in bringing the book to a brilliant, resounding, and climactic conclusion. [31]

---

with his peers while rhetoric taught him to communicate with the populace" (297). Cf. Richard McKeon's invaluable article, "Rhetoric and the Middle Ages," and Chap. IV, n. 32 above.

[30] Ten chapters precede, eleven follow the Judgment (I, chaps. XXX-XXXIII).

[31] The account of the Trojan War in Book II, while not equal to the Paris-Oenone story, is also worth reading; the remainder of *Les Illustrations,* it must be confessed, is not. The fact that the most successful section of the work, in literary terms, is also the most oratorical — and that only Book III, which contains no speeches (see above, Chap. IV, p. 101), is an artistic failure — again underscores the essentially rhetorical nature of Lemaire's talent. The reason for the falling-off as the work proceeded is of course uncertain; Lemaire's reliance on mediocre authorities may be partly responsible, though a progressive loss of enthusiasm for the task after the completion of Book I seems perhaps the most likely explanation. Lemaire's chief sources for Book II, according to Doutrepont (*JLBR,* 45, 236, and *passim*) are Dares of Phrygia and Dictys of Crete. The same critic says (41) that "Les dix-huit premiers chapitres [du premier livre] sont presque exclusivement la reproduction des histoires contées par Annius [Viterbensis]," with additional borrowings from Boccaccio's *Genealogiae,* Robert Gaguin's *Compendium super francorum gestis,* the Bible, and Jacques de Guise's *Illustrations de la Gaule Belgique, antiquitez du pays de Haynau et de la grand cité de Belges, à present dicte Bavay dont procèdent les chaussées de Brunehault,* as the title of the fifteenth-century translation (from a fourteenth-century Latin work) so resoundingly puts it. Doutrepont (193-194) speculates that "le roman de Pâris et d'Oenone" is actually "un hors-d'œuvre ... un morceau de littérature composé indépendamment des intentions politiques qui ont présidé à la confection du travail historique, proprement dit, des *Illustrations.*" He lends credence to this theory by remarking that whereas Lemaire began the work in 1500, it was only in 1506

But what is of special interest to us at this point is the triad of orations delivered by the goddesses on Mount Ida.[32] So closely are the speeches interrelated that it would be difficult — not to say pointless — to study them as distinct and separate entities.

One of the first things to strike the reader is the extremely effective way in which Lemaire contrives to make each oration appear as the product of an individual personality.[33] What is more, even were the names of the speakers suppressed, it would be astonishing if anyone reasonably well versed in Greco-Roman mythology failed to identify them. The tone of the different goddesses is unmistakably in character. Juno's is peremptory, haughty, glacial; she makes little attempt to *persuade* the judge, her language and manner are precisely those of a high and mighty princess accustomed to being obeyed without question,[34] although she does unbend so far as to address Paris in a style befitting the scion of a ruling dynasty ("Adolescent Royal, de progeniture illustre, et de tresantique generosité..." [I, 233]). Pallas, as patroness of intellectual pursuits, is every inch the bluestocking, horribly ill at ease in what cannot be dignified by any name other than that of beauty pageant. She is no more temperamentally equipped to persuade than is Juno;[35] her

---

or 1507 that Marguerite d'Autriche was entrusted with the education of the young Archduke Charles, and that it is therefore unlikely that the author desired to "orienter les *Illustrations* vers une démonstration en 'Télémaque allégorique'" before this time (Cf. Chap. IV, n. 35).

[32] There are also several magnificent descriptive passages, which will be dealt with in the next chapter.

[33] The literary re-creation of a well-known personality by composing *ex nihilo* the very words that he or she might have been expected to utter in reality is of course the traditional exercise known as *prosopopoeia* (or, in a simpler form, *ethopoeia*), to be discussed later in connection with Lemaire's use of the figures of rhetoric.

[34] Admittedly, she lacks the brutal and inimitable bluntness of a Queen Elizabeth I, whose curt missive to Dr. Richard Cox, Bishop of Ely in 1573, remains a unique epistolary masterpiece, a model of verbal economy:

> Proud Prelate:
> You know what you were before I made you what you are now. If you do not immediately comply with my request, I will unfrock you, by God.
>
> Elizabeth

[35] On the subject of "ethical" persuasion, i.e., that kind of persuasion achieved by the moral character of the speaker (*ethos*), as distinguished from the frame of mind of the audience (*pathos*) and the inherent qualities of the speech, see above, Chap. II, 67.

approach is rather the undisguised didacticism of the lecturer. The earnest and solemn Pallas is perhaps after all a kindred spirit of William Ewart Gladstone. She has that great man's unfortunate and annoying habit — which Queen Victoria found so offensive — of addressing individuals as though they were "a public meeting." Naturally, she attempts to appeal to Paris's intellect ("Enfant de bonne indole, et de tresingenieuse nature," etc. [237]). Venus, on the other hand, is — to the reader's delight — the shameless, unblushing hussy she is traditionally supposed to be.[36] One might be forgiven for claiming that the word "blandishment" is only comprehensible to one who has read and been fascinated by Venus's superlatively cajoling, tempting, enticing, and quintessentially *seductive* speech. She is the only one to make so blatantly flattering a use of the *captatio benevolentiae*; her address begins "O fleur florissante de naïue beauté [an Alexandrine, be it noted] "gentil Prince de ieunesse, le plus accomply des dons de formosité corporelle qui iamais marcha ne marchera sur terre..." (243). In contrast, Juno, even while she patronizingly assures Paris that he is worthy of the appurtenances of royal power ("tant pour lantiquité de ton origine et progeniture illustre, comme pour la magnificence de ton priué personnage mesmes" [233]), does so only after a lengthy enumera-

---

[36] I am quite unable to agree with Frappier ("Humanisme," 301), when, noting that Venus represents the sensual life, Juno the active, and Pallas the contemplative, he declares: "On sent bien que les préférences intimes de Jean Lemaire vont à la troisième déesse." It is true that he is influenced by the section of Pallas's oration beginning "Quand donques tu voudras prendre repos" (239, ll. 10-25), which is, as he justly says, a "noble programme de science et de conscience," revealing "dans sa plus pure essence la culture humaniste de Jean Lemaire." However, I would not hesitate to claim on the basis of the Judgment of Paris scene that it is the personality (and the person) of Venus, not Pallas, which fascinates Jean Lemaire. In *Les Illustrations*, the most literal indication as to where the author's favor lies is the fact that, whereas Chap. XXXI is devoted to the descriptions and discourses of both Juno and Pallas, the following chapter (which is only one page shorter) is entirely taken up with Venus alone. I believe, incidentally, that the foregoing remarks apply with equal force to P. Jodogne's reading of *La Concorde des deux langages*, when he opposes "Le Temple de Minerve" section to "Le Temple de Vénus" on much the same grounds as Frappier's (cf. *JLBEFB*, 447). The first-named passage does indeed receive the author's lip-service, but the latter gets all his loving attention. I would certainly agree that Lemaire the humanist doubtless feels that he *ought* to prefer the contemplative to the sensuous, but the poet in him gets the upper hand every time. "Video meliora proboque, / Deteriora sequor," as Ovid says.

tion of her own divinely incomparable attributes. Le Roi Soleil was later to condescend to lesser monarchs in pretty much the same vein.

From the point of view of structure, Juno's oration is the most regular and tightly organized of the three, following as it does the traditional scheme for forensic rhetoric.[37] There is a clearly defined proem (233, ll. 1-12) in which — going straight to the point — she admonishes the judge to aim for higher and better things than his present lot: "Mets ius ton ignauité rurale, pour atteindre à seigneuriant prosperité, et garde que ne te mescontes au choix des guerdons qui te seront proposez: car là gist le neu de la besongne." (Note the interesting contrast between the generally ornate, Latinizing style and the down-to-earth saying with which the citation ends.) The proem is followed by a *narratio* (233, ll. 12-25), expounding the plain facts of the matter, viz., first, that Juno's supremacy as queen of heaven is unchallengable, and second, that she (and only she) has the power to award her votaries "richesses mondaines, noblesses desirees, et haux mariages legitimes: auec les tiltres de couronnes Royales, Imperiales, et de toutes terrestres monarchies." The *confirmatio* (234, l. 1 - 235, l. 6) is an autoencomiastic development which starts out by praising the "beauté non equiparable" of the goddess, and continues as a remarkably frank exposition of the allurements of earthly power, startlingly (and doubtless intentionally) reminiscent of the manner of Satan's second temptation of Christ.[38] The marked urgency of tone achieved by the succession of a series of phrases each beginning with an imperative is a char-

---

[37] Needless to say, these speeches are hardly to be classified as forensic oratory, the only judicial aspect being the appointment of Paris as a judge of beauty. The speeches are all alike in their combination of a deliberative aim with epideictic methods. But since ancient rhetorical treatises invariably lavish by far the greater part of their theorizing on judicial oratory, the other modes are almost always considered in this light with respect to matters of structure, delivery, etc.

[38] "And the devil, taking him up into an high mountain, shewed unto him all the kingdoms of the world in a moment of time. / And the devil said unto him, All this power will I give thee, and the glory of them: for that is delivered unto me; and to whomsoever I will give it" (Luke 4, 5-6). ("Regarde la beatitude de ceux qui par moy regnent: Note la merueilleuse resplendeur doree et perlifiee, de mon throne auguste, de mon Royal diademe et sceptre immortel. Boute en ta saueur les mirifiques distillations dont les hauts Princes sont par moy arrosez. Mesure la grandeur et amplitude de la bienheuree puissance que ie leur administre," etc.)

acteristic of all three orations, though, as one might expect, Juno's use of the procedure is by far and away the most imperious. Her rebuttal (in advance) of her rivals' claims (235, ll. 7-27) occurs in the orthodox location for a *confutatio,* and consists of a twofold satire on the disciples of Pallas and Venus. Actually, perhaps only the first section should properly be termed satirical.[39] This is a devastating thumbnail sketch of the ineffectual and futile humanist, condemned to remain forever a frustrated spectator on the sidelines of power, and hence regarded with superb disdain by the patroness of men of action ("Et aussi naffiert à homme de Royale vocation muser si parfond en literature, ne tant peser le sens, ou epiloguer les diffinitions de prudence, et autres vertuz morales, et les difficultez de la conduite des choses, *par verbale garrulité seulement sans rien mettre en realle efficace*").[40] Doubtless Juno does not feel that the prudent Pallas poses a serious threat. Her portrayal of the devotees of Venus, on the other hand, is venomous to a degree which characterizes it as pure invective rather than satire, and worthy moreover of the most fanatically puritanical of Renaissance divines. ("Congnois aussi dautre part la meschance et vilité des autres encores plus mesprisables.... Et sont remplíz de luxurieuse immundicité, bannis de conuersation honneste, et tous enclins à corruption, rapine et homicide. Lesquelz tous viuans sont enseueliz en ordure mortelle, et detestable," etc.) After thus summarily disposing of the competition, Juno wastes little time on her (four-line) peroration (235, l. 27 - 236, l. 1), which, according to time-honored practice, is that part of the speech regularly reserved for a dazzling display of oratorical fireworks.[41] Juno is content to remind Paris

---

[39] "...reduis en estime lignobilité de ceux qui en oisiueté racroupie, et en contemplation solitaire, de ie ne scay quelz songes de philosophie passent inutilement leurs iours, sommeillans et baillans apres les biens de mon tresor..."

[40] The first half of this passage (as far as "...et autres vertuz morales") reads suspiciously like an acerbic commentary on the Ten Orators of *La Couronne Margaritique,* while the second, with "verbale garrulité" the antithesis of "realle efficace," might almost be considered an indictment of "empty" (i.e., epideictic) rhetoric itself. Deliberative oratory gets things done, on the contrary; it rouses men to action. Or perhaps the impatient Juno regards *all* oratory as essentially frivolous, which is richly ironic in view of the particularly high-flown rhetoric she is herself exploiting here.

[41] "...it is in the peroration, if anywhere, that we must let loose the whole torrent of our eloquence... It is at the close of our drama that we

rather curtly that the pleasure *she* can bestow upon him is "assez condigne et propice à ma hautesse et dignité, et à lequipollant de tes merites." And that, with a parting short for "lasciuité venerienne," is that.

I am not certain whether Pallas's vaunted modesty is the reason for her oration's being the shortest of the three, or if it is indicative of the (ideal) preeminence of Prudence as opposed to Puissance and Plaisance. (If the former supposition is correct, it would presumably help to explain how it happens that the brazen Venus speaks for nearly as long as both her rivals put together.) In any event, one must agree with G. Doutrepont (*JLBR*, 336) that Pallas's oration "a quelque chose de savantasse." More rhétoriqueur than rhetorician, the goddess endeavors to sway the judge by means of an excessively long-drawn-out nautical metaphor (238, ll. 5-21),[42] beginning "Nauenture point la precieuse galee de ton aage florissant au vent dambition sinistre, et de gloire vaine et desmesuree, ny en la tourmente de negoces ruïneux. Euite les perilz de tyrannique cruauté, les destroits dauarice insatiable, et le naufrage inconsideré doffension de voisins." Having by this neat innuendo given tit for tat (for the time being only; later she returns — albeit obliquely — to the offensive) to the belligerent Juno's derisive remarks about the unworldliness of her adherents, Pallas lets fly at Venus ("Ne tabandonne point à la nuict de terrienne amour: et ne te fie en lobscurté dignorance mondaine. Fuy le gouffre de vilaine lubricité" etc.). After metaphor comes medieval allegory, as Pallas encourages Paris with the prospect of the aid and comfort he will receive from "tous les soudars de ma famille: Cestasauoir, Sobre plenté, Eloquence non vaine,[43] Congnoissance historiale," and so remorselessly through an entire roll call of no less than twenty-three personifications (238-239). Pallas is much more subtle — or perhaps more self-effacing —

---

must really stir the theatre..." (*De inst. orat.*, VI.i.51-52). (But see above, n. 24.)

[42] At one point, unless I am mistaken, this becomes a slightly mixed metaphor, for when well under way (so to speak) Pallas warns Paris (ll. 15-16): "...veille à tes creneaux, desploye la meiane [i.e., "misaine"] et contremeiane de ton sens naturel." I have been unable to find a satisfactory explanation for this apparent lapse, unless of course Pallas has in mind a contemporary warship with unwieldy turreted fore- and stern-castles.

[43] An intentionally ironic touch, surely, given the final outcome of the contest.

in her self-glorification than either Juno or Venus. Aside from phrases like "seiourne les pupilles de ta circonspection discrete, au miroir de ma speciosité celeste" (238), and "aux rays de ma resplendeur, dont les yeux des ignorans sont esblouis," Pallas strictly confines herself to the panegyric of what she stands for, i.e., the "programme de science et de conscience" which so delights J. Frappier.[44] This is the climax of the prudential intellect's efforts to win the suffrages of a judge whose inclinations are anything but intellectual. Didactic to the end, Pallas holds forth — briefly, for once — on the etymology of her own names and titles[45] and rather endearingly admonishes Paris to follow "lexemple de la sage vniuersité d'Athenes, laquelle est en ma tutelle, et mexhibe vne reuerence incroyable" (240). But now comes the *pièce de résistance* as the impatient Venus, "à qui la prudente parole estoit fastidieuse" (240), is eagerly waiting in the wings, and, after the author has indulged himself in one of the most voluptuous descriptive passages of the entire work (241-243), she addresses Paris in her turn.

---

[44] See above, n. 36. ("... ma literature esclarcira tes gestes illustres, [an echo of the time-honored theme that the doughty deeds of the heroes would soon be forgotten but for the poets] mon sauoir obombrera ton chef, mes contemplations esleueront ton esprit, iusques au tiers ciel [the heaven of Venus(!), see below, n. 46], et ma rosee refreschira tes ardeurs imaginatiues. Si te seront mes tresors communiquez: et auras la congnoissance parfonde des choses secrettes, retention memoratiue des besongnes passees, cler entendement des presentes, et vtile preuision des futures. Et aussi se presenteront, pour tes familiers et domestiques en tes priuez consaulx Acuité Platonique, mesprisement asseuré de tous cas fortuits, auecques intelligence des artifices de nature, et de sa sapience, et lesclarcissement dabymes de toute science, diuine et humaine" [239]) (Cf. Rabelais's "abysme de science," in *Pantagruel,* VIII, written some twenty-two years later.)

[45] "Et par letymologie de mes noms, qui suis aucunesfois appellee Pallas, autresfois Minerue, cestadire vierge immortelle, et non corrompable: et autrefois Bellone, pour ma uertu bellique" (240). This in itself is not necessarily to be interpreted as a sign of pedantry (see above, n. 11, on the use of etymology as a *locus* of praise or blame). Juno herself does not despite etymology's aid at the appropriate moment: "... suis appellee Iuno, *Quasi iuuans omnes.* Cestadire, adiuteresse de tous: ou Lucina, pource que ie baille lumiere et entree à tous nobles coeurs" (233). Even Venus is an etymologist: "... ma planette ... laquelle est nommee Venus, pource quelle vient à toute choses. Aucunesfois aussi est appellee Hesperus, Vesperugo, ou Lucifer: cestadire portant lumiere," etc. (247). However, she also relies on a slightly less obvious method of conveying the significance of her name when she makes the alliterative rhyming pun, "Venus venuste" (244).

There can be not the slightest doubt that, if the contest between the goddesses were purely — as Ph. Aug. Becker would have us believe — a "Wettkampf der Reden und Versprechungen," to be decided as such, Venus thoroughly deserves her victory. She alone of the three has visibly taken time to study her audience psychology, which (as we saw in Chap. I above) all major authorities on rhetoric, from Plato and Aristotle on down, insist upon as crucial to successful oratory. In her discourse there is no trace of Juno's overbearing hauteur or of Pallas's rather tiresomely edifying tone. Venus senses correctly that Paris is not to be won over through an instinct for power or wisdom, because his predisposition is innately amorous, "Venerienne." Her "planette feconde et fertile" was in the ascendant at the hour of his birth: "Laquelle principalement esclaira ta natiuité, et propina à ta conception influence amoureuse, dulciloque, gaye, voluptueuse, de meditation ague, et de complexion totalement Venerienne et non euitable" (247). (During the Middle Ages, the seven inner heavens of the Ptolemaic universe were frequently interpreted allegorically to correspond to the seven liberal arts. The third heaven, that of Venus, is thus equated with rhetoric, for, as Dante writes in the *Convivio* (II, xiii), just as "... lo cielo di Venere si può comparare a la Rettorica ... che è soavissima a vedere più che altra stella ... la Rettorica è soavissima de tutte le altre scienze, però che a ciò principalmente intende. ...")[46] Needless to say, under such conditions there is really no contest: Paris is predestined to pick Venus.[47] Nevertheless, I repeat my contention that judged solely by the criterion of *persuasiveness,* her oratory is everything that it should be, whereas that of Juno and Pallas leaves much to be desired both in style and in content.

---

[46] *Convivio,* in *Opere minori,* ed. Alberto del Monte (Milan, 1960), 239-521; this citation 321. We therefore see that the presence of "rhetoricque" in "Le Temple de Venus" section of *La Concorde des deux langages* (l. 574) is nothing if not appropriate.

[47] Lemaire reproduces in chap. XXXV ("Explication tant morale comme philosophale et historiale ... du iugement de Paris, en plusieurs sortes: auec la figure du Ciel, qui fut à la naissance de Paris") Paris's horoscope, as drawn up by "Iulius Firmicus mathematique," which confirms that he was destined to "obtenir noces contentieuses, et mariage sans paix, et tout plein de malheurté, dont il se peult ensuiure merueilleux tumulte de guerre mortelle, menasses des contendans, et concitation de fureur horrible, auec grand respandement de sang humain. Et tout ce au moyen de cupidité venerique" (273).

The hallmark of this speech is its uniformly encomiastic tone. Like the previous contestants, Venus praises herself; but unlike them — apart from their passing references to Paris in the *captatio benevolentiae* and so on — she does not commit the serious tactical blunder of overlooking her one-man audience. It might even be said that her entire oration is an extended *captatio benevolentiae,* calculated to overwhelm with promises of bliss undreamed of an ardent youth, preeminently vulnerable to such an attack by virtue of both age and temperament. How could he be expected to withstand the fascination of such heady language as: "...ô perle vndoyante de blancheur arrondie, rutilant escarboucle de beauté rubicunde, surpassant toute elegance humaine, Paris le nompareil dentre le ciel et la terre, arreste ton plaisant aspect sur la speciosité dont ie suis decoree, à laquelle toute autre ne peult sortir comparaison" (246).[48] The lines in question introduce the *confirmatio* of the address, which resembles that of Pallas in one respect only, viz., the famous nautical metaphor. Venus seems to relish this opportunity to surpass her rival in florid imagery as well as in beauty, for her metaphor comprises no less than sixty-two lines (246, l. 13 - 248, l. 15), in contrast to Pallas's seventeen. (Not to mention Juno's adumbration of the same image in a scant two lines: "Dresse les voiles de ta pensee fluctuante es flotz de ieune cupidité, en vouloir hautain de sceptres maintenir" [234].) Venus devotes no one particular section (as Juno does) to an invective of her rivals. This is to be encountered *passim* in her oration, and can be distinguished from Juno's outright malevolence and Pallas's erudite gravity by a lighter touch and a skillful use of the figure comparison, to which Renaissance humanists were so partial.[49] Thus, like the good encomiast she is, she expatiates on her own illustrious ancestry, and says: "...ie croy que toutes trois approchons en equiparation conuenable, quant à ce, comme celles qui sommes sorties dun mesmes estoc: Cestasauoir de Saturne, et de Iupiter omnipotent"; but she cannot forbear to add, alluding to a significant difference which the modern

---

[48] The oration is highly poetic in nature, even to the inclusion of complete lines of verse, as this short excerpt demonstrates: "ô perle vndoyante de blancheur arrondie" (Alexandrine); "Paris le nompareil" (hemistich); "arreste ton plaisant aspect" (octosyllable). But style is a topic to which we shall return (see below, Chap. VI).

[49] See above, n. 8.

"saturnine" and "jovial" still reflect, "Mais de la festiuité elegante et proprieté Iouienne et paternelle, ie suis heritiere non degenerant. Les autres tiennent des mœurs et complexions de leur grand pere Saturne" (244). And there are glancing blows, delivered in passing, at "le pol arctique, la plage septentrionale, la froideur transmontaine, la mer congelee de continence Iunonique, et sterilité de Minerue" (247), which unpleasing prospects are at once negated by a glowing evocation of Venus's own "planette feconde et fertile." There is one instance — again within the lengthy nautical figure — of the heavy guns being brought to bear, as Venus lets fly (with devastating accuracy, moreover) at the "vent impetueux des paroles Iunoniennes[50] superbes et presumptueuses," and "limpulsion des vndes Palladiennes, pleines de strepit et garrulité" (246). By the relative length of her anti-Palladian tirade in this passage — a dozen lines compared to the four aimed at Juno — one might be inclined to the view that Venus after all finds Pallas a more dangerous rival than the queen of heaven, "pleine de grauité matronale" (254), as she is traditionally portrayed. However, I think that the author simply could not resist the temptation to amplify. And it must be confessed that the lines in question have a fine stormy "impulsion" to them, as Venus — anticipating his decision — congratulates Paris on his narrow escape from Pallas's "vagues sophistiques," which would have wrecked "ta Galee ingenieuse contre la roche brune de ses syllogismes politiques, intriquez et entouillez [= enveloppés] de timidité, mal seant à ieune Prince, pour estre absorbé en ses abymes parfondes et inuestigables: englouty au fons de ses figures de difficile intellecture, et versé au canal enigmatique de ses propositions douteuses et paraboles ambigues," etc., etc. (246-247).

Far more than her rivals, Venus deftly exploits all the possibilities inherent in the topics of encomium. Not only does she invoke External Circumstances (of lineage, etc.) as *Ad Herennium* pre-

---

[50] This epithet, with the previously quoted "Iunonique," strikes me as being somehow strangely derogatory, as "Palladiennes" in the same passage does not, doubtless because in other contexts it is invariably used by Lemaire in a laudatory sense, e.g., "l'art et estude mercurial et palladien" (*Concorde*, 3); "il mena vie palladienne; cestadire, contemplatiue" (I, 5). "Iunoniennes" and "Iunonique," on the other hand, seem to foreshadow the Rabelaisian "Sorbonicole," "Sorbonagre," etc.

scribes, but she does not fail to dwell on Physical Attributes too.[51] *Ad Herennium*'s third topic, Qualities of Character, does not — unsurprisingly — receive such close attention as the first two, but it is certainly not overlooked. After making what G. Doutrepont calls "cet aveu cynique" (*JLBR,* 337) concerning the practice (on Cyprus and Cythera, at Corinth and elsewhere) of ritual prostitution in her honor,[52] Venus insists that bloody sacrifices are anathema to her. "Car ie ne suis point Deesse sanguinolente, ny aymant occision: mais veux estre seulement seruie par offrandes de douces prieres,[53] et de fleurs bien flairantes, et par sacrifice de pur encens odoriferant: *ny autrement ne veux estre adoree"* (244).[54] But perhaps after all the best definition of her own character is contained in the sentence cited above in connection with Paris, where Venus calls him "dulciloque, gaye, voluptueuse." (One hardly needs to stress the explicit compliment in "dulciloque," as from one "sweet-talker" to another.)

Finally, this goddess produces the ultimate argument to win the allegiance of a kindred spirit, and that is of course her solemn promise to reward him with "la fruition certaine" of the consummately beautiful Helen, for, as she coolly observes, "... cest bien raison que les deux plus beaux personnages du monde soient alliez ensemble. Et aussi nous sauons assez, que la femme que tu as ores, nest pas correspondante à ton illustrité" (248). This breathtakingly cynical logic, followed by the guarantee of the aid and counsel of "mon filz Cupido," "ma niece Volupté," and "mon frere et amy le Dieu Mars" (who will ensure that Paris retains his prize against all comers),[55] and one last piece of flattery,[56] brings Venus's speech

---

[51] "Paris... arreste ton plaisant aspect sur la speciosité dont ie suis decoree... Remire la faitisse [= bien faite] tournure de ma venuste corpulence, *reflamboyant de forme seraphine* [a decasyllable]: et seiourne ton regard corporel en la clarté de ma face" (246). (Jean Lemaire, in his capacity as narrator, obeys these injunctions to the letter, and *con amore.* See below, Chap. VI, 160-161.

[52] Cf. *Concorde,* 14, ll. 160-162: "Jadis Venus, en deux temples, dont l'un / Fut corinthois, et l'autre de Sicille, / Mainte fille eut, dediée en commun."

[53] As so often with Lemaire, this line has a suspiciously (and in this instance incongruously) Biblical ring to it: "For I desired mercy, and not sacrifice; and the knowledge of God more than burnt offerings." (Hosea 6, 6)

[54] Yet another line of verse (a decasyllable).

[55] "Mars la te garantira à la pointe de son espee, enuers et contre tous" (249).

to an end. Unlike both her rivals, she exploits the use of direct emotional appeal to the judge, and this not only in the peroration, but throughout her address. In the strict Aristotelian sense, this is "bad" (though effective) oratory, because it is not the counterpart of dialectic (see this chap., n. 29). On the other hand, Cicero was famous for his emotional conclusions. One might perhaps see this as a perverted form of "ethical" persuasion in Venus (i.e., where else would one look for such overwhelmingly emotional appeal?).

We have used, with reference to Venus's oratory, such terms as "blandishments," "enticements," "allurements," all traditionally associated with the idea of temptation and hence with the diabolical.[57] A particularly striking example of the seductive (in its strictest connotation) power of the goddess occurs in I, 247, where, having just cautioned Paris to be on his guard against the "enhortemens tentatoires" (!) of Juno and Pallas, Venus encourages him to "ensuiure ma doctrine naturelle, et la propre inclination de ton sens," thereby anticipating one of the tenets destined to be so enthusiastically promulgated by François Rabelais. She continues: "*Tourne donc à gauche,* enfuis le *grand chemin* vsité de la plus part des humains." This is plainly no stern command to walk the strait and narrow path, to shun the broad highway that leads to perdition: quite the reverse.[58] It is, however, an unmistakable evocation of the ancient image of man at the crossroads of life, with the left-hand path the ill-omened way of doom, is in *Inferno* XXVI, 125-126, when Ulysses tells of his "folle volo, / Sempre acquistando *dal lato mancino*" (my ital.), a course which brought him and his companions to eternal ruin. Now the author of *Les Illustrations* knew and admired Dante (at least by reputation), but I do not think this point essential to my argument, since Jean Lemaire, immediately after Venus has finished speaking, earnestly comments on the grief that her "eloquence artificielle" will bring down on Paris and his people ("... encores en pourra il maudire les rhetoriques couleurs, qui luy seront retorquees en douleurs" [I, 249]).

---

[56] "Et de tant plus seray encline à toutes ces choses, comme tu en es mieux digne" (249).

[57] See above, n. 38, on Juno and the temptations of power.

[58] Note, a few lines below this passage, the ominous appearance of one of (the planet) Venus's titles: Lucifer.

This concludes our analysis of Lemaire's oratory studied from the point of view of structural composition. We shall now turn to a different facet of his art (yet once again a rhetorical one), namely his prose style.

Chapter VI

## SOME RHETORICAL ASPECTS OF JEAN LEMAIRE'S PROSE STYLE

O homme brutal, beste transformee, creature destinee à toute infelicité, Idole fantastique qui sembles ce que tu nes pas, vaisseau corrompu de lubricité vilaine, et sac à fiens et pourriture, mal est employee beauté corporelle en si lasche courage: mal sont assignez les biens de Dieu et de Nature en chose si desnaturee: Nas tu eu honte de preferer la vie voluptueuse et inutile, à la vie actiue et contemplatiue? Nas tu eu vergongne de postposer la pardurable à la transitoire? de laisser le grain pour la paille, la seue pour lescorce, le fruit pour les fueilles, et le gain pour la perte? De mespriser la vraye viuacité des images celestes, pour le fard coulouré et teint sophistique, dune statue plate et vuide? Et finablement de changer les tresors du souuerain fastige, et l'amas de douceur scientifique, aux fanges de toute basse souillure, et au mespris de toute infameté? Iuge ridicule et syluestre, plus leger que nest la plume au vent, prodigue de ton honneur, courage de meretrice, pollu dun leger promettre, tout vermolu dinconstance, mal sainement deliberant, aueugle choisisseur, as tu osé vomir de ton puant estomach, sentence si orde, si inique et si sanguinolente, qui te coustera la vie, et de cent mille meilleurs que toy? En cuides tu demourer impuny? Crains tu point ma puissance immensible, quand elle est addonnee à vindication? Ignores tu comment ie punis iadis ta folle tante Antigona fille de Laomedon, et sœur de ton pere Priam? Scais tu point que le malheureux visage, dont elle se glorifioit, en osant sa beauté outrecuidee comparer à la mienne, luy fut par moy transformé en vn bec de cicongne, duquel iusques à maintenant elle pesche et peschera tousiours les crapaux, et les raynes, parmy les marescages, pour son viure et sustentation?

> Ie congnois ores que ceux de ta maison ne sont nez, fors pour me faire iniure. Il me souuient du rauissement de Ganymedes, ton proayeul, qui fut fait et perpetré au desauantage de moy et de ma fille Hebé. Et nay pas oublié la rudesse que ton ayeul Laomedon feit à mon frere Neptune, en edifiant les murs de la cité de Troye. Mais ores est venu le iour, que iay trouué occasion de retribuer payement selon le merite: et de maddonner du tout à hayne et vengeance immortelle. De laquelle ie ne seray assouuie, iusques à ce que la malheureuse maison ou tu a prins origine soit exterminee par ton moyen: et le païs circonuoisin depopulé, et la nation esparse parmy le monde, ainsi que la paille dorge que les labourers ventillent au vent.
>
> (I, 258-259)

With these superbly comminatory periods thundering in the ears of the wretched Paris (who, somewhat belatedly perhaps, "se preparoit à plusieurs excuses" [I, 260]), Juno, seething with vindictive rage, and "conceuan vne hayne non appaisable encontre les Troyens" (259), takes herself off to her island of Samos, there to weave dark and bloody plots of vengeance. In Chapter V above, we examined the tirade from the standpoint of that mode of epideictic rhetoric known as *vituperatio,* or invective. I would like now to use the same piece of prose — highly charged as it is with rhetorical figures — as a convenient starting point for a necessarily brief essay[1] on Jean Lemaire's prose style in its distinctively rhetorical aspects.

It will be readily apparent that *vituperatio* in general — and Juno's speech in particular — is closely akin to apostrophe (or, more accurately, *exclamatio*). The period which begins: "O homme brutal ... mal est employee beauté corporelle en si lasche courage," etc., is strongly analogous to the numerous passages in Jean Lemaire's works where he abruptly intervenes, in person and directly, often at quite considerable length. This approach differs markedly, for example, from Dante's frequent authorial admonitions, which are quite openly aimed at the reader himself. Lemaire, on the other hand, habitually harangues his own characters, commiserating with them over their misfortunes, blackguarding them for their wicked-

---

[1] An in-depth study of Lemaire's use of rhetorical figures would, needless to say, call for an entire book, not a mere chapter. Alex. L. Gordon's *Ronsard et la Rhétorique* is a thorough-going study of this kind.

ness, and so on. In a sense, this is a subtle variant of the "distancing" technique discussed earlier, except that here the author does not place himself at one remove from the reader by the interposition of a third party to act as his spokesman, as is the case with the Ten Orators of *La Couronne Margaritique*. Instead, he attains the same end by a kind of ricochet effect: the words ostensibly aimed at the characters in his book are intended for our edification in the first place. We are obviously meant to know just where the author stands with respect to Paris, Pegasis Oenone, *et al.*, but he tells *us* by telling *them*, and thus neatly avoids giving the impression of preaching at the blameless reader. "O noble Nymphe aueuglee dambition, et desirant destre appellee femme de filz de Roy, toy mesmes tends les lacz esquelz tu seras prinse," cries the chronicler, as the fair Pegasis Oenone in all innocence contrives her husband's return to his father Priam's court and thereby seals his doom (I, 290). "Desiste toy (belle dame) si tu peux, car il me prend pitié de ton infortune. Mais faire ne se peult autrement," he continues sadly. "Il faut que les Destinees fassent leurs cours: et que pour bien faire tu ayes retribution non condigne." The moralizing intent of such an intervention is perfectly frank and undisguised. Compare the very similar warning given to Priam as, blinded by *hubris,* he allows Paris's fatal eloquence to convince him that the Greeks must be taught a lesson. The apostrophe in question is characterized by the same despairing tone on the part of the omniscient author, powerless to alter the cruel decrees of Destiny: "O Roy Priam, autrement bon Prince, et le meilleur des meilleurs, ne vois tu point que Fortune trop blandissante, laquelle ha esleué ton throne iusques aux cieux, ne t'ha ramené ton filz Paris des montaignes Idees, ... sinon à ce que son ieune conseil peu pesé en la balance de raison, preparast à ta prosperité le lacs de trebuchement merueilleux? O hauteur de courage trop magnanime, enflé de gloire prosperante ... Ne te souuient il du songe de ta femme? ... As tu oublié la premonition des Dieux? ... Certes ton heur trop resplendissant t'ha aueuglé," etc. (II, 15-16). In fact, the very chapter-headings sometimes explicitly proclaim as a forthcoming rhetorical pièce de résistance the apostrophe to be featured in the ensuing pages (thus revealing without a doubt how highly Lemaire esteems the device). The apostrophe of Priam just cited is for instance heralded in the last line (a position indicative of its climactic nature) of the title of Book II, chapter I (II, 9): "Auecques vne exclamation contre laueuglee emprise du Roy Priam." [2] Lemaire's conception of his moralizing role as historian is quite in keeping with his adherence to the Chastellain-Molinet school of Burgundian historiography.[3] It should therefore cause little surprise to discover (aside from those occasions when the author gives voice to his sympathy for the undeserved fate meted out to certain individuals)[4] apostrophe being wielded as an instrument of praise and blame, i.e., exactly in the manner of the outraged Juno in her invective. In those pages of *La Couronne Margaritique* where the writer is describing the grief of the newly widowed Marguerite d'Autriche, he eulogizes her great love by means of an *exclamatio*: "O ardant et inextinguible flambeau daffection maritale, embrasé en la poitrine pudique de ceste dame tresfortunee [sic]! Combien as tu daudace au rencontre des dangereux destroits de ton efforcement?" etc. (IV, 31). The exact counterpart to Lemaire's *laus* of womanly virtue is his vituperation of womanly vice incarnate in Helen, when at a crisis in the affairs of Troy, she refuses pointblank to return to her lawful husband, Menelaus. With admirable concision — and not without humor — Lemaire reports that "elle respondit clerement et sans feintise, quelle nauoit point nauigué iusques à Troye maugré elle: et que Menelaus allast à Dieu: et quelle nauoit que faire de son mariage" (II, 117). The cool impudence of Helen's unladylike choice of words predictably brings out the moralist ever lurking within the narrator: "O merueilleuse inconstance et terrible audace féminine! Certes aussi publiquement quelle auoit eslu Menelaus pour son mary, en la presence de tous les Princes de Grece: aussi hardiment losa elle à front eshonté, repudier deuant tous les Barons

---

[2] Cf. II, 210 (title): "De la prinse de Troye: et de la cruelle mort de Deïphobus procuree par Heleine: auec lexclamation contre icelle." (Once more the prime spot in the billing, as it were, is reserved for the *exclamatio*.)

[3] See G. Doutrepont and O. Jodogne's Introduction to Molinet's *Chroniques*: "...l'orateur Molinet... l'historien qui fait de l'histoire *ad probandum*, qui veut démontrer, qui donne ses impressions. Volontiers il prononce des discours, il apostrophe ses personnages, il exalte ou il flétrit leurs actions" (*Chroniques*, III, 186). Cf. F. Thibaut's similar remarks on Jean Lemaire (*MAJLB*, 186).

[4] Cf. an entirely conventional outburst directed at Fortune herself: "O Fortune insensee, conducteresse des Destinees! si tu eusses souffert alors que linstrument de la destruction de Troye eust esté deffait," etc. (I, 324).

de Troye" (*ibid.*).⁵ Helen in fact receives more than her fair share of apostrophe in *Les Illustrations*. So does her paramour; to the first book, which (in chaps. XXI-XXVII especially) is nothing less than an extended encomium of the innocent young shepherd Paris and his chaste love for Oenone, corresponds Book II, a great part of which is taken up with diatribes against the corrupt princeling and his iniquitous love for Helen. Thus, while most graphically describing the horrors attending Paris's treacherous attack on the unsuspecting Lacedaemonians, Lemaire paints a lurid picture of the wanton and unnatural Helen who "seoit au giron de son adultere, et repaissoit ses yeux de la flambe ardante et bruslante le patrimoine domestique de sa seule fille Hermione" (II, 77). The adulterous couple is then roundly castigated in language echoing that of Juno's vituperatio.⁶

Apostrophe, then, as used by Jean Lemaire (above all with respect to the longer examples) is essentially a highly compressed variety of epideictic oration, just as the political treatises are in reality expanded deliberative orations.⁷ The most striking feature of *exclamatio* as exemplified in Lemaire's works is the extremely high intensity of emotional appeal attained. At the beginning of this essay (p. 15) I had occasion to take issue with Ph. Aug. Becker's assertion that Lemaire's recourse to rhetorical devices is tantamount to an outright admission of artistic failure when he is dealing with

---

⁵ Cf. Lemaire's outburst against the arrogant yet falsely humble prelates who dared to depose Louis le Débonnaire: "O faulse et malicieuse pharisienne hypocrisie sacerdotale," thunders the author of the antipapal *Schismes et Conciles* (III, 276), as he begins his invective of the failing to which the clergy were traditionally reputed to be inclined.

⁶ Here is the integral text of this passage: "O cœur felon, dur et marbrin, ô courage estrangé dhonneur, aliené de raison, loingtain de pitié feminine, transformé en cruauté barbarique, ô visage angelique et venerien, ayant queüe draconique et serpentine: que tant te coustera cher le crime que tu commetz à present, que tant en seront de femmes vefues, et denfans orphenins, ains que le meffait que tu encommences soit purgé. Et toy chetif Paris, garny de vaine et inutile beauté, tu tesiouis à ceste heure, en receuant le transitoire guerdon de ton fol iugement, et ne voudrois auoir eslu les hautaines richesses de dame Iuno, ne la remuneration eternelle de la sapience et vertu de dame Pallas. Mais assez auras encores loisir de ten douloir, et maudire ta malheureuse stolidité. Dame Venus ton accointe, tha fait faire ceste nuict vn beau chef dœuure pour les premices et fruit primerain de tes vaillances, mais tard sera que tu ten repentes."

⁷ See above, Chap. II, 61.

characters and situations distasteful to him personally. Now it is perfectly true that Helen is the object of some of the bitterest *exclamationes* ever penned by Lemaire, and that his loathing for her increases in direct proportion to the accelerating Trojan calamity. But it is equally true that analogous rhetorical outbursts are inspired by one of the author's favorite characters, the sweet and touching Pegasis Oenone.[8] In short, any particularly intense emotional involvement on Lemaire's part seems to give the signal — almost as predictable as a physical reflex — for an *exclamatio*. Whether it is comminatory, laudatory, or elegiac in tone depends entirely on the circumstances, as one would expect.

Returning to the *point de départ* of this chapter, Juno's *vituperatio,* one quickly becomes aware of a highly conspicuous element therein, viz., the rhetorical question. "Nas tu eu honte de preferer la vie voluptueuse et inutile, à la vie actiue et contemplatiue? ... as tu osé vomir de ton puant estomach, sentence si orde ... ? En cuides tu demourer impuny? Crains tu point ma puissance immensible ... ? Ignores tu comment ie punis iadis ta folle tante Antigona ... ? Scais tu point," etc. (There is, I take it, no doubt whatever that Juno has not the least desire to hear any excuses that Paris might conceivably offer, but is simply bent on pointing out to her own satisfaction the miserable youth's complete worthlessness, thus assuaging her own wounded vanity. Needless to say, he does not utter so much as a syllable during the entire awesome tirade.) Well over half of the invective (26 lines out of 44, to be exact) consists of rhetorical questioning, the device being one for which Lemaire displays a marked predilection. (It is notably in evidence in his use of the apostrophe in general.)[9] Once again, there is an urgently affective impact conveyed by the staccato volley of questions, as though the speaker were genuinely incapable of containing her wrath and derision. No one, I think, has claimed that Jean Lemaire is an aloof, objective, Olympian spirit; on the

---

[8] See above, 143-144, Lemaire's sorrowful exclamations over Priam (another favorite); also 49, over the "isle de Candie," enslaved by the Venetians.

[9] As in the lamentation inspired by Priam's blind folly in relying on Paris (II, 15-16): "... ne vois tu point que Fortune ... preparast à ta prosperité le lacs de trebuchement merueilleux? ... Ne te souuient il du songe de ta femme? Nacontes tu à loracle de Delphos ... ? Mesprises tu les propheties ... ? As tu oublié la premonition des Dieux ... ?"

contrary, he constantly impresses one by an unusually high degree of involvement with his subject matter, be it contemporary politics or ancient history (or mythology). When, for instance, he is regaling the reader of *La Légende des Vénitiens* with the grisly evidence of some more than ordinarily revolting piece of Venetian treachery, and writes: "à peu me repens ie, si ce nestoit le zele de verité, qui my enhorte destre entré en labyme de ceste matiere odieuse" (III, 377), I for one am inclined to take him at his word, being persuaded that at the moment of composing this sentence, he fully believed every word of it.[10]

It is not unimportant that Lemaire resorts to the rhetorical question virtually without fail at moments of particular vehemence and animation (whether of the narrator himself or of his *dramatis personae*). This is an unimpeachable technique of classical oratory, intended to reinforce "the argument that has just been delivered" (*Ad Herenn.*, IV.xv.22), "to emphasise our point" (*De inst. orat.*, IX.ii.7).[11] Accordingly, Deïphobus's speech at the council of war held prior to the rape of Helen (II, 66-69) — a crucial oration if ever there was one — relies heavily on the rhetorical question to dispel whatever scruples Paris may still be clinging to.[12] Deïphobus (like Venus) knows his man, and his harangue — baldly stating that only the brave deserve the fair — is nicely calculated to exploit his brother's vanity and lust. Note the insidiousness of the following lines: "Voudrois tu, ie te prie, estre frustré à iamais du fruit de ton iugement...?... Car si dauenture par faute de conseil, ou de courage, tu te monstres nice et couard en ceste partie, que pourra

---

[10] See above, Chap. II, 67-68.

[11] Quintilian emphasizes his own point by citing the famous rhetorical question with which Cicero opens his *In Catilinam*: "Quousque tandem abutere, Catilina, patientia nostra?" explaining "How much greater is the fire of his words as they stand than if he had said, 'You have abused our patience a long time'" (IX.ii.7-8).

[12] Paris himself — that is to say, the new Paris, corrupted by his good fortune — is a pretty fair example of the unscrupulous orator so detested by Plato, as his cynical gloating over the glorious opportunity offered his companions and himself reveals (II, 62-63). This speech too most tellingly exploits rhetorical questions to incite and encourage. G. Doutrepont (*JLBR*, 329) aptly describes Paris in this context as "un véritable Ulysse... car il a les artifices de parole du rusé personnage de *l'Iliade*." And we know what ghastly fate Dante reserves for that arch-perverter of the divine gift of eloquence (cf. *Inferno* XXVI, ll. 46-63) among his fellow evil counselors.

on dire, sinon que point nes digne dauoir belle amie? ... Quelle autre auenture donques voudrois tu aller chercher plus preste, plus propre, ou plus naïue, pour parfournir ta conqueste que ceste cy? ... Ne faut il pas que ce fol Roy abesty soit moqué par tous les humains, de sa stolidité plus que brutale?" And so on relentlessly, Deïphobus never failing to hammer home the point, again in a series of rhetorical questions, that it is high time the overweening Greeks had a taste of their own medicine: are they alone to have licence to pillage and rape, are the long-suffering Trojans always to be taken in by "leur beau promettre sans rien tenir?" It is really a first-class exhibition of rhetorical skill utterly divorced from ethical considerations. Or, it could be argued, Deïphobus, a young and impetuous prince, has fallen victim to his own eloquence and gone much further than he originally intended.[13]

Both apostrophe-*exclamatio* and the rhetorical question (*interrogatio*) are classified by the ancient theorists as figures of thought, *figurae sententiarum*,[14] which the *Rhetorica ad Herennium* distinguishes from figures of language or diction (*figurae verborum*) as follows: "It is a figure of diction if the adornment is comprised in the fine polish of the language itself. A figure of thought derives a certain distinction from the idea, not from the words" (IV.xiii.18). As no useful purpose would be served by an over-careful classifi-

---

[13] See above, Chap. IV, 100 and n. 16.

[14] Cf. Quintilian (IX.i.17): "... There are two classes of *figure,* namely *figures of thought,* that is of the mind, feeling or conceptions ... and *figures of speech,* that is of words, diction, expression, language or style: the name by which they are known varies, but mere terminology is a matter of indifference." In the thirteenth century, John of Garland ingeniously managed to combine rhetorical instruction with pious edification in his treatise on figures of thought and language: *Exempla honestae vitae, quam debent habere praelati, coloribus verborum et sententiarum insignita.* The exceedingly vexed question of the distinction between figures, tropes, colors, etc., has given rise to countless, and often confusing, definitions on the part of critics both ancient and modern. For the latter, see W. S. Howell, "Renaissance Rhetoric and Modern Rhetoric," 305; Brian Vickers, *CREP,* 86; G. Kennedy, *APG,* 297; E. Faral, *AP,* 89-90; D. L. Clark, *RGRE,* 89-91. Quintilian himself declares that the resemblance between tropes and figures "is so close that it is not easy to distinguish between them" (IX.i.3). (His own definitions follow in his next paragraph.) D. L. Clark's discussion of the subject is the most enlightening of our day and is based upon Quintilian's, whose classification is generally acknowledged to be the best (though in the Middle Ages the *Ad Herennium* [Book IV] was the main authority; see D. E. Grosser, "Studies in the Influence," 290-291, and E. Auerbach's "Figura," 25 and 27).

cation in the present study of tropes, schemes, *figurae sententiarum et verborum,* I propose to simplify matters by referring to them all indiscriminately as "figures." Among the more commonly used figures, then — in addition to *exclamatio* and *interrogatio* — are anaphora, isocolon and parison, *accumulatio, exemplum,* simile, prosopopoeia, alliteration, assonance, *paronomasia,* chiasmus, and *descriptio* (ecphrasis). All of these (and many others: I have arbitrarily and drastically pruned what could otherwise easily become a formidable list — see n. 1 above) are employed to a greater or lesser extent in Lemaire's works,[15] and Juno's *vituperatio* by itself comprises many examples.

The goddess makes discreet use of anaphora in "*mal est employee* beauté corporelle en si lasche courage: *mal sont assignez* les biens de Dieu et de Nature..." and in "*Nas tu eu* honte...? *Nas tu eu* vergongne...?" etc. The first of these examples also exhibits isocolon, or repetition of phrases of equal length and corresponding structure; the second, in the long succession of antithetical phrases, "le grain pour la paille, le seue pour lescorce, le fruit pour les fueilles," etc., could be treated as parison, a type of isocolon comprising long phrases or clauses in parallel construction. The same artful combination of balanced, antithetical clauses with anaphora is found in *La Légende des Vénitiens* (III, 372): "Isle iadis franche et libere, maintenant asseruie es esclaue: iadis anoblie de cent citez, auiourdhuy presque deserte: iadis tant fertile et abondante en toy mesmes, et ores contrainte à stérilité...."

*Accumulatio* (a near relative of climax) is another figure much favored by Juno, as the first lines of the invective clearly reveal. A progressive sequence of notions of Paris's degradation and depravity is apparent in "homme... beste... creature... Idole...[16] vaisseau corrompu... sac à fiens et pourriture," a progression which is echoed in the series of similarly constructed phrases (parison)

---

[15] The terminology relative to figures has been vastly overelaborated, resulting in a wealth of often overlapping definitions, thanks in part at least to those who "have altered even what was perfectly sound in order to establish a claim to originality," as Quintilian severely remarks (III.i.7). Such being the case, I shall henceforth refrain from burdening the reader with a plethora of near-synonyms (see above, Chap. I, n. 31).

[16] Used here with its full etymological force: "apparence vaine," "fantôme" (Huguet).

occurring in some later lines: "... prodigue de ton honneur, courage de meretrice, pollu dun leger promettre, tout vermolu dinconstance, mal sainement deliberant, aueugle choisisseur." Mark the careful symmetry of these phrases, the first four of which — if the full value is given to the mute *e*'s (except the finals) — are all of seven syllables. Climactic too is the ominous fourfold rhetorical question: "En cuides tu demourer impuny? Crains tu point ma puissance immensible...? Ignores tu comment ie punis iadis ta folle tante Antigona...? Scais tu point que le malheureux visage... luy fut par moy transformé en vn bec de cicongne...?" An identical type of progression is evident in the passage of *Les illustrations* where the wise old shepherd is insisting on the essential nobility of the pastoral life: "Iay bien osé dire *dignité* tout à essient: et encores quand iauroye dit *maiesté,* nul ne men sauroit reprendre. Car ie soustiens, que ce labeur cy nest pas seulement *Royal,* mais plustost vne *occupation deïfique*" (I, 147).

Thoroughly characteristic of Jean Lemaire (and his times) is a fondness for the *exemplum* or paradigm, which we have already mentioned with reference to "singularitez" (above, Chap. III, n. 13). Juno herself adds force to her threats by citing the metamorphosis of the unhappy Antigona, and lashes herself to a still higher degree of vengeful fury by recalling the scandalous abduction of Ganymede by Jupiter, and the unbearably insulting behavior of "ton ayeul Laomedon" to "mon frere Neptune." The historical parallel is, needless to say, a very important form of rhetorical proof, and an acquaintance with history is one of the accomplishments demanded of a good orator by Cicero, for the obvious reason that "the mention of antiquity and the citation of examples give the speech authority and credibility." [17]

It is principally the rhetorical objectives of proof and persuasion that Lemaire has in mind whenever he introduces an *exemplum* into his narrative. Such, for instance, are the parallel cases adduced by the Ten Orators of *La Couronne Margaritique* in their common zeal

---

[17] *Orator,* xxxiv.120. Cf. the following lines from Cicero's *De partitione oratoria,* ed. and trans. H. Rackham (Cambridge, Mass., and London, 1960 [1942]), xi.40: "... the greatest corroboration is supplied to a probable truth by first an example, next the introduction of a parallel case; and also sometimes an anecdote [*fabula*], even though it be a tall story [*incredibilis*] nevertheless has an effect on people."

to miss no opportunity of honoring the princess.[18] A judicious selection of virtuous ladies serve as the first term of the comparisons; Marguerite herself provides the second. One of the best of these parallels is Chastellain's. The ancient paragon he cites is Vesta; Marguerite is "nostre seconde Vesta," and he relates an anecdote calculated to display to best advantage the princess's nice turn of sardonic humor (lauded as the modern model of *urbanité*), which never fails her even under the most trying circumstances:

> Vn autre plaisant conte fut ce pendant son nauigage d'Espaigne. Quand apres auoir passé vne nuict horrible et tempestueuse en doute de perilleux naufrage, comme le lendemain la mer fust deuenue calme et tranquille, et à ceste cause elle et ses damoïselles en passant temps par gracieuse oisiueté racontassent entre elles leurs peurs et leurs turbations passees, ainsi que cest la maniere de faire apres grans perilz eschappez, et que le propos fut mis sus, que chacune deust ditter son epitaphe, attendu quelles auoient esté si prochaines destre enseuelies es parfonds gouffres de la mer Oceane: Elle composa promptement le sien en ceste maniere:
> 
> > Cy gist Margot la gentil' damoiselle
> > Qu'ha deux marys, et encor est pucelle.[19]
> 
> Disant que si son corps fut venu au riuage, à tout le moins leust on honnoré de ce dittier sur vne tumbe. Lequel ioyeux epitaphe est si plein de vraye vrbanité, de propre gentillesse, et de noble facetie, que par iceluy seul on peult facilement auoir coniecture de la dexterité naïue de son entendement. (IV, 106-107)

The persuasive element in Lemaire's *exempla* is undeniably paramount: yet there is another important aspect worthy of remembrance, namely the gratification of the reader [20] and (need it be

---

[18] Arnauld de Villeneuve, in order to demonstrate to his audience that Marguerite is the very paragon of "Regnatiue prudence," first establishes the standard against which she is to be measured. This he does by means of the story of Rachel, who not only has a name which begins with "R" but who, for good measure, is prudence incarnate. All his confrères proceed in the same methodical manner.

[19] A joking allusion to her first "marriage" to Charles VIII and to her forthcoming one to the Infant of Spain.

[20] Cicero's commendation of the use of *exempla* (see above, n. 17) continues to the effect that they also afford "the highest pleasure to the audience" (*Orator*, xxxiv.120).

said?) of the author himself. Like many a writer of his century — Montaigne immediately springs to mind — Lemaire can never resist telling a good story for its own sake, and for this reason his prose works fairly bristle with curious items and singular anecdotes. The sort of thing that takes his fancy ranges from the intriguing account of the costliest drink in recorded history [21] to the edifying tale of the retribution meted out to a heartless scoffer, a story patently bearing the hallmark of the sermon. [22]

Juno's ferocious — yet rhetorically well-ordered — invective of Paris concludes with a simile, as she vows that her thirst for vengeance will remain unslaked until Troy is totally ruined, devastated, and depopulated, "et la nation esparse parmy le monde, ainsi que la paille dorge que les laboureurs ventillent au vent." Of particular interest to us here, insofar as Lemaire's similes, metaphors, and other figures of comparison are concerned, is his conscious and methodical imitation of ancient models. Not that his harking back to the heroically amplified comparisons of the Homeric and Virgilian epic can be claimed as innovative, since they had never completely disappeared from the literary scene: one has only to recall the art's most illustrious medieval practitioner, Dante Alighieri. Nevertheless, we have from his own pen incontrovertible evidence of Jean Lemaire's avowed admiration for Homer, [23] and many of his similes

---

[21] "Mais les deux plus singuliers chefz dœuure que nature feist onques touchant margarites perles ou vnions, Cleopatra, Royne d'Egypte les eut en possesse par le moyen des Roys d'Orient, dont par oultrageuse gloutonnie, lune dicelles fondue en tresfort vinaigre, fut par elle beüe et absorbee en vn souper, pource quelle auoit fait gageure contre le Prince Antoine Romain, de plus despendre en vn repas que luy" (IV, 65-66).

[22] Apparently a certain French nobleman named Dunois, "lequel fut exemple merueilleux," was ungentlemanly enough to make cruel jokes on the occasion of Charles VIII's tearful separation from the repudiated Marguerite d'Autriche. Not two hours later, "il receut horrible recompense de son langage derisoire: car sans benefice de confession, et sans coup ou violence exterieure, il tomba soudainement ius de son cheual tout mort..." (IV, 87-88).

[23] "...en ceste iournee il y eut vne bataille singuliere, cestadire corps à corps entre le Roy Menelaus et le beau Paris, laquelle est diffusement narree par le prince des poëtes Homere au troisieme liure de son Iliade, et bien coulouree de fleurs poëtiques... ie vueil icy marrester vn petit à descrire ledit combat, pource quil est beau et delectable, et sent bien son antiquité. Et pour ce faire, ie translateray presques mot à mot ledit Homere sur ce passage... Or dit iceluy noble prince des poëtes Grecz mis en Latin par Laurens Valle," etc. (II, 152).

are admittedly somewhat wanting in spontaneity and originality.[24] For example, the likening of the young and athletic Duke Philibert, overcome by the sudden onset of a mortal sickness, to a stricken stag (IV, 27-28) has a distinctly familiar ring to it, as is the case with other of Lemaire's comparisons.[25] But if this author's choice of imagery is not particularly impressive, what does impress is his re-creation in the vernacular of the extended epic simile, which is often of great structural complexity, and calls for the confident handling of a medium hitherto unequipped for such virtuosity. Before turning to the next topic, I will quote *in extenso* the charmingly worded image depicting how the amorous Paris succumbs to his desire for Oenone:

> Car ainsi comme il aduient aucunesfois que les pastoureaux des champs par inaduertence ont laissé vn charbon de feu entre les seiches fougieres, et il suruient aucun impetueux vent chaud et meridional, qui allume les festuz et fueillettes gisans alentour, tantost la flambe esparse prenant vigueur,

---

[24] However, during the Renaissance, as indeed throughout classical antiquity and the Middle Ages, originality and its near-relative "creation" were by no means the criteria of artistic excellence that they have become ever since the eighteenth century and particularly since the Romantic movement. In fact, as P. Spaak (*JLB*, 22) tells us: "L'originalité était alors, en poésie comme en tout art, la moindre préoccupation des artistes... C'est d'après la seule supériorité de l'exécution que se classent la plupart des œuvres de cette époque." (Cf. Castor, *Pléiade Poetics*, 86 and *passim*.)

[25] E.g., the descent of Infortune into Hell via the nearest river: "comme vn carreau de fouldre accompaigné de tonnoirre" (IV, 44); the wrestlers (Paris and Hector) hastening to come to grips "comme font deux taureaux indomptez estans aux deux cantons dun pré, lesquelz se viennent entrehurter par grand felonnie" (I, 318-319); the slight but agile Paris warily circling his brawny opponent "comme font ceux qui assiegent vne grosse tour, et affustent leurs engins de tous costez pour labatre"; and the surprised Hector's overthrow in the same context: "au tomber il sembla donner tel coup, comme fait vn grand chesne en la forest, qui par le soufflement impetueux des vents, ou d'un grand orage est abatu." These and many others like them could have come straight from Homer or Virgil. On the other hand, when Lemaire is not consciously striving for effect, figures seem to spring from him quite spontaneously. This is especially true of his correspondence. See, e.g., his passionately indignant letter to Marguerite d'Autriche, written in hot defense of the allegedly unsatisfactory alabaster he was currently engaged in quarrying for the chapel of Philibert le Beau. In somewhat self-pitying vein he observes: "Doncques ma fortune est telle que je bas tousjours les buissons et ung autre prent les oisillons" (IV, 402). And with regard to the same letter, P. Jodogne remarks that Lemaire finds "métaphores inspirées de l'architecture pour parler de son travail d'écrivain" (*JLBEFB*, 113, referring to IV, 397).

surprent ce qui luy est voisin, et ne cesse de forsener parmy les bruyeres, iusques à ce quelle ayt tout mis en cendre: Ainsi pareillement le fort mouuement de nature esmu au ieune Paris par grand calefaction damoureuse concupiscence, trouuant deuant soy obiect plaisant et propice, ne se peut onques arrester auant son emprinse acheuee.[26]

The entire Judgment of Paris sequence is a very fine illustration of what Quintilian (VI.i.25) defines as "*fictae alienarum personarum orationes,*" or *prosopopoeia* (impersonation), a figure which "lends wonderful variety and animation to oratory" (IX.ii.29). At the risk of belaboring the obvious, I will repeat my earlier observation (see above, Chap. V, 129-130) that the *dramatis personae* of the Judgment are all admirably in character, Juno an imperious shrew, Pallas a trifle over-solemn and pedantic, Venus outrageously brazen, Mercure witty and malicious, and the callow adolescent Paris hopelessly out of his depth in matters far beyond his comprehension.[27]

There is another dimension to *prosopopoeia,* one in which the power of speech is bestowed upon, *inter alia,* abstractions,[28] as in, e.g., Lemaire's Vertu (*La Couronne Margaritique*), Paincture and — most appropriately — Rhetoricque (*La Plainte du Désiré*).[29]

I will now turn to a group of figures of mainly phonetic appeal,[30] i.e., alliteration, assonance, *paronomasia,* and chiasmus. Juno

---

[26] I, 183. The first term of this comparison is in fact a somewhat amplified adaptation of a Virgilian simile (*Aeneid,* X, 405-408).

[27] Cf. the amiably prolix old shepherd of *Les Illustrations* (I, 147 ff.); his sentimental wife, in floods of tears at the prospect of losing her foster-child ("Helas, mon cher enfant Paris, que t'ay ie fait? pourquoy veux tu abandonner ta poure ancienne mere desolee? t'ay ie si mal traité, t'ay ie fait aucun desplaisir?" [I, 292]); the new-model Paris as an unctuous diplomat (II, 48-52); the young firebrand Deïphobus (II, 66-69), etc., etc. (See above, Chap. V, 124, on Jean Lemaire as a playwright born out of his time.)

[28] "Nay, we are even allowed in this form of speech to bring down the gods from heaven and raise the dead, while cities also and peoples may find a voice" (*De inst. orat.,* IX.ii.31).

[29] Cf. the brilliant personifications of *Le Roman de la Rose* (Genius, Bel Acueil, Dangiers, etc. — all, incidentally, borrowed by Lemaire for his "Temple de Venus" section in *La Concorde des deux langages*), Jean Molinet's Guerre (in *Le Testament de la Guerre*), Erasmus's renowned figure of Folly (*Encomium Moriae,* Paris, 1511), etc.

[30] I must emphasize that I am here speaking of *figures* only. Although the topic of *compositio verborum* in Lemaire's works is undeniably a rhetorical one and most worthy of a study in depth, it is far too extensive to be dealt with in the present essay. Therefore, such matters as sentence movement and structure, syntax, vocabulary, *clausulae,* etc., will not be discussed here.

makes telling, yet restrained, play with the first two, as, for example, in "malheureuse maison," "esparse parmy le monde," "ventillent au vent"; and especially in "aueugle choisisseur, as tu osé vomir de ton puant estomach, sentence si orde, si inique et si sanguinolente, qui te coustera la vie, et de cent mille meilleurs que toy? En cuides tu demourer impuny? Crains tu point ma puissance immensible..." etc.[31] Alliteration, notoriously the easiest and most overworked of all the devices of *ornatus facilis,* was flourishing in late Roman times (when the term *paromoeon* was coined for it)[32] and descended to the sixteenth century via the rhétoriqueurs. Unlike many of his confrères, Lemaire generally resists the temptation to abuse this figure.[33]

*Paronomasia* or word-play, commonly known to medieval rhetoricians as *annominatio,* is — with its potential for exploiting homophony — another figure of the sort which one might look for a writer with strong rhétoriqueur affiliations to appreciate, and indeed there are several specimens of it in Lemaire's *Œuvres.* "Val en cignes val doulx val insigne et floury" (*Épitaphe de Chastellain et Molinet,* IV, 320, l. 24) is a fairly obvious double pun on Valenciennes, in whose church of Notre-Dame de la Salle-le-Comte Georges Chastellain and Jean Molinet were buried. The city is one for which Lemaire always displays the greatest affection, having been brought

---

[31] I doubt whether I would go so far as Maurice Grammont (*Petit traité de versification française* [Paris, 1949 (1908)], 124-141) when he categorically ascribes a predetermined affective impact to the divers sonorities of the French language. Nevertheless it is hard to disagree with his statement that "les plus grands poètes ont presque toujours cherché à établir un certain rapport entre les sons des mots dont ils se servaient et les idées qu'ils exprimaient; ils ont essayé de les peindre, si abstraites fussent-elles" (125). And there is no question but that the virulence of Juno's denunciation of Paris is greatly heightened by reliance on the sibilants and the shriller vowel sounds like [i], [y], [e], which Grammont illustrates (130-131) in "la plainte aiguë, prolongée et perçante de Phèdre," and in "la colère et le désespoir qui retentissent en cris aigus" of Hermione's famous outburst in *Andromaque,* V.iii. Cf. the high-pitched crescendo scream of Juno's opening phrases and the admirably conveyed contempt in the passage beginning "Iuge ridicule et syluestre."

[32] E. Curtius notes that it "became an extremely popular piece of virtuosity in the Middle Ages" (*ELLMA,* 283).

[33] Not always, though; there are a few specimens — mostly in the poems — like the lines previously cited (Chap. II, 64) from *Les Chansons de Namur.*

up there by his revered "précepteur et parent," Molinet.[34] A careful reading of the Œuvres reveals that the author's sound judgment (or strict adherence to classical rhetorical doctrine, which here amounts to the same thing) prevents him from over-indulging in word-play of this type.[35] So far as I have been able to determine, *paronomasia* appears almost uniquely (except for expressions of this kind: "la Mort, qui mord" [IV, 37], and "la force non forcee" [I, 183]) as in the line quoted above, i.e., in puns on proper names. These latter belong to a very exclusive foursome: France, Florence, Germains, Paris (the hero, not the city). Thus in *La Concorde des deux langages,* Lemaire recalls the good old days when Dante and Jean de Meun (allegedly) were fellow-students at the University of Paris, and "France et Florence ... estoient franches, flourissans et conjoinctes," while "leur flourissance n'a oncques failly à la franchise des nostres...."[36] Lemaire's obsessive and unfulfilled dream of the reunification of Charlemagne's Empire is recalled in these lines of verse from *La Concorde du genre humain*: "Et vous, Germains, bon germe germinans, / freres germains de nous autres, Walons" (58, ll. 294-295). As for the name Paris, the writer's elaborations range from the pseudoetymological "Paris, cestadire mettant parité et accord entre les parties"[37] to the verbal extravaganza on the same theme offered by Mercure (not for nothing styled "le Dieu delo-

---

[34] See *La Chronique Annale* (IV, 481, 489, 521-522). P. Jodogne reminds us that Lemaire's earliest work, *Le Livret Sommaire* of 1498, is signed "Lemaire de Valenciennes" (*JLBEFB*, 73).

[35] Both *Ad Herennium* and *De institutione oratoria* warn against this tendency, the former (IV.xxiii.32) maintaining that whereas an infrequent and varied use of such devices will result in an agreeably brightened style, "if ... we crowd these figures together we shall seem to be taking delight in a childish style [*puerilis elocutio*]." Quintilian emphasizes the necessity of associating *paronomasia* with vigor of thought, when it will give "the impression of natural charm, which the speaker has not had to go far to find" (IX.iii.74). But, "in itself this artifice is a flat and foolish affectation" (*ibid.*) Both *Ad Herennium* and Quintilian teach that ornamentation is better suited to epideictic than to forensic or deliberative oratory (*Ad Herenn.*, IV.xxiii.32; *De inst. orat.*, VIII.iii.11-12). Such restraint is far from typical of the pronounced mannerism flourishing in late antiquity and the Middle Ages, which, as E. Curtius remarks (*ELLMA*, 279), "loves accumulated *annominatio*."

[36] P. 44, l. 275 - p. 45, l. 284. Cf. *Épître à Hector* (III, 83, l. 31 - 84, l. 1): "Chrestiens sont francz, et pour francz sont clamez. / Aussi France est de toute gent franchise: / Franche en tous cas..."

[37] I, 143. Cf. Oenone's "O noble Paris sans per, perlifié de toute speciosité corporelle" (I, 171).

quence, et dinuention"!) when persuading the goddesses to accept Paris as their judge: "Paris de Royal parentage (toutesfois sans Royal appareil) met en parité pareille, et accord pariforme, maintes pairs de pers et de parties" (I, 224). Another somewhat similar figure is chiasmus, or, as medieval rhetoricians called it, *commutatio*, the type of which occurs in *Les Illustrations de Gaule*, where it is used to suggest the extreme bitterness of Oenone's anguish when deserted by Paris: "Et quand elle se veoit esseulee, lors souspirs laggressoient, regrets lassailloient de toutes pars, *en plourant gemissoit, et en gemissant plouroit*" (II, 119).

The present-day reader might not ordinarily associate our next topic, description, with the rhetorical tradition; but, as noted in Chapter I above, description is also a figure of rhetoric, and one whose importance steadily increases with the rise to preeminence of the epideictic mode, in which it plays a central role. It is purely in this perspective that I wish to discuss the descriptive art of Jean Lemaire.

With description, as with other elements of the rhetorical tradition represented by Lemaire, there are three aspects to be considered: the ancient, the medieval, the Renaissance. Their limits are not always clearly defined, but broadly speaking it can be said that whereas description in the ancient world usually exists for its own sake, as a rhetorical tour de force, in the Middle Ages it is rarely devoid of a moralizing intent.[38] As for the Renaissance, the emphasis is primarily on imitation, i.e., in the sense both of *imitatio naturae* and of the imitation of ancient models so vigorously advocated by Quintilian. All three variants of the art of description are readily discernible in Lemaire's *Œuvres*.

As examples of the first type, the lengthy ecphrastic passages of *La Concorde des deux langages* (the Temples of Venus and Minerve sections) and of the two *Épîtres de l'Amant vert* (the Amant's Tomb and the Isles Fortunées)[39] must be passed over in silence, since our concern here is above all with Lemaire's prose. The third section

---

[38] Both ancient and medieval description are thus patently affiliated to the epideictic tradition.

[39] *Concorde*, 12-20, ll. 133-315, and 39-42, ll. 1-108; *Amant* I, ll. 192-220, and II, ll. 317-350. These passages are all variations on the theme of the *locus amoenus*.

of *Le Temple d'Honneur*[40] which is a *laus,* or rather an apotheosis, of Pierre de Bourbon, comprises, *inter alia,* a great variety of ecphrastic passages in prose: the Temple itself, situated in "ung second paradis terrestre" (ll. 669-684), which, like Dante's, occupies the summit of a spectacularly lofty mountain,[41] the "six ymages exquises," or living statues (ll. 684-702; see above, Chap. V, 115 and n. 5); a tapestry depicting the duke's "gestes memorables, ses blasons, ses armes, ses crys [ = proclamations faites],[42] ses devises, ses cerfz volans, et ses sainctures d'esperance avec tes [sic] chardons flourissans" (ll. 1086-1091); and sundry ceremonies of welcome for the new *beatus.*[43] *Le Temple d'Honneur* is Lemaire's first major literary production, and so one is not unprepared to find that the prevailing rhetorical influence here is still markedly medieval (i.e., much taken up with praise and blame). Lemaire's originality is chiefly confined to the fresh and unaffected bucolic poems with which the piece opens.

For glimpses of the author at the height of his considerable descriptive powers, one should turn his attention to the first book of *Les Illustrations de Gaule,* which is liberally studded with both scenes and portraits reminiscent of the bravura ecphrastic tradition of antiquity. One of the most delightful of these is the Botticellilike portrait of Pegasis Oenone,[44] whom Paris overtakes "legerement fuyant," while her "cheueux aureins voletoient en lair par des-

---

[40] P. 73, l. 641, to the end.

[41] As does the Temple de Minerve. Venus has to make do with the more modest "roch" (of Fourvière, in Lyons) mentioned in *Concorde,* 12, l. 134.

[42] See H. Hornik's glossary.

[43] For a discussion of the divers architectural, sculptural, and iconographical motifs employed in the work, see Panos Paul Morphos, "The Pictorialism of Lemaire de Belges in 'Le Temple d'Honneur et de Vertus,'" in *Annali dell' Istituto Universitario Orientale,* Sezione romanza 5 (1963), 5-34. Cf. *La Pompe funeralle des obsecques de Don Phelipes de Castille* (IV, 243-266), which is an ecphrastic description of late medieval pageantry.

[44] Lemaire is an authentic connoisseur of the sister arts of painting, sculpture (including goldsmithery) and music. In *La Plainte du Désiré* he specifically names, in addition to contemporary French and Flemish masters, Leonardo, Bellini, and Perugino (72, ll. 123-125). One is tempted to wonder whether he was acquainted with Poliziano's *Stanze per la Giostra* of 1475 (he quotes from the great man's *Miscellanea* in *Les Fragments de Chroniques,* IV, 441), which is said to have been the inspiration for Botticelli's *Primavera.* (Cf. Stanzas 43-46, beginning "Candida è ella, e candida la vesta, / Ma pur di rose e fior dipinta e d'erba...")

sus ses espaules" (I, 165). The highlights of this description most effectively enhance an aura of true Quattrocento delicacy, and the ethereal figure of Flora in the *Primavera* is — quite naturally — called to mind by Jean Lemaire's admirers:[45]

> ... en son beau chef elle ne portoit or ne gemmes, mais seulement pour la preseruer du hasle, vn chapeau de branches de laurier, qui est vn arbrisseau dedié à Phebus, dont les fueilles obtiennent tousiours florissant verdeur... sa venuste corpulence... nestoit absconce du regard de Paris, sinon par linterpos dune houpelande tenue et deliee, telle que les Nymphes et Fees ont accoustumé de porter. Cestasauoir de fine cotonine tissue à diuerses figures de flourettes et doiseletz... Ceinte dune riche ceinture purpurine entrelassee à nœuz damours: et retroussee par dessouz les mamellettes dont elle monstroit la forme ronde et distincte. Les vndes multicolores de cest habillement feé, flottoient iusques en terre... Et en lune de ses mains mignonnes et delicates portoit vn petit panier dosiere tout plein de diuers fruitages.
>
> (I, 166-167)

The art of word-painting here displayed in the portrayal of a lovely nymph is later carried to an astonishing pitch of sensuous realism mingled with other-worldly idealism in Lemaire's magnificent "Venus" chapters (I, 241-260), where the goddess is represented, like Goya's Maja, successively clothed and naked.[46] The first of these portraits is, as it were, the description of Oenone writ large, i.e., greatly amplified (in the rhetorical sense). It is particularly interesting for two reasons. The first is the author's rather perfunctory bow to the moralizing spirit of the late fifteenth century (to which is added the merest trace of allegory), with regard to

---

[45] See, e.g., P. Spaak, *JLB,* 119. Cf. Also Jean Frappier's brief but suggestive article, "Jean Lemaire de Belges et les Beaux-Arts," in *Atti del V° congresso internazionale di Lingue e Letterature moderne* (Florence, 1955 [1951]), 107-114, in which Jean Lemaire is seen, by virtue of his attempts to "signaler la qualité maîtresse et de caractériser le style des artistes" (in *La Plainte du Désiré* and *La Couronne Margaritique*), as the legitimate founder, however remote, of the "genre des *Salons*" (109), which was later to be "illustré" by such masters as Diderot and Baudelaire.

[46] J. Frappier ("JLB et les Beaux-Arts," 113) perceptively notes that Lemaire, "grand couturier des déesses et des nymphes," escapes from medieval allegorization and moralization "à mesure qu'il les dévêt et que diminuent le nombre et le poids de leurs robes."

Venus's "precieuse ceinture," given her by "dame Nature mesmes, à fin que la trop vagabonde lasciuité de Venus, fust cohibee et restreinte par propre vergongne, et aussi par lautorité des loix coniugales. Et en icelle auoit diuinement esmaillé ladite Deesse Nature, les figures damitié, desir, faconde, blandices, plusieurs signes damours et secrettes collocutions. Laquelle ceinture icelle Deesse Venus ne porte iamais, sinon aux noces chastes, honnestes et legitimes" (I, 242). The second point of interest lies in the explicit evidence of the direct imitation of an ancient model. We have it on Lemaire's own authority that "... en tant quil touche le iugement de Paris, quant à la structure literale, iay suiuy en partie ce treselegant acteur Apuleius, lequel en son liure de Asino aureo, descrit ledit iugement par grand mignotise."[47] Now quite early in the portrait we happen upon a painterly touch par excellence: "et estoient tous ses aornemens [i.e., clothes] de si deliee filure, que quand le doux vent Subsolanus ventillant pressoit iceux habits contre ses precieux membres, il faisoit foy entiere de la rotondité diceux, et de la solidité de sa noble corpulence" (I, 241). I think there can be little doubt as to the source of this eminently plastic image when we read in *The Golden Ass*: "... her fine and comely middle was lightly covered with a thin silken smock, and this the wanton wind blew hither and thither, sometime lifting it to testify the youth and flower of her age, and sometime making it to cling close to her to shew clearly the form and figure of her members [... *ut adhaerens pressule membrorum voluptatem graphice deliniaret*]."[48] And, needless to say, this excerpt hits off to perfection the diaphanous quality of the tunic worn by Botticelli's Flora (to hark back once again to the *Primavera*).

As for the naked Venus of pages 255-256, Lemaire's delineation is this time more sculptural than painterly. The opening lines indicate a sure grasp of the three-dimensional and a definite feeling for the *weight* of the human body: "Venus donques sestoit plantee sur le pied droit: et auançoit le gauche. La main dextre pliee sur la hanche, et lautre estendue au long de la cuisse senestre." Similarly "sculptural" are such notations as "la solidité de ses bras massifz... la polissure vnie de son ventre marbrin [an Alexandrine, by the

---

[47] I, 272. Cf. the very passage we are discussing (I, 243), where the author cites Apuleius as an authority on Venus's entourage.

[48] Trans. William Adlington (1566), revised by S. Gaselee (London and New York, 1928 [1915]), Loeb Classical Library, X.31.

way]: la grosse tournure de ses blanches cuisses: la pleine charnure de ses molz genoux."[49] There is no need to expatiate on the author's keen observation of a classic studio pose, nor to dwell on such key terms as "polissure vnie" and "marbrin."

This concludes our discussion of rhetorical figures. In Chapter I, we had occasion to touch upon the classical doctrine of the three styles, each with its appropriate rhetorical function. And we have noted (Chap. I, 38) how medieval theorists misinterpret this in a characteristically hierarchical fashion. However, with the humanistic revival of classical culture, the style levels begin again to reflect purely aesthetic considerations, as Jean Lemaire's explicit statements in the context of *La Légende des Vénitiens* (see above, Chap. III, 89) conclusively demonstrate.

What level of style then should the reader look for in a work like *Les Illustrations de Gaule?* Insofar as medieval rhetorical convention is concerned, the answer is simple. Since the subject of the book is nothing less than the august *matière de Troie* (whose characters are gods, heroes, and the like), the appropriate style can only be the sublime; and Lemaire visibly believed he had written in the sublime mode. (On the other hand, classical treatises of rhetoric clearly stipulate the plain style for a didactic work, and it has been suggested with some plausibility that *Les Illustrations* is to a certain degree didactic in intent [see Chap. IV, 107, above]. However, we have already noted [Chap. IV, 104 and n. 27] the distinction, actual and intended, between the styles of *Les Illustrations* and Lemaire's polemical tracts.) But the most successful achievement of Lemaire's prose, the story of Paris and Oenone[50] in the first book of *Les*

---

[49] Frappier rightly points to "la persistance d'une tradition médiévale," i.e., "le portrait suit l'ordre descendant, depuis le front jusqu'aux pieds" ("Humanisme dans la poèsie de JLB," 282-283). But the tradition is in actual fact much older than that, dating back at least as far as Aphthonius (fourth century A.D.). The description of the naked goddesses may well owe something to Burgundian pageantry of the fifteenth century, in which nudity was prevalent (and whose favorite theme just happened to be the Judgment of Paris). Cf. J. Huizinga, *WMA*, 315-316.

[50] The Idyll of Paris and Oenone has been far too long neglected, owing no doubt to its concealment in the somewhat forbidding mass of *Les Illustrations de Gaule*, just as *Manon Lescaut* would in all likelihood be lost to the twentieth-century reader were it still published as a mere interlude of the interminable *Mémoires d'un homme de qualité*. A separate edition would seem to be called for.

*Illustrations* — while ornate, rhythmic, rich in rhetorical figures — cannot be considered truly sublime: that is, grand, impassioned, intended to move the audience. Rather, it is a delight to read, and thus exactly fulfills the function assigned by the ancients to the middle style.[51]

---

[51] In an illuminating piece on precisely this subject, Erich Auerbach states that: "The first elegant and pleasing middle style to be met with in a European vernacular occurs in the courtly *roman.*" He then proceeds to elaborate in terms which, *mutatis mutandis,* might well be applied to the Paris-Oenone chapters in Lemaire: "... there is a strong accent on remoteness in space and time, on the exotic, miraculous, and adventurous; on the other hand the treatment is so rich in psychological aperçus and social and vestimentary detail that the characters lose their legendary remoteness and superhuman stature and become members of contemporary feudal society, fashionable ladies and gentlemen, good to tell stories about" (*LLP,* 207-208). See also above Chap. I, n. 57.

Chapter VII

AN OVERVIEW OF PRE-RENAISSANCE RHETORIC:
*LA PLAINTE DU DÉSIRÉ*

It is common knowledge that Jean Lemaire's literary career got off to a singularly unpromising start. At the turn of the sixteenth century, while still only in his twenties, he was in the service of Pierre II, duc de Bourbon, in the official capacity of "clerc des finances." This was not, on the face of it, an ideal post for a budding poet, but nevertheless provided a safe haven where the young writer's talents might be expected to develop in relative security. But it was not to be, for Pierre de Bourbon died on October 10, 1503, and his passing was duly lamented in Lemaire's first published work, *Le Temple d'Honneur et de Vertus*. The poet quickly found himself a new patron, Louis de Luxembourg, comte de Ligny; [1] but again to no avail, since on December 31, 1503 — less than three months after the death of Lemaire's first noble benefactor — his second likewise succumbed.

The poet had dedicated *Le Temple d'Honneur* to de Ligny, which may strike us as somewhat lacking in taste. But in our day, what with copyright laws, royalties, motion-picture rights, etc., as the acknowledged perquisites of the successful literary person, we tend to forget what was — until all too recently — the writer's lot. Samuel Johnson — who knew what he was talking about — bids us "mark what ills the scholar's life assail, / Toil, envy, want, the patron, and the jail." All but the last were to assail Jean Lemaire de

---

[1] Although P. Jodogne surmises that Lemaire was already in de Ligny's employ when Pierre de Bourbon died (v. *JLBEFB*, 170-171).

Belges at one time or another, and it is only too possible that he may actually have died in abject poverty.

I do not wish to dwell on these depressing thoughts, but mention them as a preamble to what follows.

Just as he had done for Pierre de Bourbon, so Jean Lemaire now composed a *déploration* in honor of Louis de Luxembourg. This was entitled *La Plainte du Désiré* (i.e., Regretté, or "loved one," as J. McClelland suggests [*op. cit.*, 6]), and was not in fact published until some six years later (at Lyons, c. 1509, by Jehan I$^{er}$ de Vingle, according to Yabsley's Introduction, 61). At this stage in his career, Lemaire was approaching the height of his artistic powers. *La Première Épître de l'Amant Vert* — and possibly *La Seconde* also (cf. Jodogne, *JLBEFB*, 254-255) — was written in 1505; *La Couronne Margaritique,* though not published until 1549, was completed — that is, as far as it ever was to be completed — by March 1505 (cf. Jodogne, *JLBEFB,* 215); the first volume of Lemaire's magnum opus, *Les Illustrations de Gaule et Singularités de Troie,* was published in the spring of 1511; *La Concorde des deux langages,* in 1513. Yabsley, in the Introduction to her edition of *La Plainte,* observes that Lemaire apparently devoted a great deal of care to the work, which he revised thoroughly and in minute detail, particularly, it would seem, in the search for "une épithète plus juste." As an example, she cites the expression "Hystoire doulce et voluptueuse" in the manuscript, compared with the definitive printed version "hystoire fructueuse," the epithet "doulce et voluptueuse" having now been transferred to "la musique" (62), as being more appropriate thereto. From this and other instances of careful reworking, Miss Yabsley concludes reasonably enough that "l'attention que l'auteur, au bout de six ans, porte à cet ouvrage de circonstance, semble indiquer une prédilection spéciale pour *La Plainte du Désiré*" (62).[2] Accordingly, the final version of *La Plainte* could with-

---

[2] Revision of the type thus described is not of course unusual *per se.* Lemaire himself refers to it fairly frequently. In one of his letters to Marguerite d'Autriche, written in 1509, he includes a catalogue of works in progress which begins: "Le deuxième livre de la Couronne margariticque, lequel est tout minuté; ne reste que *le mettre au net.* Les trois livres des Singularitez de Troye, qui sont à *corriger et parfaire* ..." (IV, 395). Cf. *Épître à Charles le Clerc* (IV, 322) in which, again speaking of *Les Illustrations,* Lemaire mentions que Marguerite has commanded him to "recorriger et amplijer [sic] bien exquisement ains les mettre en lumiere."

AN OVERVIEW OF PRE-RENAISSANCE RHETORIC    165

out undue exaggeration be claimed to represent its author's mature and fully evolved thought regarding literary theory. The truth of this claim is in no way invalidated by the possibility that Lemaire may in fact have revised *La Plainte* at an earlier date — say, immediately after its composition — since the work was held in such high esteem by the poet, and was published in its definitive form during his own lifetime, and indeed while he was at his artistic peak.

From our own rather specialized viewpoint, the most interesting feature of *La Plainte du Désiré* is Lemaire's preoccupation with what he calls "l'art de bien dire" (82, l. 187). This phrase is patently an exact rendering of the ancient conception of rhetoric expressed, for example, in Quintilian's comprehensive definition (of which I here cite only the key section), "... *ostenderemus rhetoricen* bene dicendi scientiam ... *esse*" (VIII.Pr.6). In fact, as I believe, *La Plainte du Désiré* may well be considered an adumbration of Lemaire's own "Art de Rhétorique" — and in this context "rhétorique" stands not only for the art of the Grands Rhétoriqueurs, but also for "rhetoric" proper.

*La Plainte* is by no means exceptional among Lemaire's literary productions in the extraordinary degree to which it is permeated by illustrations of rhetorical theory and practice; they are simply the more noticeable, not to say remarkable, in that they are concentrated within so narrow a compass.

The piece is, then, a *déploration* or *complainte*,[3] an elegaic form which the rhétoriqueurs, in their dual capacity as court poets and historiographers, were frequently called upon to practice. Miss Yabsley's Introduction (25-30) provides an informative account of the evolution of the *déploration,* from the primitive popular lament "chanté sur un air simple et monotone" to the "élégies recherchées des Grands Rhétoriqueurs," by way of such intermediary versions as Eustache Deschamp's *lai* on the death of Bertrand Du Guesclin and Christine de Pisan's *Ballade sur la mort du Duc de Bourgogne*. The term *déploration* and its derivatives are met with fairly often

---

[3] Lemaire's original title reads as follows: "C'est la *plaincte* du désiré, c'est a dire la *deploration* du trespas de feu monseigneur Loys de Luxembourg, Prince d'Altemore, duc d'Andre et de Venouze, Conte de Ligny, etc."

in Lemaire's *Œuvres*.[4] On the other hand, the long lament uttered by the distraught Pegasis Oenone (in Book II of *Les Illustrations*), which is a formal and highly lyrical monologue, is called by the nymph herself "ceste complainte" (II, 123), a more general, less technical term than *déploration*. The shortest of Lemaire's three major *déplorations*, *La Plainte du Désiré* is in many respects the most original and the most interesting. Like both *Le Temple d'Honneur* and *La Couronne Margaritique,* it belongs to a hybrid genre, part prose, part poetry, which Georges Doutrepont, giving examples dating back to *Aucassin et Nicolette,* terms "le *vers-prose*" (*JLBR*, 355). Henry Guy (102-103) tells us that the rhétoriqueurs were particularly fond of this form, and reserved it for their most portentous productions.[5] It is therefore no great wonder to see it exploited in such important occasional works as the *déplorations*.

The subject-matter of *La Plainte* is quite simple and straightforward. The poet is in Lyons, where he comes upon a pitiful spectacle, "ung noble corps gisant mort tout de fraiz, estendu sur ung lit de camp." Beside the body stand the grief-stricken "Dame Nature naturée" and two of her most cherished handmaidens, "Paincture parée" and "riche Rhetoricque." Paincture delivers a funeral oration in which lamentations over the loss of Nature's "si noble chief d'euvre" are mingled with a vituperation of Mort and recriminations against Nature herself for letting such a catastrophe occur in the first place ("Et vous, helas! Nature, noble dame, / Ou estiez vous? Que faisiez vous alors?"). Paincture then calls upon her "alumnes modernes" (Leonardo, Bellini, and Jean de Paris, among others) to portray Nature in her affliction.[6] After going into some fascinating

---

[4] Cf., e.g., "Pour deplorer ces tristes funerailles" (*Plainte*, 79, 1. 103); "Jay deploré la perte de Ligny," *Traité des Pompes funèbres* (IV, 270, 1. 3). In Book II of *Les Illustrations,* the word is given its full etymological force of "weeping" or "wailing": "Or apres longue deploration, la pompe funerale fut faite" (II, 87).

[5] E. R. Curtius, *ELLMA* (151) discusses the medieval Latin predecessor of "le *vers-prose*," which was called "*prosimetra*"; and P. Jodogne reminds us that "le genre des œuvres mixtes, en vers et prose" enjoyed especially high favor among writers of the Burgundian school (*JLBEFB*, 313).

[6] De Ligny was a bona fide patron of the arts ("Painctres prudens, le deffunct vous aymoit" [74, 1. 201]), which is the point Lemaire has chosen to highlight in the *déploration,* rather than following the established mode of exalting with outrageous hyperbole the civil and/or military virtues of the deceased. Henry Guy comments approvingly on the originality of this approach (*HPF16*, I, 180-181).

detail relative to the painter's art, Paincture suddenly realizes the futility of attempting to depict Nature's desolation in visual terms ("Non! Laissez tout! Vous n'y scauriez toucher: / Vous n'y pourriez a mon gré satisfaire"), and calls upon her sister Rhetoricque to express the inexpressible through the medium of language.

The apparent humility with which Rhetoricque then begins her own oration ("Qu'en diray je, moy, lasse, povre, humblette, / Peu affluente aux biens que vertu preste, / Et peu duysant a grant chose assener? / Mon sens petit et ma langue sobrette / Ne suffiroit a si haultaine emplette," etc.), comparing herself unfavorably with her "doulce seur germaine," Paincture, and in short proclaiming herself unequal to a task which has already defeated her sister, is a perfectly conventional — and conventionally insincere — use of the affected modesty formula combined with the closely allied inexpressibility topos. Nevertheless both Henry Guy and Abel Lefranc take the statement at face value. "La Rhétorique... avoue tristement son impuissance, déclare que son règne décline, et pressent que l'avenir n'est pas à elle," writes Guy (181), while Lefranc ("Les Grands Rhétoriqueurs," 729) merely echoes this hasty judgment. Paul Spaak, much less prejudiced towards the rhétoriqueurs, sees quite correctly that Rhetoricque's self-abasement is simply "une plaisante règle" of the rhétoriqueurs (*JLB*, 29-30), in no way intended to be taken seriously, and in fact contradicted by the text itself. Indeed it is: one has merely to glance at *La Plainte du Désiré* to realize that whereas Paincture's harangue comprises 248 lines — in octaves — of decasyllabic verse, ending, as mentioned above, with a confession of failure ("Or doncq, ma seur, il fault bien qu'on desploye / Vostre tresor, car mes sens y deffaillent: / Ma main refuit, mon engin se reploye: / Si est besoing que vostre langue employe / Les motz dorez" etc.), Rhetoricque produces 34 decasyllabic quatorzains (476 lines), nearly double the space allocated to Paincture. I suppose this could be interpreted as a satire on rhetorical prolixity as opposed to the economy of the visual arts, but nothing else Lemaire wrote in any way serves to confirm such an opinion. Moreover, as Yabsley notes in her Introduction (54), the quatorzain is a very unusual and extremely complex strophe demanding great technical skill of the poet, and displaying in this instance "une dignité convenable au sujet."

In her oration, Rhetoricque deplores the loss of her faithful disciples from Virgil to Octovien de Saint-Gelais and invokes the aid of music ("Ung grave accent, musicque larmoiable, / Est bien seant a ce dueil piteable, / Pour parfournir noz lamentations") and of contemporary musicians. De Ligny was the patron par excellence ("Qui ayma plus paincture sumptueuse, / L'art de bien dire, histoire fructueuse, / Musicque aussi, doulce et voluptueuse, / Ou qui mist plus son estude en tous biens?"), a sincere devotee of all the arts; and consequently it is up to their representatives to "adoulcir ce dueil qui autre passe," because their combined power is irresistible. Rhetoricque commands a simultaneous invective against Mort and an encomium of the departed, then commissions another invective to be aimed at Envie. Finally, after divers considerations on the mutability of Fortune, she exhorts her "clers orateurs" to put the finishing touches to "du Désiré la plaincte." The crowd of bystanders is not completely persuaded by her admonition to forget their grief, and, as Nature and her handmaidens vanish, those who remain charge the poet (who is still holding the pen with which he composed *Le Temple d'Honneur*) with "ceste seconde matiere funebre," and the piece ends with his reluctant consent.

Paincture and Rhetoricque are introduced at the very outset of the work as radiantly beautiful young women ("deux cleres nymphes"), each designated by an alliterative epithet, "Paincture parée" and "riche Rhetoricque." The use of such formulas is a device of great antiquity, as the expression "epic (or "Homeric") tag" indicates. "Golden Aphrodite," "ox-eyed Hera," the "wine-dark sea": phrases of this type are commonplaces to readers of the *Iliad* and *Odyssey*. Lemaire is thus following a time-honored tradition; but we are not to believe that so self-conscious a writer is following it merely for its own sake, although the force of tradition, of "toute ceste belle antiquité" (I, 14), cannot lightly be discounted when we are dealing with a self-confessed lover of "aulcune chose estrange, merveilleuse et anticque" (*Concorde*, 36, ll. 177-178). Undoubtedly, there is a certain numinous, ritualistic quality to phrases like "riche Rhetoricque" and "Paincture parée," a quality which is intensified by the alliterative and rhythmical quality of Lemaire's prose.[7]

---

[7] Miss Yabsley demonstrates that almost the entire passage in question is composed "dans un style rythmique qui est presque de la poésie pure" (In-

If we now concentrate our attention on Rhetoricque, we soon discover that she is graced by several contrasting epithets in the course of *La Plainte du Désiré*. She is, variously, "la noble nymphe Rhetoricque," "la pucelle Rhetoricque," "la celeste perle Rhetoricque," "la precieuse perle mondaine." The first two appellations plainly serve to establish the allegorical identity of Rhetoricque as a comely maiden of high degree, but with the two "pearl" allusions [8] we are in the domain of medieval rhetoric and its equation with embellishment and ornamentation — in short, with honeyed words and aureate language. This peculiarly medieval concept of the function of rhetoric is taken for granted throughout *La Plainte du Désiré*. Paincture, for example, appeals for the aid of her sister "*tresclere rethoricque, / Bouche dorée et langue melliflue,*" and again insists that she "*desploye / Vostre tresor...*" because Paincture alone cannot succeed in describing Nature's grief: "*Si est besoing que vostre langue employe / Les motz dorez que les haulx dieux luy baillent.*" Rhetoricque herself summons her "*poetes bons, et bons musiciens*" to "*Prester du sucre ung chascun de sa casse, / Pour adoulcir ce dueil qui autre passe, / Et pour aider mes rhetoriciens.*" [9] These repeated allusions to gilding, brightness, sweetness, sugared words, and the like are part and parcel of the one-sided medieval notion of eloquence inherited by the rhétoriqueurs. Expressions of this kind constantly appear in Lemaire's works, both verse and prose. [10]

---

troduction, 57), pointing out that most phrases contain an even number of syllables (4, 6, or 8); that long periods often close with a perfect decasyllable, e.g., "qu'on percevoit en sa dolente face"; and that there are so many syllabic verses in the passage that it could well be taken for a strophe beginning: "Aupres d'elle (3) / Estoient deux cleres nymphes, (6) / Ses plus privées damoiselles (8) / Et pedissecques, (4) / Dont, comme je fuz adverty, (8) / L'une avoit nom Paincture parée (9) / Et l'autre riche Rhetoricque (8)" (57-58).

[8] Note that "celeste" does not, as would at first sight appear, negate "mondaine." The latter adjective has here its old connotation of "bright," "noble," or "perfect," rather than the modern "mundane, worldly" (as is the case in *La Première Épître de l'Amant vert* (6, l. 24) and again in *Concorde* (34, l. 124).

[9] Ll. 194-196. On poetry's debt to music see above, Chap. III, 73-74. It is of interest that Lemaire here specifically differentiates between "poetes" and "rhetoriciens," which is not always his practice (see Chap. III, Section 2 above).

[10] Cf. *Plainte*, 78, l. 74: "Tu me diz *clere*, et de beaulx motz me *dores*" (Rhetorique is speaking); "Tu scez et vois que papier je ne *dore* / Ny em-

*La Plainte du Désiré* belongs to rhétoriqueur art in a number of other ways as well. Though many of the techniques employed are rhetorical in the strictest interpretation of the term, such features as a notable predilection for alliteration, apostrophe, enumeration (the most obvious form of *amplificatio*), definitions, hyperbolic comparison, and the affected modesty formula [11] are all highly typical of pre-Renaissance "rhétorique." The use of the words *rhétoricien* and *orateur* to designate "writer," "author," or even "poet" is similarly a hallmark of the rhétoriqueur. However, *La Plainte du Désiré*, though it does demonstrate skillful handling of the difficult quatorzain, is conspicuously lacking in rhétorique's most characteristically flamboyant trait: viz, the bravura versification, the extraordinarily complex and subtle rhyme-schemes, *rhétorique à double queue, rimes batelées, enchaînées, équivoquées, rétrogrades,* and so on, examples of which occur in *Le Temple d'Honneur, La Couronne Margaritique,* and *L'Oraison et double virelai.* It was of course precisely this "frivolous" attitude toward poetry, this treatment of it as a courtly game, an opportunity to display one's dazzling virtuosity, which provoked the wrath of the truculent young Pléiade poets and inspired Du Bellay's dismissal of Rhétorique and all its works (with the solitary exception of Jean Lemaire) as mere "episseries" (*Deffence,* II, iv, 7). There is, to be sure, rhythmical prose in plenty in *La Plainte du Désiré,* but none of that jingling, rhyming prose (traditionally invented by the illustrious Gorgias of Leontini) which Lemaire resorts to in passages like the following: "affin que vous

---

*belliz* de riens..." (IV, 269, ll. 7-8); "desploye icy la *suauité* de ton eloquence" (IV, 62); "la Princesse Marguerite... dont la bouche *mellifluente* est toute arrosee de pure eloquence naïue et *tressouefue faconde*" (IV, 104-105); "maistre Iean Robertet... Orateur de langue *dulcifluente*" (IV, 77-78); "langue bien exprimant et *suauiloquente*" (III, 406). And cf. especially the liminary verses to *Le Temple d'Honneur.* These are the composition of one who was in his own lifetime among the most admired of the rhétoriqueurs, and a man whom Jean Lemaire greatly respected (as may be deduced from the extremely flattering dedication of *Les Illustrations* [II, 255-257]), Guillaume Cretin. Note particularly ll. 4 and 11: "Par motz *dorez* et *azurez* canticques," "Car le *doulx myel* que ta plume distille" (*Temple,* 45 and 46).

[11] H. Guy, never a very tolerant man, is at his most waspish on the rhétoriqueur fondness for this convention (*HPF16,* I, 75-76): "L'un des [lieux communs les] plus inévitables est celui qui consiste, pour l'écrivain, à se déclarer, dans les premiers et les derniers vers de son ouvrage, absolument incapable de traiter le sujet qu'il a choisi. Et il ne s'agit point de se montrer simplement modeste: il faut se proclamer idiot."

veissiez vos crys dedans escriptz en couleur de douleur, plains de tous plaintz, et que voz soulas qui sont las et voz rys qui sont perilz prinssent quelque source de ressourse; affin, aussi, que l'honneur de Bourbon bon resplendist en triumphant, triumphast en flourissant, et flourist en acroissant par la diuturnité de tous sieclez advenir" (*Temple*, 44-45).[12] Also inherently rhétoriqueur in the *déploration* is its explicit acceptance of the doctrine of poetry's utility. Hence the marked fondness for the moralizing tone, the proverb, the "dicts prouffitables," the use of such expressions as "pour *explaner*... / Du désiré les faitz nobles et preux"; "pour *blasmer* la Mort et ses tenailles"; "Vous formerez une forte *invective* / Encontre Mort... / Et puis apres... / Vous *blasmerez* Envie detractive / Et ferez tant, par *art demonstrative*, / Qu'on congnoistra son pervers dampnement."

This latter sequence, with its thematic terms *blasmer* (its counterpart *louer* is after all what *La Plainte* is really about, i.e., singing the praises of the good Comte de Ligny), *invective*, *demonstrer*, etc., reveals the work's most palpable connections with classical rhetoric, albeit of the later period, for it is a panegyric: i.e., a piece of rhetoric in the epideictic (or demonstrative) mode, whose function is essentially to allocate praise and blame. Description, particularly description with a didactic or moral intent, is as we have seen intrinsic to the epideictic mode; and it is worthy of remark that Paincture instructs her "alumnes modernes" to *portray* Nature's inexpressible grief.[13] Dame Rhetoricque, as one might expect, urges her disciples to *persuade*: "Vueillez en oultre a toutes nobles dames, / ... / Persuader de leurs plaintz abolir," and Lemaire makes much of the *power* (*efficace*) of "le parler rhetorical," which, however, on this occasion proves unequal to the superhuman task

---

[12] A much more sophisticated, restrained, and effective use of rhyming prose occurs in Venus's tour de force of "eloquence artificielle": "... tu auras mellifluence sans male influence, douceur sans douleur, autorité sans austerité, honneur sans horreur, et luisance sans nuisance" (I, 248).

[13] See, e.g., 69, l. 37: "Elle a changé sa belle pourtraicture"; 75, ll. 225-232: "Pourtraiez la, si vous scavez entendre, / Comme une tourbe ayant adversité, / ... / Pourtraiez la comme la grant cité / Jherusalem Machabee plaignant, / Ou Romme autour du corps Cesar seignant." Edmond Faral observes that: "dans toute la littérature du moyen âge, la description ne vise que très rarement à peindre objectivement les personnes et les choses et... [elle est] toujours dominée par une intention affective qui oscille entre la louange et la critique" (*AP*, 76).

it faces, since the grief of the mourners is not completely dispelled, in spite of Rhetoricque's most strenuous exhortations.[14]

When "Paincture la noble pucelle" begins to address Nature and the assembled mourners, the exact manner in which she goes about it is minutely described: "Paincture..., de la piteable voix yssant de son gosier christallin feit resonner la region circumjacente, et rengrega le pleur et la commiseration de tous les assistens." Rhetoricque's preparations to speak are even more painstakingly observed: "Et lors la pucelle Rhetoricque... disposa sa contenance ainsi que pour parler, et commenca a entrouvrir sa gracieuse bouche.... Adoncques la celeste perle Rhetoricque, d'une voix tremulente et d'ung accent resonant, dressa son doulx langaige...." All this, I venture to assert, amounts to far more than a meticulously realistic description of every last detail of the Comte de Ligny's obsequies (as, for instance, in *La pompe funeralle de Phelipes de Castille*). In the precise notation of the actual *manner* in which the funeral orations are delivered, I believe it is not too fanciful to discern a preoccupation with the fifth qualitative part of rhetoric, namely *pronuntiatio*, delivery (see above, Chap. 1, 26-27).

Lastly, we may take note of the most glaringly apparent of all the rhetorical features of *La Plainte du Désiré*; the fact that of the work's 25 pages, no less than 20 are given over to the orations delivered by Paincture and Rhetoricque.

As previously noted in Chapters I and III above, literary critics and historians of the past few decades have suggested with a persuasiveness which should prove gratifying to a teacher of rhetoric that the key to the Renaissance lies in a fuller understanding of the centrality of rhetoric to humanism. "The humanists' modes of argument from example and from authority, their emphasis on 'verisi-

---

[14] The appearance here of such terms as "persuader" and "efficace" would seem at first sight to indicate that *La Plainte du Désiré* has deliberative overtones in addition to its basic epideictic function, as Prof. John A. McClelland observes in his interesting paper on the work. "Previous *complaintes* had always assumed the efficacy of the genre as a piece of deliberative rhetoric. Words could reduce grief by being marshalled together under the topical arguments of consolatory eloquence," etc. ("Rhetoric and Catharsis," 7). I seriously doubt, however, that such an assumption was ever taken to be more than the merest literary convention, or that the genre was intended actually to *purge* the mourners of their grief, in the sense of a true catharsis, as McClelland suggests (10-11). Lemaire's purpose was not after all to compose a tragedy, but a *déploration*, which is by definition essentially lyrical.

militude,' on variety, and on vividness, their insistence on representing general types or conveying universal lessons through the concrete, the visual, the emotionally convincing — all these bear both a formal and a substantive relation to rhetoric." Thus Gray ("Renaissance Humanism," 506), writing on the pervasive influence of rhetoric on humanistic thought and modes of expression, in a passage whose appositeness to Jean Lemaire is unquestionable.

In this chapter as well as in the course of those preceding, I have attempted a fairly detailed demonstration of the degree of Lemaire's adherence to the rhetorical tradition in its several evolutionary stages, classical, medieval, and Renaissance. There are of course no clearly defined lines of demarcation between the three rhetorics as such, the tradition as a whole being endowed with remarkable powers of endurance and cohesiveness. What is often characterized as a particularly medieval outlook, for instance — a certain tendency to equate rhetoric with aureate language pure and simple — does indeed reflect the preoccupations of the most influential medieval theorists, but is really a gross over-simplification of the facts insofar as medieval *practice* is concerned, and quite fails to take into account such important phenomena as the rhetoric of preaching and (in the case of late medieval French literature) the establishment and development by Alain Chartier of a highly complex form of oratorical prose.[15] It is nevertheless broadly true that

---

[15] It has been authoritatively stated (E. Auerbach, *LLP*, 205) that intricate sentence structure in French prose was virtually unknown before Alain Chartier, and the modern editor of *Le Quadrilogue invectif* (1422) does not hesitate to claim that its author remains in effect without imitators throughout the fifteenth century: "Je ne vois... que quelques pages de Gerson qui puissent être comparées à la prose de Chartier" (E. Droz, introduction to *Le Quadrilogue*, vi). This judgment is perhaps a trifle partisan in its enthusiasm, ignoring in a distinctly cavalier fashion the highly oratorical prose of, notably, Georges Chastellain and Jean Molinet. However, Chartier is not only frequently singled out for special praise among the "poëtes, orateurs et historiens" whom Jean Lemaire loves to honor (see, e.g., *Temple*, 89, l. 1118; *Plainte*, 79, l. 109; and I, 60, III, 246; IV, 381), but in one instance, indeed, is quoted *in extenso*, "de mot à mot." This is in the polemical *Schismes et Conciles*, whose author borrows the closing paragraphs of Chartier's *Traité de la Consolation des Trois Vertus, Foi, Espérance, Charité* (Chartier, *Œuvres*, ed. by André du Chesne [Paris, 1617], 388-390 cited by Lemaire in III, 355-357), as being a most forceful and elegant expression of Lemaire's own indictment of ecclesiastical corruption. Incidentally, Lemaire himself refers to the work as "Lexil" (cf. du Chesne's editorial comment [*op. cit.*, 851]: "L'Inscription de ce Liure est diuerse entre les Autheurs qui l'alleguent. Car Iean le Maire de

whereas deliberative and judicial oratory (which lay particular stress on *inventio*) are predominant in classical antiquity, the Middle Ages is quintessentially the period of the epideictic mode (with its insistence on *elocutio*). During the Renaissance, deliberative rhetoric once more comes into its own. It is therefore largely a matter of emphasis — or rather of over-emphasis — at different periods, on this or that facet of what is actually a unified and perennial tradition.

This point is neatly exemplified in the *Œuvres* of Jean Lemaire. To reduce a complex problem to its simplest terms: medieval (in the looser sense) is his conception of rhetoric as "suauiloquence" and "motz dorez" (above all in the *déplorations*); classical is his correct application of the doctrine of the three levels of style and his conscious imitation of the best available models, while his effective use of deliberative oratory in the polemical writings bears the distinctive stamp of the Renaissance. A cardinal element of Lemaire's rhetorically oriented literary approach is his use of the oration. As we observed earlier (see above, Chap. IV, 106), no less than the ballad, the rondeau, or the sonnet, the oration is a literary *form,* with its own highly individual conventions. Like all other genres it is subject, in the wrong hands, to woeful abuse (just as Plato feared), whereas for a master craftsman its potentialities are almost endless. In his finest orations, Lemaire succeeds in giving to prose some of the organizational density and the lapidary quality of poetry.

And yet there still persists in some academic circles an unfortunate misconception as to the very nature of rhetoric, which is all too often airily dismissed as the antithesis of literature (instead of receiving due recognition as lying at its foundation). It is this attitude which has long bedeviled scholars working in the area of the French pre-Renaissance. No unbiased critic could conceivably deny that the rhétoriqueurs, Jean Lemaire included, produced in their time vast quantities of empty compliments, insincere flatteries, and wild hyperboles, all of which are monotonously — and erroneously — characterized as "rhetoric." But the blame for these ex-

---

Belges... luy donne le nom d'*Exil*. Au contraire, Maistre Pierre le Feure [Fabri], Curé de Meray, le cite souz le tiltre d'*Esperance*, en son art de vraye Rhetorique. Et i'en ay un Exemplaire escrit à la main, qui l'appelle, Traité de la Consolation des trois vertus, Foi, Esperance, Charité.")

cesses is not primarily attributable to rhetoric at all, but rather to the proverbially chronic financial insecurity and degrading client status of the court poet. There is a world of difference between, for example, the dutifully solemn eulogizing of much of *La Couronne Margaritique* and the charming exuberance of the Idyll of Paris and Oenone (in the oratorical passages no less than in the narrative proper). One would not be far off the mark, I suspect, in believing that the former work — despite its author's very real affection for his patroness — labors under the curiously deadening influence of the literary commission: compare, e.g., the generally perfunctory tenor of many of the Birthday Odes, New Year's Day Odes, Odes for St. George's Day, etc., produced by British Poets Laureate over the centuries.[16] As for the finest chapters of Jean Lemaire's prose, it seems plain that, commissioned or no, he composed them above all for his own delight.

From the perspective of French literary history, perhaps the most important point to be made is that a writer like Jean Lemaire does not suddenly spring into being — like Pallas Athena from the head of Zeus — a fully formed pre-Renaissance man quite distinct from his medieval predecessors. He represents, on the contrary, a stage (a very significant one, to be sure: even, possibly, a culmination) in the evolution of French *prose oratoire* which begins with Alain Chartier and continues in direct line through the three succeeding generations represented by Georges Chastellain, Jean Molinet, and Jean Lemaire himself.

---

[16] For a fairly representative sampling of the Laureates from John Dryden through John Masefield, see Kenneth Hopkins, *The Poets Laureate* (New York, 1955), 200-280.

# BIBLIOGRAPHY

I. EDITIONS OF JEAN LEMAIRE'S WORKS

Lemaire de Belges, Jean. *La Concorde des deux langages,* ed. Jean Frappier. Textes Littéraires Français. Paris: Droz, 1947.
———. *La Concorde du genre humain,* ed. Pierre Jodogne. Brussels: Palais des Académies, 1964.
———. *Les Épitres de l'Amant Vert,* ed. Jean Frappier. Textes Littéraires Français. Geneva: Droz, 1948.
———. *Œuvres,* ed. Jean Stecher. Louvain: Lefever, 1882-1891. 4 vols.
———. *La Plainte du Désiré,* ed. Dora Yabsley. Paris: Droz, 1932. (Univ. of London M.A. thesis, 1929).
———. *Le Temple d'Honneur et de Vertus,* ed. Henri Hornik. Textes Littéraires Français. Geneva: Droz, 1957.


II. ANCIENT AND MEDIEVAL TREATISES OF RHETORIC AND POETICS

Aphthonius. *Progymnasmata,* trans. Ray Nadeau, *Speech Monographs* 19 (1952), 264-285.
Aristotle. *The Poetics,* trans. W. Hamilton Fyfe. Loeb Classical Library. Cambridge, Mass.: Harvard Univ. Press; London: Heinemann, 1965 [1927].
———. *The "Art" of Rhetoric,* trans. John H. Freese. Loeb Classical Library. Cambridge, Mass.: Harvard Univ. Press; London: Heinemann, 1959 [1926].
[Cicero]. *Ad C. Herennium de Ratione Dicendi (Rhetorica ad Herennium),* trans. Harry Caplan. Loeb Classical Library. Cambridge, Mass.: Harvard Univ. Press; London: Heinemann, 1954.
Cicero. *Orator,* trans. H. M. Hubbell. Loeb Classical Library. Cambridge, Mass.: Harvard Univ. Press; London: Heinemann, 1939.
———. *De inventione,* trans. H. M. Hubbell. Loeb Classical Library. Cambridge, Mass.: Harvard Univ. Press, 1960 [1949].
———. *De oratore,* trans. E. W. Sutton and H. Rackham. Loeb Classical Library. Cambridge, Mass.: Harvard Univ. Press; London: Heinemann, 1959 [1942].
———. *De partitione oratoria,* trans. H. Rackham. Loeb Classical Library. Cambridge, Mass.: Harvard Univ. Press; London: Heinemann, 1960 [1942].
Daretis Phrygii. *De Excidio Troiae Historia.* Bonn: Weber, 1837.

Deschamps, Eustache. *L'Art de dictier et de fere chançons,* etc. [1392], ed. Gaston Reynaud. Société des anciens textes français. Paris: Didot, 1891. In vol. VII of *Œuvres complètes,* 266-292.

Fabri, Pierre (Le Fevre). *Le Grand et Vrai Art de Pleine Rhétorique,* ed. A. Heron. Société des Bibliophiles normands. Rouen: Lestringant, 1889-1890. 3 vols.

Hermogenes of Tarsus. *Progymnasmata,* trans. Charles S. Baldwin, in his *Medieval Rhetoric and Poetic* (q.v.), 23-38.

Horace. *Ars poetica,* trans. H. Rushton Fairclough. Loeb Classical Library. Cambridge, Mass.: Harvard Univ. Press; London: Heinemann, 1961 [1926].

John of Garland. *Exempla honestae vitae,* ed. Edwin Habel, *Romanische Forschungen* 29 (1910-1911), 131-154.

———. *The Parisiana Poetria of John of Garland,* ed. Traugott Lawler. Yale Studies in English, 182. New Haven and London: Yale Univ. Press, 1974.

Langlois, Ernest. *Recueil d'arts de seconde rhétorique.* Paris: Imprimerie nationale, 1902.

Latini, Brunetto. *Li Livres dou Tresor,* ed. Francis J. Carmody. Berkeley: Univ. of California Press, 1948.

Martianus Capella. *De Nuptiis Philologiae et Mercurii et de Septem Artibus Liberalibus.* Book V (*De Rhetorica*), trans. Lou W. Conklin. Ithaca, N.Y.: unpublished Cornell Univ. M.A. thesis, 1928.

Molinet, Jean. *Art de Rhétorique,* in E. Langlois, *Recueil d'arts de seconde rhétorique* (q.v.), 214-252.

Plato. *Gorgias,* trans. W. R. M. Lamb. Loeb Classical Library. London: Heinemann; New York: Putnam's Sons, 1932 [1925].

———. *The Dialogues,* trans. Benjamin Jowett. New York: Oxford Univ. Press; London: Henry Frowde, 1892 [1871]. 5 vols.; vol. I contains *Phaedrus.*

Quintilian. *Institutio Oratoria,* trans. H. E. Butler. Loeb Classical Library. Cambridge, Mass.: Harvard Univ. Press; London: Heinemann, 1963-1968 [1920-1922].

———. *On the Early Education of the Citizen-Orator. Institutio Oratoria,* I and II, chaps. 1-10, trans. (1856) John Selby Watson, ed. James J. Murphy. Library of Liberal Arts. Indianapolis and New York: Bobbs-Merrill, 1965.

———. *Opera,* ed. Nicolas Eloi Lemaire. Paris: Bibliotheca Classica Latina, 1825. 7 vols.

Rockinger, Ludwig. *Briefsteller und Formelbücher des eilften* [sic] *bis vierzehnten Jahrhunderts.* New York: Burt Franklin, 1961 [1863-1864]. 2 vols.

III. OTHER WORKS CONSULTED

Abelson, Paul. *The Seven Liberal Arts.* New York: Teachers' College (Columbia), 1906.

Apuleius. *The Golden Ass (The Metamorphoses of Lucius Apuleius),* trans. William Adlington (1566), rev. S. Gaselee. Loeb Classical Library. London: Heinemann; New York: Putnam's Sons, 1928 [1915].

Auerbach, Erich. *Literary Language and Its Public in Late Latin Antiquity and in the Middle Ages,* trans. Ralph Manheim. London: Routledge and Kegan Paul, 1965 [1958].

Auerbach, Erich. "Figura," trans. Ralph Manheim, in *Scenes from the Drama of European Literature*. New York: Meridian Books, 1959 [1938].

Baldwin, Charles S. *Ancient Rhetoric and Poetic Interpreted from Representative Works*. New York: Macmillan, 1924.

———. *Medieval Rhetoric and Poetic (to 1400) Interpreted from Representative Works*. Gloucester, Mass.: Peter Smith, 1959 [1928].

———. *Renaissance Literary Theory and Practice*, ed. D. L. Clark. Gloucester, Mass.: Peter Smith, 1959 [1939].

Becker, Ph. Aug. *Jean Lemaire, der erste humanistische Dichter Frankreichs*. Strassburg: Karl J. Trübner, 1893.

Benôit de Sainte-Maure. *Le Roman de Troie*, ed. Léopold Constans. Société des anciens textes français. Paris: Firmin-Didot, 1904-1912. 7 vols.

Bolgar, R. R. *The Classical Heritage and Its Beneficiaries*. New York: Harper Torchbooks, 1964 [1954].

Boskoff, Priscilla S. "Quintilian in the Late Middle Ages," *Speculum* 27 (1952), 71-78.

Bryant, Donald C. "Rhetoric: Its Function and Scope," in *The Province of Rhetoric*, ed. J. Schwartz and J. A. Rycenga (q.v.), 3-36.

Caplan, Harry. "Classical Rhetoric and the Mediaeval Theory of Preaching," *Classical Philology* 28 (1933), 73-96.

Castor, Grahame. *Pléiade Poetics*. Cambridge, England: Cambridge Univ. Press, 1964.

Chamard, Henri. *Histoire de la Pléiade*. Paris: Didier, 1961 [1939]. 4 vols.

———. *Les Origines de la Poésie française de la Renaissance*. Paris: de Boccard, 1920.

Champion, Pierre. *Histoire poétique du XV$^e$ siècle*. Bibliothèque du XV$^e$ siècle, 17 and 18. Paris: Champion, 1923. 2 vols.

Charland, Thomas M., O.P. *Artes praedicandi: une contribution à l'histoire de la rhétorique au moyen âge*. Paris: Vrin; Ottawa: Institut d'études médiévales, 1936.

Chartier, Alain. *Œuvres*, ed. André du Chesne. Paris: S. Thibaut, 1617.

———. *Le Quadrilogue invectif*, ed. E. Droz (2nd ed.) Les Classiques français du moyen âge. Paris: Champion, 1950.

Clark, Donald L. *Rhetoric and Poetry in the Renaissance*. New York: Columbia Univ. Press, 1922.

———. *Rhetoric in Greco-Roman Education*. New York: Columbia Univ. Press, 1966 [1957].

———. "The Rise and Fall of Progymnasmata in Sixteenth and Seventeenth Century Grammar Schools," *Speech Monographs* 19 (1952), 259-263.

Clarke, Martin L. *Rhetoric at Rome: a Historical Survey*. London: Cohen and West, 1966 [1953].

Chastellain, Georges. *Œuvres*, ed. Kervyn de Lettenhove. Brussels: Huessner, 1863-1866. 8 vols.

Cousin, Jean. "Rhétorique latine et classicisme français," *Revue des Cours et Conférences* 34 (1933), 502-518; 589-605 (1$^{re}$ série); 34 (1933), 159-168; 234-243; 461-469; 659-672; 737-750 (2$^e$ série).

Curtius, Ernst R. *European Literature and the Latin Middle Ages*, trans. Willard R. Trask. New York: Harper Torchbooks, 1963 [1948].

Dante Alighieri. *Convivio*, in *Opere Minori*, ed. Alberto del Monte. Milan: Rizzoli, 1960, 239-521.

Daru, Pierre. *Histoire de la République de Venise*. (2nd ed.) Paris: Firmin-Didot, 1821. 8 vols.

Doutrepont, Georges. *Jean Lemaire de Belges et la Renaissance*. Brussels: Lamertin, 1934.
Du Bellay, Joachim. *La Deffence et Illustration de la Langue Françoyse*, ed. Henri Chamard. Société des textes français modernes. Paris: Didier, 1966 [1948].
Faral, Edmond. *Les Arts poétiques du XII$^e$ et du XIII$^e$ siècle*. Paris: Champion, 1923.
Frappier, Jean. "L'Humanisme dans la poésie de Lemaire de Belges," *Romance Philology* 17 (1963-1964), 272-284.
————. "L'Humanisme de Lemaire de Belges," *Bibliothèque d'Humanisme et Renaissance* 25 (1963), 289-306.
————. "Jean Lemaire de Belges et les Beaux-Arts," *Atti del V$^o$ congresso internazionale di lingue e letterature moderne*. Florence: Valmartina, 1955 [1951], 107-114.
Frye, Northrop. *Anatomy of Criticism. Four Essays*. New York: Atheneum, 1968 [1957].
Gilmore, Myron P. *The World of Humanism*. New York: Harper Torchbooks, 1962 [1952].
Gilson, Étienne. *Les Idées et les lettres*. Paris: Vrin, 1955 [1931].
Gmelin, Hermann. "Das Prinzip der Imitatio in den romanischen Literaturen der Renaissance," *Romanische Forschungen* 46 (1932), 83-359.
Gordon, Alex. L. *Ronsard et la Rhétorique*. Geneva: Droz, 1970.
Grammont, Maurice. *Petit traité de versification française*. Paris: Colin, 1949 (13th ed.) [1908].
Gray, Hanna H. "Renaissance Humanism; the Pursuit of Eloquence," *Journal of the History of Ideas* 24 (1963), 497-514.
Griffin, Robert. *Coronation of the Poet: Joachim Du Bellay's Debt to the Trivium*. Berkeley and Los Angeles: Univ. of California Press, 1969.
Grosser, Dorothy E. "Studies in the Influence of the *Rhetorica ad Herennium* and Cicero's *De inventione*." Ithaca, N.Y., unpubl. Ph.D. dissertation, Cornell Univ., 1953.
Guy, Henry. *Histoire de la poésie française au XVI$^e$ siècle*. Paris: Champion, 1910. 4 vols (Vol. I: *L'École des Rhétoriqueurs*).
Hall, Vernon, Jr. *Renaissance Literary Criticism*. New York: Columbia Univ. Press, 1945.
Harding, Harold F. "Quintilian's Witnesses," in *Historical Studies of Rhetoric and Rhetoricians*, ed. R. F. Howes (q.v.), 90-106.
Haskins, Charles Homer. *The Renaissance of the Twelfth Century*. Cleveland and New York: Meridian, 1967 [1927].
Hefele, Charles-Joseph [Karl-Joseph von]. *Histoire des Conciles d'après les documents originaux*, trans. Dom H. Leclercq, O.S.B. Paris: Letouzey et Ané, 1907-1913. 10 vols.
Hopkins, Kenneth. *The Poets Laureate*. New York: Library Publishers, 1955.
Howell, Wilbur S. "Renaissance Rhetoric and Modern Rhetoric: a Study in Change," in *The Province of Rhetoric*, ed. J. Schwartz and J. A. Rycenga (q.v.), 292-308.
Howes, Raymond F. (ed.). *Historical Studies of Rhetoric and Rhetoricians*. Ithaca, N.Y.: Cornell Univ. Press, 1961.
Huguet, Edmond. *Dictionnaire de la langue française du XVI$^e$ siècle*. Paris: Champion, 1925-1964.
Huizinga, Johan. *The Waning of the Middle Ages*. Garden City, N.Y.: Doubleday Anchor, 1954 [1924].

Hulubei, Alice. *L'Églogue en France au XVIe siècle.* Paris: Droz, 1938.
Humpers, Alfred. *Étude sur la langue de Jean Lemaire de Belges.* Bibliothèque de la Faculté de Philosophie et Lettres de l'Université de Liège, Fasc. XXVI. Liège: Vaillant-Carmanne; Paris: Champion, 1921.
Irsay, Stephen D'. *Histoire des Universités françaises et étrangères des origines à nos jours. I. Moyen Age et Renaissance.* Paris: Auguste Picard, 1933.
Jaeger, Werner. "The Rhetoric of Isocrates and Its Cultural Ideal," in *The Province of Rhetoric,* ed. J. Schwartz and J. A. Rycenga (q.v.), 84-111.
Jodogne, Pierre. *Jean Lemaire de Belges, écrivain franco-bourguignon.* Mémoires de la Classe des Lettres, 2e série, T. XIII, Fasc. 1. Brussels: Palais des académies, 1972.
John of Salisbury. *Metalogicon,* trans. Daniel D. McGarry. Berkeley and Los Angeles: Univ. of California Press, 1962.
Kennedy, George. *The Art of Persuasion in Greece.* Princeton, N. J.: Princeton Univ. Press, 1963.
―――. *The Art of Rhetoric in the Roman World.* Princeton, N. J.: Princeton Univ. Press, 1972.
Kristeller, Paul Oskar. "Humanism and Scholasticism in the Italian Renaissance," in *Renaissance Thought.* New York: Harper Torchbooks, 1961 [1955], 92-119.
―――. "The Moral Thought of Renaissance Humanism," in *Renaissance Thought II.* New York: Harper Torchbooks, 1965, 20-68.
Lanham, Richard A. *A Handlist of Rhetorical Terms.* Berkeley and Los Angeles: Univ. of California Press, 1969 [1968].
Laumonier, Paul. *Ronsard, poète lyrique.* Paris: Hachette, 1909.
Lefranc, Abel. "Les Grands Rhétoriqueurs," *Revue des Cours et Conférences* 19 (1910-1911), 721-730 (1re série).
―――. "Jean Lemaire de Belges," *Revue des Cours et conférences* 19 (1910-1911), 769-777; 19 (1911), 97-106; 145-149 (2e série).
Lewis, C. S. *The Discarded Image.* Cambridge, England: Cambridge Univ. Press, 1967 [1964].
McClelland, John A. "*La Plainte du Désiré*: Rhetoric and Catharsis in the Early Renaissance." Unpubl. paper read before the 1972 convention of the MLA.
McKeon, Richard. "Rhetoric in the Middle Ages," *Speculum* 17 (1942), 1-32.
Molinet, Jean. *Chroniques,* ed. Georges Doutrepont and Omer Jodogne. Classe des lettres et des sciences morales et politiques. Collection des anciens auteurs belges. Brussels: Palais des Académies, 1935. 3 vols.
Morphos, Panos Paul. "The Pictorialism of Lemaire de Belges in 'Le Temple d'Honneur et de Vertus,'" *Annali dell' Istituto Universitario Orientale,* Sezione romanza 5 (1963), 5-34.
Munn, Kathleen Miriam. *A Contribution to the Study of Jean Lemaire de Belges. A Critical Study of Bio-bibliographical Data.* Scottdale, Pa.: Mennonite Publishing House, 1936. (Columbia Univ. Ph. D. dissertation).
Murphy, James J. *Rhetoric in the Middle Ages.* Berkeley, Los Angeles, and London: Univ. of California Press, 1974.
Ong, Walter J., S.J. "The Province of Rhetoric and Poetic," in *The Province of Rhetoric,* ed. J. Schwartz and J. A. Rycenga (q.v.), 48-56.
*Oxford Companion to French Literature,* ed. Paul Harvey and J. E. Heseltine. Oxford: Clarendon Press, 1966 [1959].
Paetow, Louis J. *The Arts Course at Medieval Universities.* Champaign, Ill.: Univ. of Illinois Studies III, 7, 1910.

Pasquier, Étienne. *Œuvres choisies,* ed. Léon Feugère. Paris: Firmin-Didot, 1849. 2 vols.
Patterson, Warner F. *Three Centuries of French Poetic Theory.* Ann Arbor, Mich.: Univ. of Michigan Press, 1935. 2 vols.
Picard, Raymond. "Les grands rhétoriqueurs," in *Tableau de la littérature française I* (q.v.), 186-195.
Sandys, John E. *A History of Classical Scholarship.* Cambridge, England: Cambridge Univ. Press, vol. I, 1921 [1903], vol. II, 1908.
Schwartz, Joseph, and Rycenga, John A. (eds.). *The Province of Rhetoric.* New York: Ronald Press, 1965.
Seigel, Jerrold E. *Rhetoric and Philosophy in Renaissance Humanism.* Princeton, N.J.: Princeton Univ. Press, 1968.
Spaak, Paul. *Jean Lemaire de Belges, sa vie, son œuvre et ses meilleures pages.* Paris: Champion, 1926.
Spencer, John R. "Ut Rhetorica Pictura," *Journal of the Warburg and Courtauld Institutes* 20 (1957), 26-44.
Sperduti, Alice W. "Petrarch on Poetry," Ithaca, N.Y.: unpubl. Ph.D. dissertation, Cornell Univ., 1947.
Spingarn, Joel E. *A History of Literary Criticism in the Renaissance.* New York: Harcourt, Brace (Harbinger Books), 1963 [1899].
Stecher, Jean. *Notice sur la vie et les œuvres de Jean Lemaire de Belges.* Louvain: Lefever, 1891. (Forms an appendix to vol. IV of Stecher's edition of Lemaire's *Œuvres* [q.v.], pp. i-cvii).
*Tableau de la Littérature Française* I, Paris: Gallimard, 1962.
Tassoni, Alessandro. *De Pensieri Diversi di Alessandro Tassoni Libri Dieci.* Venice: Barezzi, 1646.
Thibaut, Francisque. *Marguerite d'Autriche et Jean Lemaire de Belges.* Paris: Ernest Leroux, 1888.
Thurot, Charles. *De l'Organisation de l'enseignement dans l'Université de Paris, au Moyen-Age.* Frankfurt: Minerva G.M.B.H., 1967 [1850].
Ullman, Berthold L. "Leonardo Bruni and Humanistic Historiography," in *Studies in the Italian Renaissance.* Rome: Edizioni di storia e letteratura, 1955, 321-344.
Vickers, Brian. *Classical Rhetoric in English Poetry.* London: Macmillan, 1970.
Vier, Jacques. *Histoire de la littérature française: XVI$^e$-XVII$^e$ siècles.* Paris: Armand Colin, 1959.
Voltaire. *Œuvres Complètes.* Paris: Garnier, 1878.
Weber, Henri. *La Création poétique au XVI$^e$ siècle en France.* Paris: Nizet, 1956.
Woodward, William Harrison. *Studies in Education during the Age of the Renaissance, 1400-1600.* Classics in Education, 32. New York: Teachers College Press, 1967 [1906].
Yates, Frances A. *The Art of Memory.* London: Routledge and Kegan Paul, 1966.

# INDEX

Alberti, Leon Battista, 32n
Aphthonius, 30-31, 117
Aristotle, 21, 22, 25, 42, 46, 67, 106n, 125n, 139
*Artes dictaminis,* 34
*Artes praedicandi,* 33-34
*Arts poétiques* (medieval), 31, 33, 36-37, 41-42
*Arts de seconde rhétorique,* 38-39; see also Molinet, Fabri
Averroës, 42
Benoît de Sainte-Maure, 111
Boccaccio, 48, 78, 84, 120n
Boncompagno of Bologna, 127
Bracciolini, Poggio, 43
Bruni, Leonardo, 54-55, 67, 106
Castiglione, Baldassare, 88
Cato, 22
Chartier, Alain, 19, 47, 48-49, 78, 81, 83, 173, 175
Chastellain, Georges, 19, 47, 48, 49-52, 78, 173n, 175
Christine de Pisan, 40n, 165
[Cicero] *Rhetorica ad Herennium,* 23, 25, 26-27, 29n, 41-42, 45-46, 71n, 87, 114-115, 117, 121, 125, 137-138, 156
Cicero, 21, 24, 32n, 42, 44, 78, 82, 121n, 139, 147, 150, 151; *Brutus,* 23, 42; *De inventione,* 22, 23, 25, 41-42, 45, 46, 114; *Orator,* 23, 26, 42; *De oratore,* 23, 34-35, 37n, 42, 67; *Partitiones oratoriae,* 23
Cretin, Guillaume, 17, 72, 169n
Dante Alighieri, 31, 40, 48, 68n, 139, 142, 147, 152
Dares of Phrygia, 105, 128n
Demetrius Phalareus, 22

Demosthenes, 20
Deschamps, Eustache, 38, 39, 41n, 73n
Description, 29-32, 157-161, 172
Dictys of Crete, 105n, 128
Du Bellay, Joachim, 35n, 75n, 80n, 83, 170
Erasmus, 108n, 154n
Fabri, Pierre, 38
Fichet, Guillaume, 43, 44
Ficino, Marsilio, 79, 81, 108
Filelfo, Francesco, 42, 108
Gaguin, Robert, 43, 45, 55, 81, 97n
Gautier de Coincy, 40n
Geoffroi de Vinsauf, 36, 37
George of Trebizond (Trapezuntius), 42
Gorgias of Leontini, 21
Gui de Cambrai, 40n
Hermogenes of Tarsus, 30-31, 117
Herodotus, 106
Heynlin, Jean, 44
Homer, 20, 83, 101, 105, 152
Horace, 32, 35n, 39, 80n, 84, 124n
Isocrates, 23, 82
John of Garland, 29n, 34n, 36, 38n, 74, 118n
John of Salisbury, 69, 107n
Landino, Cristoforo, 108
Latini, Brunetto, 35n, 36-37
Legrand, Jacques, 40n
Lemaire de Belges, Jean, 45, 47, 57-58, 68, 163-164; and the Bible, 104, 131, 138, 139; born out of his time, 17-18, 124; critics' opinions of, 15, 56-57; as encomiast and polemicist, 58-68, 83-85, 102-103, 111, 114-128, 136-138, 171-172; and imitation, 82-83, 100,

# INDEX

101, 152-154, 168; dialogue in, 92; education of, 45-47; and ethical persuasion, 67, 129, 139; feminism of, 99n; and *furor poeticus*, 79-80; ideas on history, 81-85, 102-108, 110; literary heir of Chartier, 19, 47-54, 173-175; and pastoral, 121-124; on poetry and music, 73-74, 168, 169n; and *pronuntiatio*, 86-88, 172; as Renaissance "orator", 55, 56-68, 174; rhetorical cast of thinking, 71, 83-85, 102; and *rhétorique*, 17, 72-74, 167-170, 174, 175; short verse by, 92; and status of poet, 77-81, 103, 170; terms for "writer," 75-83; and urbanity, 87-88, 117-119

Lemaire, style of, 88-91, 110-111, 120-121; *accumulatio*, 149; alliteration/assonance, 155; amplification, 110, 157; anaphora, 149; apostrophe/*exclamatio*, 142-146; description, 29n, 30n, 86, 123-124, 157-161; *exempla*, 109, 118-119, 122, 150-152; isocolon/parison, 149; levels of style, 104, 120-121, 161-162; metaphor and simile, 122-124, 133, 136, 137, 152-154; *paronomasia*, 155-156; prosopopoeia, 129, 154; rhetorical questions, 146-148; virtuosity, 170

Lemaire, works of: *Les Chansons de Namur*, 64, 155n; *La Chronique Annale*, 58, 59, 63, 64; *La Concorde des deux langages*, 40n, 48, 62, 63, 73, 77, 79, 81, 82, 89, 94, 102, 130n, 137n, 156, 157; *La Concorde du genre humain*, 62, 79, 90-91, 102, 114, 115n, 126-128, 156; *La Couronne Margaritique*, 46n, 48, 57n, 59, 68n, 71, 78, 80, 84, 85, 87-88, 92, 102, 111, 114-119, 120, 143, 159, 164, 166, 170; *Les Épîtres de l'Amant Vert*, 72, 73, 82-83, 94, 123, 157, 164; *Épître à Charles le Clerc*, 45-46, 58, 60n, 164n; *L'Épître du Roi à Hector de Troie*, 59n; *Les Fragments de Chronique*, 46, 59; *Les Illustrations de Gaule et Singularités de Troie*, 15-18, 45, 58, 63, 65, 75, 78, 85, 86, 90, 91, 92, 96-101, 103, 104-106, 108, 109, 110, 115n, 119-121, 128-162, 164; *La Légende des Vénitiens*, 59n, 60-61, 75, 89, 95, 104, 110n, 147, 161; *La Plainte du Désiré*, 59, 79, 84, 85, 86n, 88, 93, 102, 154, 158n, 164-173; *Le Temple d'Honneur*, 72, 77, 79, 80, 82, 88-89, 93, 105n, 115, 158, 165, 166, 170; *Le Traité des Pompes funèbres*, 84, 172; *Le Traité des Schismes et Conciles*, 48, 59, 60-62, 75, 95-96, 103n; *Les Trois Contes de Cupido et d'Atropos*, 94-95, 114

Le Queux, Regnaud, 79
Lucan, 35n
Marot, Clément, 101
Martianus Capella, 25, 36n
Matthieu de Vendôme, 31, 36, 37
Milton, John, 28
Molinet, Jean, 17, 19, 38, 39, 41, 46, 48, 52-54, 66, 74, 78, 83n, 84, 144n, 154n, 156, 173n, 175
Oration, parts of, 34, 61, 124, 126-127, 131-133, 136; defined, 27
"Orator," Renaissance, 53-59, 81-82, 174
Oratory, types of, 20, 25, 117n, 174; deliberative, 61, 109-110, 126-139, 145; epideictic, 35, 53-54, 111, 115-126, 136, 141-142, 171; forensic, 113, 131
Oresme, Nicolas, 40
Ovid, 35n, 100, 103, 130n
Pericles, 20
Petrarch, 39, 48
Plato, 21-22, 34, 79, 84, 91
Plutarch, 32, 44
Poliziano, 46
Priscian, 31
Proofs, rhetorical, 67, 127; enthymeme, 119n; ethical persuasion, 67, 139; plausibility, 106-107
Quintilian (*De institutione oratoria*), 20, 22, 24, 26, 27, 28, 30, 32n, 35, 42, 44, 71n, 74, 83, 87, 101, 110, 118n, 121n, 147, 148n, 154, 156, 157, 165
Raoul de Tours, 34
Rhetoric, parts of, 25, 34; *dispositio*, 25, 121, 131; *elocutio*, 25-26, 29-31, 35-40, 64, 49-51, 88-91 (*see*

*also* Lemaire, style of); invention, 25, 33-34, 106, 117-118, 137-138; *memoria*, 26, 114-115; *pronuntiatio*, 26-27, 86-88, 172
*Rhetorica ad Herennium:* see [Cicero]
Rhétoriqueurs (rhétorique), 16-17, 40-41, 73, 133, 167, 169-171, 174
Robert de Basevorn, 33n
Ronsard, Pierre de, 39
Saint-Gelais, Octovien de, 17, 79
Salutati, Coluccio, 54
Second Sophistic, 29
Seneca, 35n, 48
Shakespeare, William, 28, 80n
Sidonius Apollinaris, 31
Socrates, 21-22
Statius, 35n
Style: *see* Rhetoric, parts of, *elocutio*; Lemaire, style of
Tassoni, Alessandro, 55-56
Thucydides, 106
Valla, Giorgio, 42
Van Eyck, Jan, 50
Virgil, 35n, 38, 103, 121, 153n
Voltaire, 18
Waleys, Thomas, 33n
William of Moerbeke, 42

The Department of Romance Studies Digital Arts and Collaboration Lab at the University of North Carolina at Chapel Hill is proud to support the digitization of the North Carolina Studies in the Romance Languages and Literatures series.

www.ingramcontent.com/pod-product-compliance
Lightning Source LLC
Chambersburg PA
CBHW022022220426
43663CB00007B/1180